SAVVA

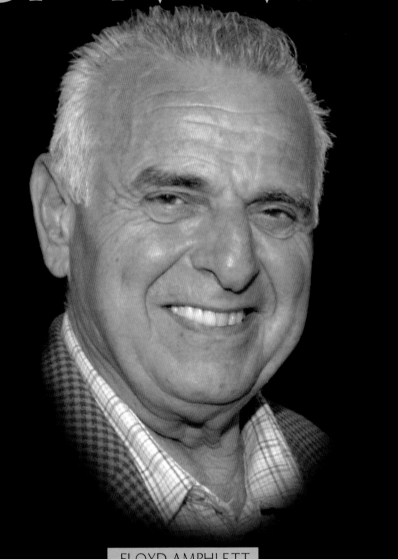

FLOYD AMPHLETT

NICK'S DEDICATION

Dedicated to my parents Savas and Xenou, who I thank for any virtues
I inherited, and any success that came because of them.

First published in 2011

Greyhound Star
PO Box 49, Letchworth
Herts, SG6 2XB.

Cover photography and many other pictures courtesy of Steve Nash.

ISBN
978-1-906305-56-7

Printed and bound in China through Printworks Int. Ltd.

CONTENTS

Acknowledgements   4

Foreword   5

Chapter 1   FAST AWAY   6

Chapter 2   SOON LED   14

Chapter 3   WESTMEAD HO   24

Chapter 4   WINNING TIMES   52

Chapter 5   SIMPLY THE BEST   81

Chapter 6   POSITIVES AND NEGATIVES   113

Chapter 7   HAWK FLIES IN   131

Chapter 8   MY WAYS   147

Chapter 9   THE MATING GAME   180

Epilogue   203

Appendix 1   ROLL OF HONOUR   205

Appendix 2   WESTMEAD LITTERS 1968-2010   208

Acknowledgements

As someone who never reads acknowledgments, I am delighted that you have taken the time to read this. Until I started to write this book, I had assumed they were simply a device for authors to thank people rather than paying them. I was only half wrong!

Seriously, without the patience of our respective wives, Mandy and Natalie, for putting up with countless trips away, and in Natalie's case, numerous invasions of her lounge and kitchen, this book would never have happened.

I also owe a massive debt to the wider Savva family, particularly Nick's brother Peter, and to his wife Andrula, who is quite simply the best cook in Cyprus.

Closer to home, I will forever owe Gail May, who kindly agreed to act as referee between myself and himself on assorted editorial squabbles. She did a remarkably fair job considering, as I was often reminded, 'you do know he is a legend, don't you?'

Indeed had the legend not been so popular, it would have been impossible to pressgang all the staff and friends, past and present, who willingly contributed so much of the literary colour in the pages to come.

Then, when I needed that extra push over the winning line, I was able to call on John Sellers and Sarah Williams at First Stone Publishing.

The cover design was Sarah's brainwave, along with the lay-out, and everything else is down to John's expertise. I have often said that anything I ever learned about journalism, I learned from John. (I await a solicitor's letter.) In the meantime I only hope we sell enough books to cover any legal costs and/or an impending drinks bill.

Last of course, I have to thank the man himself. Nick Savva is quite simply my hero. What's more, he is also a very special friend.

Compiling this book has been, and I am sure, will always be, the pinnacle of my journalistic career.

'It doesn't seem fair to call it work', I often reflected over a coffee or beer on a balcony in Cyprus, listening to the man who I regard as the greatest of all time.

Floyd Amphlett
October 2011

Foreword

Mention the name Nick Savva anywhere in the world of greyhound racing, and heads will shake in disbelief at the extent of his achievements. He is truly a remarkable man.

I have been involved in greyhound racing for over 60 years as secretary of the Greyhound Breeders Forum, as breeders representative on the BGRB and on the newly-formed GBGB. During that time I have followed the progress of Nick Savva from his earliest days in the sport.

In 1970 he showed his first home-bred pups at the Greyhound Breeders Festival at Northaw in Hertfordshire and I was privileged to be there on that day. They were magnificent-looking greyhounds, yet no-one could possibly imagine the many triumphs that the future would hold.

At that time British greyhound breeding was held in low esteem, as most of the champions were bred in Ireland. When Nick came on the scene all this was to change.

The British have always loved racing, and it has been a large part of our lives in the sporting world, whether horses or greyhounds.

For over forty years, Nick has consistently bred champions and has put British Breeding on the map. He has inspired younger breeders and has given countless pleasure to racegoers with the exploits of his greyhounds. He has bred winners of all the classics. He has won numerous Category One races, including our own Breeders Forum Produce Stakes run annually, a record nine times.

The pinnacle of his career was winning the English Greyhound Derby with his British bred greyhounds in three consecutive years – Westmead Hawk in 2005 and 2006 and Westmead Lord in 2007.

Nick is a most unassuming man, a rare quality in someone so successful. He is always willing to give advice, and, through his efforts and dedication to detail, he is admired the world over. British bred greyhounds can now take on the best and win!

Bob Gilling
September 2011.

CLASS ACTS: Nick with double Derby winner Westmead Hawk

Chapter 1

FAST AWAY

If our destinies are pre-ordained, then Nick Savva's route to greyhound greatness must rate among the Almighty's most curious game plans. The unlikely first scene is set in 1934 in Rizokarpaso in northern Cyrus. Study a map of the country and Nick's birthplace is very near the end of the 'pointy bit' closest to Turkey.

Nick's birthday is recorded as April 27, though there are some doubts about his true whelping date.

He said: "My mother would write down the date on the back of the door when she remembered and register you when she got around to it. Birthdays weren't considered as being particularly important. I never realised how significant they are considered to be until I first came to England.

"Originally, my mother was going to register my birthday as April 1, because they weren't sure. Three of us were born in April and my brother Peter ended up with that date."

It was 18 years later that Nick first set foot on a greyhound track. The place was Harringay some time in 1952 and Nick, newly arrived in London, was dragged there by his brother-in-law Sotoris, a compulsive gambler.

Within a few weeks Nick was hooked on the dogs too – a lifetime addiction that would eventually lead him to the pinnacle of the sport both as a trainer and breeder.

It was a long journey from the North London track that was bursting at the seams with punters during greyhound racing's golden age.

Nick said: "The first thing that really amazed me were the people and their reactions to the dogs winning or getting beat.

"They would be 'effing this' and 'effing

that' and always had good excuses as to why they didn't win – quite often in Greek, of course. That part of London had a massive Greek population.

"It wasn't very long before I was going twice a week and for trials on my day off. I had become 'one of them'.

"I soon found myself going racing every night. If it wasn't Harringay it would be Stamford Bridge, Clapton, New Cross, Walthamstow, Wandsworth or White City.

"Unlike many of the punters, I didn't listen to tips or just back favourites, I began studying the dogs, and became interested in them individually.

" I also attended all the trial sessions and, to amuse myself, bought a stop watch and soon became very proficient.

"Then something strange started to happen. I found that every so often, I would be wildly out on my timing. Instead of being to within three to four spots, I might be .40 or .50 out. Almost always I would have the trial winners that much quicker than the trial results sheet.

"So I started to gamble those trial winners first time out and found I was backing winner after winner at big odds. In fact, had I been a bit shrewder, I would also have followed the dogs who were finishing second and third in the trials.

"I don't want to accuse anybody of anything, but I became very successful and seldom had a losing night. I was also studying the dogs closely; I knew their running styles and, unlike the trainers, I wasn't biased in my opinions. I remember one night backing seven out of eight winners.

"The beaten dog finished second and I had a saver forecast. I arrived at the track with a fiver and won over £400 that night. That was a lot of money back in the early 1950s.

"Unfortunately, my system for backing dogs off trials came to an end when GRA instigated a 'rule' whereby racing managers were supposed to get every newcomer beaten first time out.

"I continued to win at Harringay, but

CONFORMING: The registration card issued by the British to Nick's father. Note the best 'guesstimate' in the spelling of the names into English and no actual date of birth.

being young and stupid, was blowing all my winnings on the other tracks or on the horses."

Nick did, however, devise a very unusual system for winning at Walthamstow. He said: "I wasn't a regular there; it was a trickier track than Harringay, and I didn't know the dogs. But there were people who did. I used to stand near where the Chandler wives were sitting.

"I would get in the tote queue behind them and try to listen to what they were backing. It worked. I won money at it."

Nick's grasp of English had clearly improved from that of the young man who arrived from Cyprus in 1951 to make a better life for himself.

He said: "I came on a £30 fare. The War had only been over six years and there was still rationing. Jobs were very scarce.

"I came to stay in North London with an uncle, who had agreed to be my sponsor. Although Cypriots were British citizens, the authorities insisted that the immigrants should not be a burden on the country.

"I stayed with my uncle and with two of my sisters who were already living here. I was very very homesick

"I managed to get a job working in an engineering factory but the wages were only two pounds and ten shillings per week.

"In the end I decided that the best place to work was a hotel, at least I would get enough food to eat.

MUM: Nick had a close bond with his mother Xenou. She successfully reared her own litter of seven.

"I started out working in the kitchens, but then became a waiter, earning eight pounds per week.

"I thought about going to Australia on the £10 assisted scheme but the queue to sign up was massive. I queued for eight hours, then gave up."

Rizokarpaso was a typical poor farming village, of between 5,000 and 6,000 inhabitants, situated midway along a peninsula of one of the most beautiful and fertile parts of Cyprus.

The majority, Greek Cypriots, lived alongside their Turkish neighbours in comparative calm.

Nick recalls: "My father had quite a few dealings with the people in the Turkish village, which was seven miles away, and we would often use them to transport crops on their camels.

"We lived apart, but there was no bad feeling between the two villages. They were very hospitable to us.

"Sometimes us kids would go to their festivals which seemed very colourful and exciting. There was never animosity between the two communities, despite the fact that they were predominantly Moslem and we were Christians."

Living conditions were at best 'basic', bordering on primitive. Nick's home was a clay building with just a single room inside for the entire family. There was a sectioned-off area at one end, for when the cattle came inside in the winter.

For much of the year there would also be the stench of tobacco leaves being stored and only the most basic furniture, including a table to eat at, beds, and a spinning wheel to make yarn for clothing. Water came from two wells.

The family, like most in the area, were poor but kept themselves fed through hard work on the land.

Nick said: "We had around two to three acres of land at home, and a second house with some land about four miles away which we used in the summer.

"We grew all our own vegetables and for meat we had chickens, pigs, rabbits and goats. We would also eat wild fruit and berries when they were in season, and catch fish.

"If we were hungry we would just go into the garden and pick something to eat from the growing vegetables. As kids we would drink milk straight out of the cows.

"There wasn't a lot to spare, but looking back, I'd have to say it was a very healthy diet and, remember, it was wartime. Crime was virtually non-existent."

Interestingly, Nick's early days had a major influence in his outlook on life. By no means 'political', Nick has always tried to live his life according to socialist principles.

He said: "Nobody ever starved. If they were hungry, you would give them something to keep them going.

"I remember a man once tried to buy a marrow from my mother. He only had a penny, but it had to be a big marrow to feed his family of seven.

"My mother told him to go and pick the biggest marrow he could find and keep his money. That was the way people were."

From his earliest days, Nick was always surrounded by animals. He says: "We had donkeys and oxen for working in the fields

LONELY: 16-year-old Nick arrived from Cyprus having spent most of the journey with seasickness and most of the next two years pining for home.

SCHOOLING TRACK: Harringay, a perfect place to learn bilingual cursing.

plus four or five mongrels.

"We also grew tobacco, at the summer house, though that was just a cash crop to pay for my sisters' dowries. It was by far the worst of the crops to grow and pick. It stunk and made you feel ill.

"To dry the leaves, we had to thread them one by one on to pieces of string, which were then attached to six feet long poles. For completing a whole pole, my father would give us a penny."

Nick remembers his father 'Savvas' fondly as a tall good looking man with, unusually for Mediterranean stock, bright blue eyes.

He says: "He was a very hard worker and amazing with his hands. He could make anything that was needed for the home or the land. He was also a very determined man, a very strong character and completely honest.

"He wasn't educated but was a great observer of life, very wise. I remember he advised me: 'never keep money in the bank. Always invest it'.

"Whenever he had a pound to spare, he would buy a piece of land. Although he was never rich, when he died he owned quite a bit of land scattered around."

Nick's father did his utmost to transmit his strict life values to his offspring. Nick says: "I remember a time when a friend and I each had a baby goat. We gave them some leaves off some corn plants that belonged to someone else.

"In his mind it was theft, and to punish me, he made me walk through a patch of thistles in my bare feet."

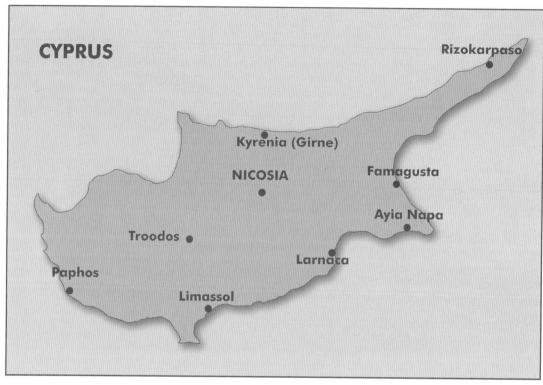

DIVIDED ISLAND: Nick hasn't visited his home village of Rizokarpaso for many years though he has a holiday home in Limassol.

He says: "Although I didn't look anything like my father, in temperament I think I was the most like him of all his sons.

"We were both determined and obstinate and very slow to forgive anyone who did us any wrong.

"Our father was notorious. If someone ripped him off, he would never even speak to them again. I am very similar."

Nick was the eldest of four sons, followed in age order by Theo, Andrew and Peter with three older sisters, Sophia, Anastasia and Maria.

Nick's three brothers all spent time in England at one stage or another, though all have since returned to Cyprus. The three sisters have either stayed or returned to Britain to spend their later years.

Peter and Andrew have followed Nick's success with interest, though it was Theo who came to achieve his own fame in greyhound racing, winning the Derby in 1995 with Moaning Lad.

At this stage it might be worth clearing one query for the record; why was Theo's surname Mentzis and not Savva?

Nick replies: "In Cyprus it is not unusual to have four surnames, including nicknames, which can be used to distinguish you from other people with similar names.

"Theo didn't want to confuse people when he got into the greyhound game and originally called himself under the full surname of Hajisavva, but then soon changed it to one of the nicknames, Mentzis."

In fact, if Nick had chosen to use the most accurate family name, neither the name Savva nor Mentzis would feature on the Derby winner's role of fame. But there would be five 'Hajisavvas'.

In fact, even that might be slightly misleading, as Nick's father's identification papers spell the name as 'Hadjisava'.

Nick said: "It was the best approximation in English of the way the words are spoken in Greek."

The 'Haji' prefix is quite interesting in its own right. It is given to people, in the time of distant forbear, who had made the pilgrimage to Jordan and been baptised in the Nile.

Nick's first cousin Pannos is of a similar age to Nick and lived within 100 yards of the Savva family. Pannos also emigrated to England, and in in later years, became a highly successful businessman. He also retains an astonishing memory for the events of the village back in the 1940s.

He said: "The Savva family were very close and very, very hard-working. Nick's parents toiled like slaves to feed their seven children.

"I remember Nick as being very serious. As the oldest son, he shouldered a lot of responsibility.

"Nick's father was also incredibly strict and a traditionalist, but he had Theo to contend with! Theo was always in trouble and was urged on by his uncle Lazaris.

"Lazaris was the black sheep of the family. He was a thief and had many girlfriends. He also had 14 children and far from frowning on his extra marital activities, his wife encouraged him to go with other women to leave her alone. She even helped arrange some of them.

"It was possibly because he had so many children and struggled to feed his family that Lazaris used to steal goats or chickens.

"One day he persuaded Theo to steal a goat which they then ate in the countryside. Nick's father would have gone mad if he had known"

Nick can recall the day when Lazaris arrived on the doorstep with a pile of stolen meat. He and the meat were thrown out, and he took a clip around the ear from Nick's outraged father.

By the time Nick was 15, he had decided that he didn't want to follow the life of a peasant farmer.

He said: "I had looked around and saw no future. I had no education or trade and would be expected to marry a village girl and live like my father. I decided I wanted something better..."

Chapter 2

SOON LED

Around the Greyhound tracks of London, Nick's aspirations were growing, as was his interest in the open race scene. He says: "I loved my graded racing at Harringay but soon began to appreciate the open racers. Pall Mall winner Home Luck always struck me as a very good dog.

"One of my other favourites was Galtee Cleo. He was owned by George Flintham, who I knew. I watched the dog run at Hackney and thought he was exceptional. In fact he would have won the 1953 Derby final if he had been drawn on the outside.

"In later years, I was a bit of a fan of Spectre. In his style, he could almost have been a 'Westmead' – Derby class, but could stay as far as marathons in top class. I only ever missed one Derby final."

Nick became more and more fascinated with the behaviour and characteristics of individual dogs. He loved to go to the paddock and just marvel at racing's superstars.

He said: "I decided that I wanted to be part of the greyhound industry.

"I applied for a kennelhand's job at GRA's main kennel complex at Northaw. I wasn't accepted. It might have been because I was a foreigner, or maybe just because they were very selective and I had no background in greyhounds. Northaw was very much a 'closed shop' in those days.

"I had a long chat with myself. I decided that I would need to make some money and buy my own dogs, but at that stage, I didn't have a clue how to go about it.

"Looking back, if you had told me that one day I could be associated with dogs of the calibre that I used to watch and admire, I would have said you were mad."

So often, it is the major life changes that are the most difficult to predict and Nick's jolt on to a different course came about through a strange opportunity.

He said: "As I was working in hotels, I decided to go on a three-month working holiday to Jersey.

"There was a Jewish family from the East End who were staying as guests and they were a real pain in the arse. I was working as a waiter and one day they just pushed me too far and I finally lost my temper with them.

MODEL: Spectre pictured with trainer his trainer Jim Hookway was the sort of dog that Nick had always admired. Derby class over four bends but with enough stamina to win a TV Trophy.

"Incredibly, it was all sorted out and I got on really well with them from then on. Before they left, they offered me a job working as a presser in their clothes factory back in London, earning £8 per week."

The work was hard and very long hours, but Nick soon found himself serving an apprenticeship in the rag trade.

The next stage came when he joined brother-in-law John and sister Maria, who had a small business making clothes.

He said: "I have always been the sort of person that if I take an interest in something it absolutely absorbs me. I have to learn as much as I can about it.

"I soon had enough knowledge to set about making clothes; specifically, I was able to 'cut make and trim' the basic procedure in the manufacture."

More importantly, Nick realised that this was the opportunity that he had craved – a chance, one day, to create a new life, owning and training his beloved greyhounds.

The plan simply involved making as much money as was necessary and moving to the countryside as soon as he could.

He said: "Suddenly I had a purpose in my life. I gave up gambling, not that I was ever addicted, and began economising. I became single minded on achieving my ambition. I would work as hard and for as many hours as was necessary."

With his apprenticeship completed, Nick set out on his own, making clothes in a small workshop in Warren Street, central London.

Nick said: "We were creating middle class women's clothing and we soon had plenty of orders."

A bigger workshop followed. Among his employees was younger brother Theo, who followed his older sibling into the rag trade, as he would into the greyhound industry.

Nick, meanwhile had expanded his expertise, too. He said: "I wasn't able to design clothes, but I knew how to copy and I had a very good understanding of the whole clothing production process."

With an ever expanding order book, Nick eventually bought a factory in Tottenham and was turning out 6,000 garments a week. He handed over the smaller workshop to Theo, who wanted to go it alone.

With his business career on the up-and-up, events were also unfolding in his personal life. In 1957, he was introduced by a friend to a lady who would change his life forever, Natalie.

They first met on a blind date set up by one of Natalie's friends at the bank where she worked.

She said: "My friend had a flat in Hampstead and wanted to spend the evening with her boyfriend. But her father was very strict and the only way that she could do it, was by having a female friend there at the same time.

"I wasn't that keen, but she said that her boyfriend would bring along a friend of his to even up the numbers and I went along with it. That friend turned out to be Nick."

So what were her first impressions of her new suitor?

She said: "I can't really remember. His English wasn't very good, but we got on quite well. I suppose we must have done because we met again the next day."

It was a little over four years later, on August 19th 1961 that they married in Paddington, in the same church where Natalie had been christened.

Unsurprisingly, the marriage did not meet with widespread approval from Nick's family. Natalie said: "It was quite understandable. They wanted Nick to marry a girl from a similar background. It didn't help matters that the part of the family who were living in England did little to reassure them."

Natalie eventually met her mother-in-law and they got on well together. But it wasn't until after the birth of their first daughter Lisa, in 1969, that Natalie met Nick's father for the first time. It was Natalie's first visit to Cyprus and it came as quite a shock.

She said: "Nick's father and brother Peter came to meet us at Nicosia airport, but within a couple of miles we were already driving on dirt roads."

Nick soon introduced Natalie to his other great love, greyhound racing, with a trip to Hendon dog track.

So when did Natalie first realise the full depth of her boyfriend's obsession with greyhound racing?

She replies: "When it was too late."

Nick and Natalie lived in Tuffnel Park for a short period before moving to a small house in Colindale, where Nick began to fulfil his dream and become a backyard greyhound trainer.

He bought his first two greyhounds to train and built a small kennel in the back garden. They were bought as pups for £50 each.

He said: "One was a son of Town Prince who turned out to be a fighter. I refused to accept it originally and took him to three different schooling tracks.

Pincano

f b (Clopook-Dungooly Chariot, Apr 64)

Pincano's racing career was spent almost entirely on the independent circuit (see chapter 2) though she did win a couple of 510 yard opens at Rayleigh during a brief spell there.

She was the first brood to produce a litter at Westmead. The date was January 1968. By Maryville Hi, the litter featured Westmead Villa.

However, it also contained open winners, Westmead Mono, Westmead Brook and Westmead Hi who contested the Trafalgar Cup Final before a promising career ended prematurely in the 1969 Yorkshire Puppy Derby Final. Hi later threw marathon star Westmead Mia.

Pincano's second litter were by Irish Laurels winner Boro Parachute but featured nothing of note. The Deneholme Hunter litter included Westmead View, who would later be mated to Westmead County to produce Drynham Star.

A top class open racer during the mid 1970s, Star won the 1976 Spring Cup, Jubilee Stake and Gold Vase, and also finished runner-up in the '75 Pall Mall and the '76 St Leger. The fawn broke the Harringay 660 clock, twice broke the Wimbledon 660 clock and also set new records

at Hackney (523m) and Derby (590m).

Pincano's final litter was to Discretions and included the minor open racer Johnny Wood.

He was sent over to Australia and eventually went to stud, where his progeny included the 1977 Melbourne Cup winner Milepost.

Nick says: "Nicky Kervick warned me not to breed with Pincano because she wasn't a hundred percent genuine – at least on the outside hare.

He told me 'She'll break your heart!' But she was fast and good looking so I went against his advice. But I made sure that I went to a dog that I always considered a 100 per cent hard chaser – Maryville Hi. I had watched him in the Derby and liked his style of racing.

"Whether it was him who made the difference or not I don't know, but the litter were all very genuine, none more so than Westmead Villa."

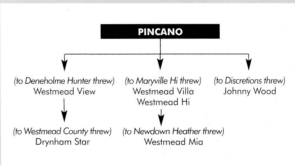

PINCANO

(to Deneholme Hunter threw)
Westmead View

(to Maryville Hi threw)
Westmead Villa
Westmead Hi

(to Discretions threw)
Johnny Wood

(to Westmead County threw)
Drynham Star

(to Newdown Heather threw)
Westmead Mia

Cricket Dance

f b (Prairie Flash-Juggie, March 66)

One of the original three broods that would put Westmead on the breeding map, Cricket Dance produced eight litters.

But it was the first, by Clonalvy Pride and featuring Westmead County, Pride, Lane and Silver that set the benchmark against which all other litters would be measured.

While County and Lane (see separate) went on to sire many fast hounds, it was left to Silver to keep the dam line going.

After a small, ordinary, batch by Faithful Hope, Cricket Dance's third litter were by Laurels winner Carry On Oregon and featured two exceptional dogs who both, for some reason, loved Slough.

Delroney Leader would win the '74 Buckinghamshire Cup and set a new 660 track record. Westmead Valley, trained by McEntyre, would win the '74 Scurry Gold Cup and finish runner-up in the Oxfordshire.

There were another pair of high class Westmeads in a versatile Always Proud litter. Early paced 'Border' reached a string of finals, winning the Midland Flat and setting track records for 430 metres at Bletchley and 420 at Derby.

Brother 'Land' was more of a stayer, winning two decent competitions and setting a six bend clock at Bristol. One of the litter, 'Glide', won over 890 metres.

Clohast Rebel, the sire of Dance's next litter was an abject failure at stud. The best of the Westmeads was Westmead Choice, who won the 1976 Champion Stakes at Shelbourne Park.

Another member of the litter, 'Mink', finished runner-up to half brother Land in the Whitbread Final at Portsmouth.

Dance's daughter, Westmead Silver, had already produced a decent Mels Pupil litter, so there was great interest when her mum was crossed by the same dog.

The best bitch in the litter was Westmead Dance who won the East Anglian Derby and set a 462 metre clock at Yarmouth that would remain untouched for 20 years.

The best dog in the litter was Westmead Special. In 1977 he won 15 opens and reached a string of finals, including the Scottish Derby and the Essex Vase, where he finished fifth.

Last but not least was Cricket Dance's Feb 76 litter by Fionntra Frolic. The most notable member,

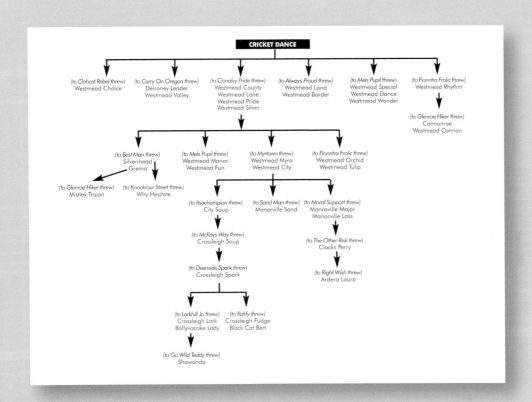

CRICKET DANCE

(to Clohast Rebel threw)
Westmead Choice

(to Carry On Oregon threw)
Delroney Leader
Westmead Valley

(to Clonalvy Pride threw)
Westmead County
Westmead Lane
Westmead Pride
Westmead Silver

(to Always Proud threw)
Westmead Land
Westmead Border

(to Mels Pupil threw)
Westmead Special
Westmead Dance
Westmead Wonder

(to Fionntra Frolic threw)
Westmead Rhythm

(to Glenroe Hiker threw)
Cannonroe
Westmead Cannon

(to Best Man threw)
Silvermead
Grema

(to Mels Pupil threw)
Westmead Manor
Westmead Fun

(to Myrtown threw)
Westmead Myra
Westmead City

(to Fionntra Frolic threw)
Westmead Orchid
Westmead Tulip

(to Glenroe Hiker threw)
Mistley Trojan

(to Knockrour Street threw)
Why Hesitate

(to Itsachampion threw)
City Soup

(to Sand Man threw)
Manorville Sand

(to Moral Support threw)
Manorville Major
Manorville Lass

(to McKays Way threw)
Crossleigh Soup

(to The Other Risk threw)
Clocks Perry

(to Deenside Spark threw)
Crossleigh Spark

(to Right Wish threw)
Ardera Laura

(to Larkhill Jo threw)
Crossleigh Lark
Ballyvocoke Lady

(to Ratify threw)
Crossleigh Fudge
Black Cat Bert

(to Go Wild Teddy threw)
Shawanda

Westmead Rhythm, would go on to throw Produce Stakes winner Westmead Cannon and Romford Puppy Cup winner Cannonroe.

If there was one daughter who, above all others, would extend Cricket Dance's influence, it was Westmead Silver, from that first amazing litter.

Silver's first litter to Myrtown included the headline-grabbing Westmead Myra, but it would be her minor open race winning sister Westmead City who would have such a major effect on Irish breeding.

Trained by Ernie Price and sold on to Irish farmer Paddy Doran, City would throw one of the leading sires of the early 1990s, Manorville Sand, plus his half brother and sister Manorville's Major and Lass.

In April 1975, Silver threw her second litter, this time by Mels Pupil. The star was Westmead Manor who contested the 1977 Derby final won by

Balliniska Band. The following year he won the Hunt Cup and Steel City Cup. His littermates included Cesarewitch finalist Westmead Fun.

In May '76, Westmead Tulip was born, from a mating between Silver and the kennel's new sire, Fionntra Frolic. The brindle went on to win a stack of opens for Terry Atkins and finished runner-up in both the Super Trapper and Rochester Derby. Sister 'Orchid' ran third in the 1978 English Oaks and Scurry finals.

Silver's final litter was to coursing sire Best Man. Although there was nothing of note, two of the bitches went on to produce well. One produced Lifford Derby winner Why Hesitate.

The other, when mated to Glenroe Hiker, threw Mistley Trojan, who Nick trained to win the 1984 Classic Select Stakes and Anglo-Irish International at Wimbledon.

HITCHED: Nick and Natalie marry in the church where she was christened.

"In the end I realised that they couldn't all be wrong and I eventually gave him away for coursing. The other dog, David, was too slow to win a race.

"He actually did win one, flapping at Watford, but it was a photo finish. They didn't actually have a photo and the result went against us."

Natalie said: "David was a lovely dog and we kept him for the rest of his life. When I think back now as to how we trained him, it isn't any surprise that he couldn't win a race.

"We used to feed him a washing-up bowl of food absolutely dripping in gravy. It was only as we listened and learned that we realised our mistakes."

To hear Nick talk, you would be amazed that he ever trained a winner when he first started out.

He said: "I don't think Natalie was being completely fair. In those days all kennels fed slop. David was just not very good, irrespective of my training abilities. I sent him to a professional trainer at Harringay and he was too slow to grade.

" Although I was very amateurish, I listened and I read everything I could as I tried to learn. But very soon I realised that good dogs don't need top trainers - and I was proof of it."

Nick's luck changed thanks to a visit to a local schooling track.

He said: "A guy was moaning about a bitch that he owned that had obviously let him down the previous night. He asked if anyone would give him £30 for her, which I did.

"I sent her to a trainer at Rye House and she never got beat in graded or open races. Then I had her home to train myself.

"Her name was Pincano and she was a great little bitch for me. I discovered that she was an inside hare specialist. On the McKee, she would just run with them.

"She let down the guy at Rye House on a couple of occasions, but despite my lack of experience, she never let me down.

"I flapped her all over the country and she won loads of opens, including the Rye House Derby. It was my first taste of success."

"I remember taking Pincano to Worksop one night and leading her around myself. Fortunately, she was in trap one which meant once I had put her in the traps I had chance to dash over to the bookies.

" I had £20 at 8-1 on her, and then ran back on to the track ready to catch her at the pick-up – and she won."

Like many novice trainers, Nick eventually turned to the dark side and decided to stop one of his runners for the first and only time in his life.

He said: "Pincano was very well known at Watford and was always very short in the betting.

"I decided I would stop her, hoping that I might get a better price next time out. I listened how it should be done from the other trainers.

"It was a warm day, and instead of leaving Pincano in her kennel, I let her run around the garden to her heart's content. I also left her with a couple of bones, hoping she would tire herself out.

"We got to the track and sure enough she opened up at even money. The bookies soon realised that she was a non-trier and pushed her out to 10-1.

"She absolutely flew and did the fastest

time of her career. When I realised what had happened all I could do was laugh."

With the business doing well, Nick fancied owning a really top class greyhound. He contacted Phil Rees who, in turn, put Irish agent Nicky Kervick on the case. He came up with an unraced pup called Cricket Dance for £500.

Nick said: "That was decent money back in the early 1960s but she looked worth the money in her trials.

"She went straight into the Puppy Oaks and reached the final. Unfortunately, she badly damaged a gracilis muscle and was never the same again.

"We sent her to Crayford, which was a peat track. It helped with the problem and she did win a few races, but could never fulfil her original potential."

Nick took advice off many people in his early days, but few were more influential than Kilkenny bookmaker Patsy Browne, the man behind the 'Dogstown' prefix.

Nick said: "I went over to Ireland with someone who worked for me and he took me to various breeders who had dogs for sale.

"I didn't realise it at the time but I was being recommended a lot of bad dogs and the guy who was supposed to be helping me was getting back-handers from the breeders.

"Among the people we visited was Patsy, who my kennelman had also worked for. I was introduced to Patsy and he soon realised what was going on.

"He took pity on me and we became great friends. Apart from being a bookmaker and breeder, he was a great judge of a dog. He found many good dogs for me, the first being

NO.1: Ivy Hall Jewel became the kennel's first winner.

Ivy Hall Jewel who I bought for £500.

"Patsy came to England to stay with us for a few days. He wanted to see the set-up and offer any advice to help me. But he was extremely eccentric, very loud and with some very colourful language.

"I remember taking him down to my local and within 10 minutes he had cleared the place.

"But we stayed until about 3am drinking brandy and champagne and the landlady made more money than she would have done with a full pub.

"I remember taking him flapping to Rye House and he headed straight for the paddock. He walked straight in and began examining the dogs, but no one batted an eyelid."

"Patsy knew that I had ambitions to set up a breeding kennel and one day he offered me a bitch for sale for £300. He said: 'She's wristy. She won't do much on the track, but she will make a great brood bitch.' Her name was Hacksaw."

Natalie says: "'Eccentric' wouldn't even begin to describe Patsy. We dropped in on him at home at one stage. The place was a real tip, and he was the first to say, 'Surely you could have found somewhere better to have a cup of tea!'

"I remember he took us for a meal to a nice hotel and he turned up in wellies covered in cow muck.

"On another occasion when he came to see us, he asked to see Lisa in her pram. He peered at her for a few moments and said: 'Be lucky! Be lucky!' He then threw a £5 note into the pram.

"Patsy was a character alright, and he was a very nice man too."

By now, greyhounds had become a welcome distraction from business.

At its peak Nick employed around 100 staff at his factory in Tottenham. They made dresses to order, but the factory would also produce its own garments. It was an expanding, profitable business.

Nick said: "I think my greatest ability involved incorporating the design of the patterns to make best use of the available material. So although the profit on an individual dress was small, by careful design I could keep the cabbage (waste material) to a minimum and possibly get three garments from the material allowed for two.

"I would also wait to see which was the latest hit design, and, before anybody else, I would buy the material and make copies.

"But I was working very long days under immense pressure. Inevitably, my health was suffering. I needed a bottle of whiskey or brandy to unwind at the end of the day.

"But 12 years after first devising my plan, my savings had increased to a point that I was ready to take the next step towards achieving my dream."

Chapter 3

WESTMEAD HO

By the mid-sixties, Nick's efforts to find a place to train had become frenetic. He bombarded estate agents with requests for details of properties with land within reasonable access of London.

In 1967, he was offered a ramshackle fruit farm in Edelsborough, a small village near Dunstable – 'Westmead'. Price £9,000.

Nick says: "It was completely overgrown, a house that was uninhabitable, a pig-sty and a couple of outbuildings.

"My first job was to convert one of the outbuildings, that is now a whelping kennel, into temporary accommodation for Natalie and myself while we renovated the house. We also built kennels for the brood bitches.

"Outside, the big job was uprooting 500 prune trees and making the ground suitable for greyhounds. Although I had some help,

uprooting the trees nearly killed me and took its toll on my back.

"Eventually we built the racing kennels. They were only ever meant to be temporary but we never got round to replacing them."

For a city girl like Natalie, the prospect of living in the Bedfordshire countryside was as big a culture shock as Nick's move to England.

She says: "Although I was brought up in London, I never liked the place and couldn't wait to live in the country.

"I fell in love with Westmead straight away, even though the whole place was a complete wreck. The surveyor took one look at it and said: 'Don't buy it.'

"But we just got on with it, living in London during the week and staying at Westmead over the weekends getting the place ready.

PLUM POSITION: The Westmead fruit farm soon to be transformed.

"The part to be finished first was the whelping kennels and that was where we slept.

"The house was gutted from top to bottom, with only the four walls remaining. It was a huge job."

Within a year, Westmead was ready to whelp its first litter of pups and in January 1968, Pincano produced 4 dogs and 5 bitches from a mating to Maryville Hi. Nick originally had no major plans for breeding. He primarily just wanted to train greyhounds.

He said: "I decided that I should try to breed my own due to the number of times I was ripped off buying dogs in Ireland."

But soon after the first litter was born, Nick realised that he had stumbled on something that would change his life forever.

He said: "I would get up early in the morning, in the summer, as soon as it was dawn and take the pups out into the fields or nearby countryside.

"Just to watch them running and playing was wonderful. I used to play hide and seek with them. I was like a child.

"I would then have to drive to London and do a full day's work and then take the pups out when I got home.

"They were very long days, but I don't think I ever had more enthusiasm and energy in my life. The greyhounds became my life force. Natalie felt the same; she took to the puppies with just as much enthusiasm as I did."

Natalie would regularly join Nick to take the pups on to the Downs for exercise at 5am in the morning. The pair would stand around half a mile from each other and call the pups from one side of the valley to the other.

ON TRACK: The schooling circuit was an early addition to the kennel.

Nick said: "The ground was chalky and very rough but the pups never hurt themselves."

Natalie said: "I loved looking after the pups and the brood bitches. Pincano was my special favourite in the early days. Nick would leave early for work and let her into the house.

"She used to come upstairs to the bedroom, get into bed beside me and go to sleep."

As he waited for his first home bred runners, Nick's earliest runners from his new kennel were on the flaps. He also had runners as an owner at various NGRC tracks.

Unfortunately, prior to Patsy Browne's intervention, he had been sold one expensive flop after another.

Nick says: "My brother-in-law and I spent £15,000 on around six to eight dogs, all at the recommendation of Bill O'Hare. Two of the most expensive were a dog called Badge Of Combat, and a Quarrymount bitch who had won the Munster Puppy Cup and cost £3,000.

"Badge Of Combat was sent to Phil Rees at Wimbledon, but wasn't good enough and was transferred to John Coleman at Romford.

"We waited until he was in bottom grade and had a punt to get our money back. He led into the third bend and broke a hock.

"The Quarrymount bitch was also disappointing and while her breeder, John

Mackey, was in England, he asked to see her trial.

"We took her to Beaverwood and she ran into a stray piece of inside fence and broke her neck on the spot. Mackey made various promises to replace her but it never happened."

The one bright spot was former White City runner Franks Tower. Owned by brother Theo, he had been treated for a broken hock by Paddy Sweeney before joining Theo.

Tower, who looked as though he would have made a good class stayer prior to the injury, came back over four bends at Luton and won nine in a row.

The kennel had its first two NGRC runners on April 26 1969. Given Nick's full-time work commitment, the trainer's licence was in Natalie's name and would remain so for almost 30 years.

Quarrymount Mink was the first to traps in heat four of the Gold Collar at Catford. He finished fifth. But 15 minutes later, it was the turn of Ivy Hall Jewel. The former White City top heat runner 'soon led' and duly became the first of many thousands of winners to be sent out by the kennel.

The unknown 'Savva – Private' successfully steered her runner to the Gold Collar Final. An 8-1 chance in the betting, Jewel led to the run-in before being beaten half a length by Surprising Fella. Jewel went on to reach a string of finals, including the Oxon and Golden Crest.

Nick has learned a great deal from many people in the greyhound racing world, but in the early days, few people influenced him

HANDS ON: Nick achieved his first success as a breeder/trainer with the talented Westmead Villa.

more than Paddy O'Shaunnessy.

A native of Glin in Limerick, Paddy was a trainer at Wandsworth for 21 years until it closed. He trained the last ever winner there, before moving on to Charlton, which then also closed.

Nick says: "I was very amateur in the early days and one day I asked my local steward Ken Guy if he could recommend someone to help me.

Ken was the former head of racing for South London Stadiums and he recommended Paddy, who he had known from their Wandsworth days.

Westmead County f d

(Clonalvy Pride-Cricket Dance, Jan 70)

County was 19 months old when he made his NGRC open race debut in the Eclipse puppy stakes at Hall Green.

Before the end of the year, he had contested 11 races and had won the consolation final of the Cesarewitch in a quicker time than the final. He had also finished down the field in the West Ham's Junior Cup Final, having won the fastest semi.

The fawn hit the ground running in early 1972 winning five of his first seven opens, clocking 29.36 for Wembley's 525 yards in a semi of the Evening Standard Trophy. He finished third in the final at Wimbledon.

He stayed at Plough Lane for the local Produce Stake where he finished runner-up (5-4f) to Deneholme Chief.

The fawn's next date was the English Derby. He won his first two heats, clocking 28.76 in the second round but contested 'the heat of death' in round three.

County finished fourth, behind the brilliant Super Rory, whose 28.36 was the fastest of the night by more than four lengths. Scintillas Gem took second, with the last remaining place going to a dog called Patricia's Hope. County went on to finish third in the consolation behind Suburban Gent.

But the Savva-trained runner then returned to his beloved Wembley for the Summer Cup in which he beat Silver Skipper in a time of 29.56.

He re-appeared two weeks later in the Select Stakes where he was taking on the second, third and fourth from the English Derby final. But they had no answer to County's pace as he produced the performance of his career to win in 29.23 for the 525 yards.

It would be his last run over the standard. He made a six-bend debut next time out, winning by nine lengths.

County started as ante post favourite for the 1972 St Leger and dominated the event with fantastic runs in the first round (39.76) and semi (39.77), before breaking a hock in the final when well clear.

Nick says: His hock went just in front of the Wembley tunnel. To make matters worse, I could see he was lame but the crowd started booing him.

"I think that was the lowest point I have even experienced in greyhound racing. I felt hollow inside. But journalist Alan Lennox came to console me. He said, 'Don't worry, it will turn out for the best. I am convinced he will do exceptionally well at stud."

County's leg healed, but didn't mend straight. Nevertheless Nick decided to bring him back for the following year's St Leger.

In fairytales, County would have come back to win the race at the second attempt. In real life,

County reached the semis but split a web.

Nick says: "He was a dog without a fault. If I had to choose the dog most like him that I've trained it would probably be 'The Hawk.'

"It was only after he was injured that I really realised what I had lost. He is the main reason that our interest grew in breeding.

"I was very much an amateur when County came along but he still performed brilliantly, no matter how many mistakes I made in his feeding and training.

"He had great track craft and back-straight pace and won the Select Stakes coming from the back of the field. I still believe that he and Move are the best stayers that we bred.

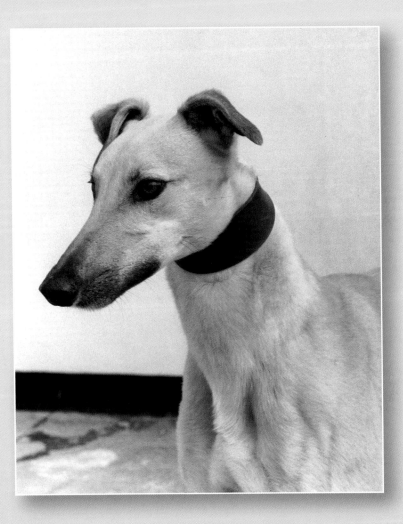

"As a stud dog he passed on so many of his good traits to his offspring. In my opinion, he was an outstanding stud dog. He died of a heart attack as a ten year old on April 21, 1980 and is buried in the garden."

County sired the winners of two Scottish Derbys, three TV Trophies, two St Legers and two Gold Collars.

He was particularly good to his own breeder - three of his offspring, Westmead Power, Special Account and Westmead Champ – are profiled in this publication.

Other County progeny included Westown Adam, 'Decoys' Duke, Ranch, Ranger, and Sovereign, Cormacruiser, Weston Blaze, 'Westmeads' Bound, Bounty, Melody, Gem and Ruby plus Keep Moving and Drynham Star.

Westmead Lane bd d

(Clonalvy Pride-Cricket Dance, Jan 70)

The 77 pound brindle and white made a successful open race debut in a 640 yard event at Slough when still only 17 months old. He returned to four bends to run fourth in the 1971 British Breeders final over 440 yard at Catford.

1972 was a busy year for Lane, who contested 34 opens, winning 12 on nine different tracks. He reached a string of major finals, including the Midland St Leger, Gold Cup and Gold Collar.

The strong-galloping dog finished fourth in the Collar final, just 24 hours after winning a heat of the Wimbledon British Breeders Stakes.

Towards year end, the new Brighton 785-yard record holder was finally put over extended distances and landed the kennel its first classic, the 880 yard Cesarewitch at Belle Vue. That was soon followed by victory in the Test over the Stow's 880 course.

1973 would prove disappointing. Lane built up a big winning sequence but was beaten in London Marathon Championship by litter brother Westmead Pride and was then retired through injury.

He went to stud in England, but was in the shade of brother County and eventually went to Ireland, where he died prematurely at Jack Mullan's Newry range.

Thankfully, before he left, he produced a litter out of Hacksaw that included the great Westmead Satin.

Nick says: "I'd forgotten running him in the Gold Collar the night after running at Wimbledon, but I was very indiscriminate in those day. I'd had him flapping from 12 months of age.

"Whatever Lane achieved was down to natural ability, and had very little to do with his trainer."

Paddy came along for an interview and over lunch I offered him the job. I said: 'I want you to teach me to become a better trainer'. He replied, 'after seeing the condition of the dogs and the kennels, I think it is you who should be teaching me!' which I took as a great compliment.

"I can't speak highly enough of Paddy. He was very knowledgeable and very kind to the dogs. I remember one day we had a very badly behaved young dog, quite nasty.

"The dog did something bad, I can't remember what, he probably attacked another dog and Paddy slapped him. As soon as he did it, he was full of remorse.

"I'm so sorry, boy" he kept saying to the dog. He didn't see me, but it made me smile, he was such a gentle man.

"He was also one of the most honest men I came across. He was practically a saint. When he had been at Wandsworth he had a string of time finding local enquiries and had never been able to explain why.

"They were always dogs off trials and his explanation was always accepted. We'll never know, but I'm convinced that there were odd things going on in the racing office, just as I had experienced at Harringay at the same time.

"They knew Paddy was the straightest trainer at the track so they would hold a few lengths from the trial times and back them first time out. Paddy was so naïve about such things that he never ever considered it."

But tragedy struck in October 1977.

Nick says "Paddy was taken ill with stomach pains and I pleaded with him to go and see a specialist. I offered to send him to Harley Street.

Hacksaw

f b (Hack Up Chieftain-Meteoric, Jan 67)

Bought specifically for breeding, Hacksaw's race career was very brief due to a wrist injury. She produced her first litter by former marathon open racer Franks Tower in April 1970. The star of the litter was Westmead Tower, who ran third in the Cesarewitch and fifth in the 1972 Irish TV Trophy.

Hacksaw's following litter to Newdown Heather produced nothing of note on the track,

but Westmead Damson went on to become the 1978 Dam of the Year.

Damson's first litter included double classic winner Westmead Power and the prolific open race stayer Westmead Fair.

To Fionntra Frolic, Damson would throw Regency runner-up Playfield Royal, Coronation Stakes winner Westmead Velvet and the useful Westmead Trophy. There was also an Edinburgh

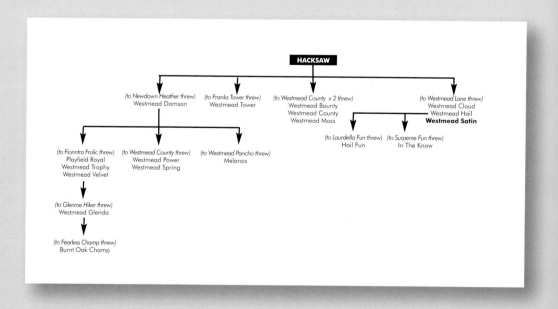

Cup finalist in her litter by Westmead Pancho.

In the meantime, her mum, Hacksaw, was producing litters by Westmead brothers County and Lane. To the former she threw the leading stayer of winter '74/'75, the Arnold Mobley-trained Westmead Bounty. The Lane litter would include the legend that became Westmead Satin.

A repeat mating to County produced yet another superstar in Westmead Champ. There was little of note in her second litter by Lane.

"But he was determined to go on holiday in Ireland and see a doctor there. That was the last I ever saw of him. He developed peritonitis and died in Ireland. He was 68 and had worked for me for 10 years and I was very sad to lose him."

Natalie said: "I can still remember Nick taking the phone call. It just wouldn't sink in. Paddy was a lovely gentle man. We all thought the world of him."

Eventually, the first Pincano litter reached schooling age and Nick took them to Henlow, a flapping track popular with local breeders.

Nick says: "I took them along for their first look. They were fanatically keen so I handslipped them. They all went first time. I thought they would be pretty good, but I didn't think much beyond that and decided to send them off to John Horsfall at Catford"

On May 26 1969, a Bank Holiday morning meeting, the 'Westmead' prefix appeared on a racecard for the first time.

Westmead Villa was beaten in the 570 yard graded race, but after a couple of defeats gave her proud breeder his greatest moment in the sport to date.

Nick says: "It was only a graded race, but I was absolutely thrilled. I wanted to climb the paddock fence just to give her a big hug. It was a wonderful moment that I've never forgotten."

Villa would prove the best of the litter and she soon landed the kennel's first trophy, the Catford Breeders Produce Stakes when leading home Westmeads Hi (2nd) and King (5th), who were trained by Natalie.

TEAM SAVVA: Natalie played an invaluable role in the rearing and handling of the early litters.

Another four littermates had been bought by Pauline Wallace and were sent to race in the USA.

Natalie says: "I remember the day that Pauline Wallis bought the pups. I took them out for a walk and then cried my eyes out. I didn't want them to go."

Eventually, Nick decided to bring Villa home so that he could train her himself.

He said: "She won first time out for me in an open at Walthamstow and I had £20 at 33-1."

More success soon followed in the shape of the 1970 Cobb Marathon at West Ham. During Nick's first season as a trainer, Villa won eight opens, reached the final of the Greenwich Cup and ran third in the Crazy Paving Stakes.

The following year she would break the 700 yard track record at West Ham and land the consolation final of the Cesarewitch.

Nick had no doubt that Villa was destined to be a fantastic brood. Unfortunately, she smashed a hock, developed gangrene, and had to be put to sleep.

It was a tragic end for a fine bitch, but a remarkable debut litter for Westmead Kennels.

The early days at Westmead were among the toughest times, physically, of Nick's life. Not only was he trying to develop the kennels and facilities, he was running a factory and two shops, training a small open race string, and rearing litters, as well as being the father of a young family.

Nick says: "In the very early days, Natalie was able to help out with the pups and brood bitches, but when the girls came along, they took up most of her time."

Staff came and went. Paddy O'Shaugnessy shone through, but he was a non-driver and Nick either had to employ someone to transport Paddy and dogs around the country or do it himself.

He said: "I would be up early in the morning and in the summer would take the pups out at 4am to give them a gallop. I would then either beat the traffic into London by leaving at 7am or leaving it until after 9am depending on what I had on during the day.

"I would do the same thing in the evening in terms of beating the traffic, but it had to be an early day if we were going racing."

Quite often Nick would set off for a Northern destination during the early afternoon with the back seat of the Jaguar laid flat and three or four dogs in the back, with a three or four hour drive and a 6pm kennelling deadline.

After the meeting, a similar journey to arrive back home in the early hours of the morning, put the dogs away, eat, sleep and then the same routine again.

Nick says: "Sometimes I was so tired that I would have to stop on the way home for 15 minutes sleep because it was too dangerous to keep driving.

"The business suffered too. Things were missed because staff weren't doing their jobs and stock went missing, but it was impossible to monitor everything."

In the meantime, Natalie had battles of her own. The Savva's first daughter, Lisa, had been born in October 1969 followed by Nicola two years later.

Natalie found herself torn between feeding her own babies and helping out the young mothers and offspring outside in the whelping kennels and paddocks.

She said: "I don't think I ever got the bottles of milk mixed up! Looking back it was exciting, but very tiring, with long hard days. I would never want to do it again."

Family holidays came as another distraction for Nick with races to be won, a factory to be monitored, kennels to be built and a million other jobs, but Nick remembers those days fondly.

"I discovered that the English must have their summer holidays. I have great memories of taking the girls away and spending time as a family."

Yet despite the huge commitment, Nick never had any thoughts about giving up his greyhounds.

He says: "It never entered my head. Looking back, I wouldn't have done anything differently."

Clearly though something had to go and Nick decided it would be the business. He sold off the factory in 1975, but kept the shops, which were run by Natalie, to subsidise the kennel.

He said: "We needed the income. I knew there was no money in the greyhound breeding and rearing business."

The Pincano litter had been barely two years old when Cricket Dance came into season. Nick was undecided about which sire to choose.

He said: "Her breeder had originally said that if I sent her back to him, he would go to Yanka Boy and rear me a sapling.

"I decided to ask Patsy's opinion and he advised to use Yanka Boy's father Clonalvy Pride who was getting on in years and would not be around forever. I could always go to Yanka Boy next time."

Westmead Satin

bd b (Westmead Lane-Hacksaw, Aug 73)

Westmead Satin was whelped in August 1973 from a Westmead Lane/Hacksaw litter that included Westmeads 'Cloud' (Gr London Challenge Trophy), 'Gale' (TR 764m Derby), and 'Patrick', who would win opens over four, six and eight bends.

A small brindle, Satin began her open race career in early 1975. She ran dual distance opens and was still a pup when she went unbeaten to the final of the 600 metre Ebor at Leeds, where she finished third.

Seasonal breaks plus lameness restricted Satin to 16 appearance in that first season, though she also won opens at White City and Wembley. She was kept in training over the winter and in January '76 she contested the final of White City's Longcross Cup, where she ran Sallys Cobbler to within a length as he set a new 680 metre track record.

A month later, and over the City's 730 metre trip, Satin beat the country's top stayer, Glin Bridge, in both semi and final of the GRA Stakes.

Her third major final of the year was Wimbledon's Spring Cup, where she finished down the field as kennel-mate Drynham Star set a new 660 metre record.

Once again, Satin spent the summer on the sides lines, and after a six month lay-off, reappeared in the 620 metre Milton Keynes Derby. In the final Drynham Star (2-5f) again stood in her way, but Satin took her revenge with a three length

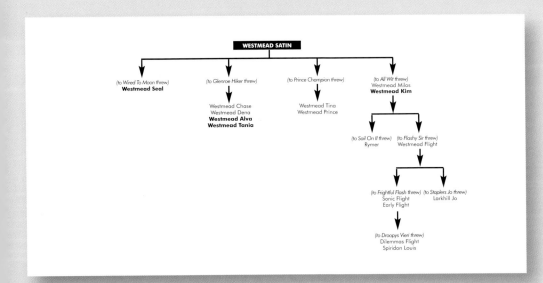

WESTMEAD SATIN

(to Wired To Moon threw)
Westmead Seal

(to Glenroe Hiker threw)

Westmead Chase
Westmead Dena
Westmead Alva
Westmead Tania

(to Prince Champion threw)

Westmead Tina
Westmead Prince

(to All Wit threw)
Westmead Milos
Westmead Kim

(to Sail On II threw)
Rymer

(to Flashy Sir threw)
Westmead Flight

(to Frightful Flash threw)
Sonic Flight
Early Flight

(to Staplers Jo threw)
Larkhill Jo

(to Droopys Vieri threw)
Dilemmas Flight
Spiridon Louis

win from Weston Oak. Star finished fourth.

A runner-up spot in her fifth final of the year, Hall Green's Winter Trophy, saw Satin complete 1976 with eight wins from a mere 22 outings.

Satin came into season in early 1977 and was mated to the former De Mulder-trained stayer Prince Champion.

The litter featured Canada Dry Marathon winner Westmead Tina and the incredibly versatile Westmead Prince.

In his first season, the black reached a couple of stayers' finals. The following year, he emulated his dam by winning the Milton Keynes Derby and also finished runner-up in Leicester's Midlands Grand Prix before, as a veteran, he embarked on a successful hurdling career.

Over the years Nick has used some poor stud dogs. But by his own admission, his choice of Wired To Moon for Satin's second litter was among his worst decisions. The former Hove open racer was a disaster at stud, yet Satin still managed to produce two fine greyhounds by him in Feb 1979.

The outstanding dog in the litter would be the 1982 Guys And Dolls winner Westmead Badger; his sister was Westmead Seal.

When Nick put Glenroe Hiker across Satin, it was another story of 'hope over expectation'. In fact, the litter of six bitches would put Hiker on the breeding map – none more so than Westmead Tania.

For her fourth litter, Satin was booked in for a mating to Sail On II. But due to a breakdown on the way to the ferry, Nick chose the lightly-used All Wit instead.

The litter would feature Westmeads Milos and Kim. Litter brother Westmead Sound did 29.00 at Wembley before breaking his hock. Another sister, Westmead Grace, finished runner-up in the Henlow Derby and made the final of the Golden Jacket at Harringay.

There was a repeat mating to Glenroe Hiker though sadly their arrival at Westmead coincided with that of parvovirus.

Westmead Satin died on 17 January 1985 – the first of the great Westmead bitches to reproduce in the breeding paddocks what she was capable of on the track.

Westmead Myra bd b

(Myrtown-Westmead Silver, Jul 74)

Very few bitches are able to compete with the top middle distance dogs. Westmead Chick did it – but Westmead Myra did it first.

The brindle gave her first glimpse of a special ability when, at 22 months old, she ran away with a Wembley open in 29.24 for 490 metres on grass. The track record was 29.12.

She was still a pup at the start of the '76 English Derby, but surprisingly scraped though to reach the final.

A 20-1 outsider, she ran well to finish third, albeit six lengths behind winner Mutts Silver.

Her career seemed set for further and she duly went on to land the 600 metre Essex Vase by just under four lengths as a short priced favourite.

There was a renewal of hostilities in the Select Stakes next time out when the slightly nervy brindle again ran third to the Derby winner.

Connections reckoned they could have given Phil Rees' dog a much closer run but for being impeded at the traps by Two PM.

The challenge was accepted by the Derby winner's connections. There would be a two-runner match over 484 metres at Southend, with each side pledging £2,000.

Mutts Silver went to traps at odds on, but was led up by Myra. The favourite hit the front at the second bend, but couldn't shake off the 6-4 chance.

Off the last bend Myra drew alongside and then pulled away for a famous three quarter length win in a new track record of 29.47 (-20).

Two nights later, she went to traps at Shawfield for the first round of the Scottish Derby and won again. By the final there were two unbeaten finalists, Myra and Flip Your Top. The latter had nine spots in hand on semi final form and duly franked it in the decider.

The pair met again in the quarter finals of the St Leger and Myra had her revenge. Unfortunately she went lame in the semis.

Following a three month lay-off she returned to win the £1,000 British Breeders Championship comfortably at White City. She finished the year with 12 wins from 29 races and fourth in the prize money table. She raced briefly into 1977, but was sold to Australia and died before she had chance to produce pups.

Nick said: "Over the years I haven't produced too many who have been so highly strung as Myra.

"She was a bit 'iffy' as a pup and had a brother Westmead Romeo. He was every bit as fast as Myra and never actually did anything wrong. He could catch any dog in the English Derby and I think he could have made the final.

"But he was giving racing manager Bob Rowe absolute kittens with the fear that he might ruin a race and so I withdrew him in the latter stages. I blame his breeding for the ungenuine trait. In my opinion there was definitely a kink in the Myross Again sire line."

The litter was whelped in January 1970 and would quickly establish Nick and Natalie among Britain's top breeders.

However there were many scrapes and twists en route.

By the time the litter was around nine months old, Nick realised that he had overstretched himself financially and he decided to sell some of them. Six of the ten saplings went.

He said: "It was all very random. We used to get people here on a Sunday to trial dogs on the schooling track and I let it be known that there were for sale for £150 each.

"I think Theo had the first pick, with the dog who turned out to be the worst in the litter. I didn't choose the four I kept, they were the last four that nobody wanted."

Then one of the quartet, the good looking light fawn dog, broke a stifle while exercising, having almost certainly been barged into a gate post by his littermates at full gallop.

The dog spent six weeks in a cast. Nick was gutted, but the pup was not written off. It would mean that he would have to be schooled after the rest.

At 12 months, Nick couldn't wait to get the litter schooled and within a month they were winning races on the flapping tracks.

Nick says: "It was madness but I didn't know any better at that time. I was lucky to have any pups left intact."

At 15 months old, they were sent to Hall Green where their qualifying trials were overseen by the bright young racing manager Bob Rowe.

They made an immediate impression and Nick gradually began to realise that, due to sheer good luck, the three littermates that he had been left with, were actually better than the six who were sold.

All three, Westmeads Lane, Silver and Pride were soon racing in puppy opens. The crocked fawn dog had begun his schooling and was going well. Nick was offered £200 for him and agreed the sale.

He recalls: "The guy was a flapper who said he would be along with the money on Sunday but he never arrived."

By this time Bletchley had switched to NGRC racing and the fawn was graded in.

Nick recalls: "He had shown some ability on my schooling track but was beaten on his first four or five races. I was annoyed that he never seemed to get a clear run and was ready to take him away.

"Then racing manager Bob Beckett said 'Give him one more graded race' which I agreed to do.

"He was downgraded a little bit and managed to lead up. Once he hit the front it was all over and he won a long way. We never looked back after that."

That fawn would become arguably the most important British bred male greyhound of the 1970s - Westmead County.

In fact, the four unsold pups all won major events. The 81 pound brindle Westmead Lane won a dozen opens in 1972 including the Cesarewitch and Test, setting a new track record for Brighton's 725 yards.

"The plodder" Westmead Pride, who was then sold on to the Mobley family, was a pure marathon specialist and won 21 opens.

That left the enigmatic Westmead Silver. As a pup, she was entered in a 645m open at Hall Green and became a very rare Westmead indeed – one with red ink in her book.

Nick says: "I remember her going to the first bend in a good position and a dog came straight across her and gave her a massive thump in the side.

"She was knocked back to last place and must have been 20 yards behind the leader. She showed fantastic pace to catch the pack. She then attacked the dog who had hit her at the first bend, before going on to win the race.

"She never did anything like it before or since and I've often wondered what was going through her mind when she fought.

"I eventually re-qualified her and she went on to win many opens. In fact, she was never beaten on the inside hare, though she was always a bit hesitant on the outside lure. It is quite possible that she was faster than County."

Indeed Silver went on to win the Christie Stayers Trophy, breaking the Leicester 700 yard track record, and she also ran second in the '72 Spring Cup at Wimbledon.

As the kennel built, Sundays became a great social event at Westmead. Nick would stage trials for owners to see the progress of their pups and they soon became mini meetings.

Jimmy Rhodes, one of Nick's connections in the rag trade and joint owner of Westmead Myra, began to fancy himself as a judge.

That developed into him becoming an unofficial bookie, taking bets on the results of individual trials.

Things went well for a few weeks until Nick decided to have a bit of fun at Jimmy's expense.

The shrewd layer suddenly looked shaky as one good thing after another was turned over in trials. In the end, exasperated, Jimmy hung up his metaphorical satchel.

TOP CLASS: Possibly the only picture of Westmead County (T2) in action, during a morning trial session at White City.

So what went wrong?

"I took one of the rubber mats out of the traps" Nick chuckles fondly. "I then gave strict instructions on which dogs should go into that particular trap knowing that Jimmy would make them favourite.

"I don't think he ever found out how he had been stitched up, but some of the other owners had a good laugh about it."

But while things were starting to come together at Westmead Kennels, the Savva family's whole world turned upside down in 1974.

News broke that Turkey had invaded Cyprus and had annexed the Northern section. Thousands of Greek Cypriots fled their homes or were thrown out by the Turkish army to become refugees in their own country. In the meantime, thousands of southern-based Turkish Cypriots headed north into the captured area and took over the homes and property of their countrymen. Most are still there.

Nick says: "To begin with, we couldn't find out any information. We eventually discovered that the Turks had rounded up all the young men, including my brother Andrew, and taken them as prisoners to Turkey.

"My parents were left behind, but were having a very bad time of it. All the windows in the house were smashed and they were threatened."

Defiant until the last, Nick's father Savvas remained in his home until eventually dying in the early 80s.

Nick's mother eventually came to Britain to

Westmead Champ

(Westmead County-Hacksaw, Apr 74)

After beginning his career in graded company at Hackney, Champ was soon on the open race scene, contesting the likes of the '76 Wood Lane Stakes (runner-up) and Pall Mall.

His first major win for trainer Pam Heasman was in the Regency at Brighton, when he beat local champion Glin Bridge in a new 670 yard track record of 39.78. (He also had a 29.08 on his card for the 500 metres- TR 29.03).

A dog of true class, within a month he was contesting the '76 English Derby Final after winning the fastest semi in 29.35, but he finished fifth behind Mutts Silver.

Back over six bends he landed the '76 St Leger. Then, just 19 days later, he won his second classic, when going unbeaten through the Gold Collar, where he smashed the 555-metre Catford track record in the second round.

The best dual distance dog of his era, he won 20 of his 35 races in 1976 and was voted joint Greyhound of the Year with Mutts Silver.

The blue fawn Champ had originally been sold for £250 to owner Steve Constanti and in his early days showed little promise in graded races.

Nick says: "I only had Champ up to the schooling stage before he joined Pam Heasman. He was beaten in his first few races at Hackney and I was very surprised and disappointed.

Nick says: "I knew he was better than his Hackney form and I said as much to Pam. I don't know what she did to turn things around, but suddenly Champ found his form and never looked back.

"I always thought Champ would be a stayer so I was surprised when he reached the Derby Final. Later on he beat me in the St Leger Final, where I had Drynham Star who finished second, beaten by half a length.

"There was also a litter brother who was bought by Freddie Warrell at the Hilton auction. He looked very good in schooling but was injured soon afterwards."

A year or so after he had left the kennel, Nick was in the racing paddock when he was spotted by Champ.

Nick said: "He was quite a shy dog, but he went beserk when he saw me, wagging his tail and pulling on his lead to get to me. It was a nice moment; I'd assumed he might have forgotten me."

Champ went to stud but was not particularly popular with breeders – his sire Westmead County was still at stud. He nevertheless threw Cesarewitch winner Linkside Liquor.

stay with her daughters. However, when she realised that she was close to dying, she asked Nick to take her back to Cyprus. She died within a fortnight of arriving.

Nick had been expecting an invasion, though he was still shocked when it occurred. He says: "The Turks had drawn up the plan to invade 10 years earlier and were looking for an excuse. Eventually, they engineered the unrest and then moved in."

Nick's brother Andrew spent the first month in prison within Cyprus and, following protests from the United Nations over prisoner conditions, another two months in a Turkish cell.

When the prisoners were eventually returned to Cyprus, they were made to report to a police station twice a day, and had to apply for a licence to travel outside the village.

The Hajisavva family were fortunate that they did not suffer directly at the hands of the Turkish invaders, though there was violence.

Andrew says: "There was no trouble from the Turkish Cypriots; the troublemakers came from mainland Turkey."

After the worst of the trouble died down, Natalie took her young daughters to visit their grandparents in Turkish controlled Rizokarpaso.

She said: "When we got to the village, we were told that we would have to be escorted by two Turkish policemen to Nick's parents' house.

"Partition was very new back then and things were quite strict. Yet when we got

Westmead Power f d

(Westmead County-Westmead Damson, Aug 75)

Westmead Power, a bit like the modern Hawk, was a dog who took a while to show his true class. He started off over four bends and made his open race debut at Henlow at 20 months old. He soon won a small final over 430 metes at Bletchley.

Overall though, he won just 10 of his 36 opens in 1977. He broke the track records at Leeds (650m), Hall Green (606m) and Ipswich (620m), but failed by a neck to reach the St Leger final. His only major victory was the Gold Collar at Catford, where he beat a field that included Black Legend and El Cavalier in 34.98.

The following year he was beaten a short head in the Ebor at Leeds, and ran third in the Gold Cup. But he was awesome in the St Leger, going unbeaten through to the final where he beat Rhu by three lengths in 39.67 for the 655 metres. He also added to his track record tally with the 600 metre clock at Romford (twice).

Following retirement, Power went to stud, though like Westmead Champ, would be in the shade of his sire.

He nevertheless threw a number of decent open racers, most notably the early-paced Oakfield Tracey and Golden Bonzo.

Nick says: "We started him off at Milton Keynes, but he was totally unsuited to the track. He went to Geoff De Mulder at Hall Green and took off, and then came back to me.

"I think he was a typical 'Westmead' in many ways with plenty of stamina and a very genuine temperament."

How genuine? On one occasion, Nick wanted to give Westmead Power a run around his track, but didn't want him to extend himself so he arranged a trial behind the trolley, but without the lure attached.

Not only did Power record a sensational time, he chased the trolley until it stopped and then attacked it.

there, instead of resenting the policemen, Nick's parents invited them into the house to eat with the family."

The Turkish invasion didn't just hit the family emotionally, they had all their land taken away. It remains within the Turkish controlled area to this day.

There was a further twist for Nick who, back in the late 1960s, had decided to invest some of the profits from his thriving dress factory on property in Famagusta.

The rapidly-growing coastal town was booming and the plan should have guaranteed a tasty nest-egg in his later years.

Unfortunately, the thriving town was just inside the border line drawn up by the Turkish government.

At the time of writing this book, Famagusta remains derelict and off limits, as do Nick's two houses, currently worth an estimated £1.5m between them.

Nick's other piece of land, a three-acre site on the shore line worth around £1m, was even closer to the border. Indeed, when we visited it during the writing of the book, Nick discovered that he had an unusual squatter – a United Nations security tower. So much for old Savvas' advice about investing in property!

In 1975 Nick decided that he had to sell his major source of income, the factory in Tottenham and commit full time to his greyounds.

He said: "The factory hadn't been making money awyway since I hadn't been able to give it my full attention.

"I have no doubt that the clothing business could have become very big, but I was never fully committed to it."

Nick also owned two dress shops, run by Natalie, one in Hemel Hempsted and one in Luton. He had supplied them with stock from his own factories, supplemented with products bought in from other manufacturers.

He said: "We kept the shops as a safeguard because I already knew that the greyhound game would never pay its way. How could it when all I could get for nine month old saplings was £150?

Looking back, Nick regrets getting out of the clothing trade when he did. He says: "I had it made really. I had learned everything I needed to know and this was before the days when the markets became flooded with cheap imported goods.

"If I had stayed in it for another five years I have no doubt that I could have become a multi-millionaire

"Although money was never my driving force, I hadn't foreseen the problems that were about to hit the greyhound industry, with widespread closures.

"Five more years would have given me the cash to buy my own dog track, which is something I would have liked to put my energies into."

By the mid-1970s, the 'Westmead' brand was firmly established in the premier league both for breeding and training. Nothing emphasised that better than the kennel's first two English Derby finalists, Westmeads Myra and Champ, who both reached the 1976 decider. (Manor would make the '77 final)

Myra ran third, but would soon be recognised as the best middle distance bitch in training. Champ kicked on to be the country's top stayer for Pam Heasman by landing the Leger/ Collar double.

PLOTTED UP: The UN watchtower in the buffer zone has its own beach cove and is precisely where Nick planned to build a luxurious holiday home. (We were stopped by a UN guard when taking this photo).

During a brilliant era, only Glin Bridge stood between the Westmeads and total domination of stayers events, with Drynham Star and Westmead Satin taking one major stake after another. The decade brought the kennel's only two TV Trophy winners, Stage Box ('74) and the giant Westown Adam ('78)

The kennel supplied its first Scurry winner in the Hugh McEntyre-trained Westmead Valley. The Mobley kennel won White City's two top stayers events, the GRA Stakes and Longcross Cup with Westmead Champ's older brother Westmead Bounty. In Ireland, Westmead Choice was proving a prolific stakes winner for Ger McKenna.

In 1978 Nick finally laid his St Leger bogey

to rest. Just six years after the gut wrenching disappointment with 'County' (see page 28), Westmead Power vindicated his sire by completing a Collar/Leger double. Although Champ had already won his Leger, this one stayed in the kennel.

Viewing the decade as a whole, if there was one single night when the kennel showed that it really could compete against the very best it was 26 March 1977.

Ladbrokes had decided to stage an entirely new event, a challenge to the top six kennels in the country – the Trainers Championship.

Interestingly, Nick found himself competing against three handlers whom he held in particular respect: George Curtis and Geoff De Mulder, whose dogs he had admired long before the days of Westmead, and Phil Rees who had trained Cricket Dance for him.

The night started well when Westmead Power, still only 21 months old, ran a gallant second to George Curtis's Get To Town. There were two Westmeads in the first stayers division. Westmead Fun managed to secure a second for her breeder, with Westmead Top, representing Geoffrey De Mulder back in fourth.

Westmead Court finished fourth in heat three, before Westmead Wonder ran a very creditable third in the sprint behind crack sprinter Foxy Copper and Derby winner Mutts Silver.

Ka Boom provided the kennel's first winner in the next stayers event, followed by a fourth for Westmead Leader in heat six.

The traps failed to open for the penultimate heat, leaving the whole competition due to be decided on the last heat – the 'top standard'.

Westmead Special was the complete outsider at 20-1, but when he edged out favourite Sean Na Gaisce for second slot, he secured enough points to see Natalie and Geoff De Mulder share the £750 first prize with 38 points each.

Although Nick was still considered primarily as a breeder, the kennel's continued success saw them take on a small number of non-Westmeads.

Among them was Ka Boom, owned by Doreen Maude (Cobbold). During 1976, the brindle had 32 opens, winning 13 including the Whitbread Trophy and the consolation final of the Golden Jacket.

She broke the 485 metre clock at Henlow, the 600 metre clock at Monmore and equalled the 620 metre record at Milton Keynes.

Nick said: "She was very fast, but not a very nice bitch in the kennel. She hated other greyhounds and she would have to travel on her own."

The Savvas and Cobbolds became good friends and would holiday together. Ka Boom returned to Decoy Farm and was to win the Dam of the Year title in 1982 and 1983, both as a result of litters by Westmead County.

Despite the kennel's success during the decade, Nick couldn't overcome an unshakable dread that the kennel would inevitably go bust.

He said: "I didn't expect us to last. Natalie was very concerned and I thought I would have to go back to the rag trade.

"It was for that reason that I didn't build new kennels. I also let some of the bitches go that I would have liked to breed with."

So what changed?

Nick said: "Most of my better dogs had always gone to Bob (Morton) because he gave me a complete free hand to do with them as I pleased. It was almost like owning them myself.

"But as a result, I didn't ask very much money for them, even the top open racers. Bob recognised what was happening and offered to give them back to me for nothing when their racing careers were over. That made a big difference.

"I also bought the stud dogs and they helped the finances just enough to keep us going."

Westmead County was particularly popular with breeders and following the success and then the death of his sire Clonalvy Pride, he even attracted 16 bitches from Ireland.

One of the Irish bitches arrived at the kennel in very poor condition. She also had an internal infection. There was no way that Nick was going to allow County to cover her.

Nick says: "I was in a very difficult position. Her owner was one of Ireland's top breeders; how could I possibly tell him that I thought his bitch wasn't fit to be mated?

"In the end I decided that I would put her on antibiotics and get her cleared up. I then told her owner that it had been a bad mating and not to bother to pay the stud fee. He could pay me if she produced a litter, but I wasn't hopeful.

"I thought no more about it until about three months later when a cheque for the stud fee arrived. The bitch had whelped a litter and the breeder wanted to register them. "I can only leave you to draw your own conclusions as to what happened"

Westmead could not have thrived without owners – and not just to pay kennel bills. From the very earliest days, the kennel has been supported by greyhound lovers who have pitched in to do everything, from walking dogs to taking them open racing, and all jobs in between.

Nick says: "Derek Jones was one of my earliest owners. He was a builder who lived in London and he bought Delroney Leader from me as a pup.

"He would leave home early every morning and come and help me walk the dogs before he went to work.

"The NGRC allowed him a licence, even though it was against the rules because he was an owner in the kennel, and Derek

paraded many dogs for me.

"He had such a determined nature that I am sure it transmitted itself down the lead. He expected to win every time and in many cases we won races that I didn't expect to win.

"Derek really embraced everything that I felt for greyhounds. He was passionate about the game and a genuine enthusiast."

David Sharp, the owner of Westmead Bound, also became another very close friend. He lived locally and spent a great deal of time helping out, whether it was schooling, walking dogs or taking them racing.

"Like Derek, he had tremendous enthusiasm for the game and the dogs really responded to him."

And very often, the helpers find themselves dragged into some of the dramas that accompany handling livestock.

Nick says: "I remember one day Derek Jones came into the yard with four dogs including Stage Box. At that time we had a couple of cats who we had inherited from builders who had been working on the kennel.

"That particular morning the male cat ran into the yard and within reach of the four dogs. The first I knew was Derek screaming his head off as the dogs attacked the poor cat.

"Suddenly, the cat's sister came running from the nearby garage and attacked the four greyhounds. She was so brave that she distracted the dogs long enough for her brother and herself to escape. I couldn't believe my eyes. She showed the sort of qualities of selflessness that only special humans are supposed to exhibit."

MADE IT: Proof that the Savvas could train with the best of them came in the first ever trainers'
championship. The result was a dead heat with long-time friend Geoffrey De Mulder.

"I took the male cat to the vets who did his best but did the kindest thing and put him to sleep. The female learned to stay out of the way of the dogs and lived with us until she eventually died of old age."

Kennel stalwarts Paddy Dunne, David Sharp, Derek Jones and the longest serving supporter of them all, Bob Lowth, all shared Nick's ideals.

Bob was a welder by trade, but also a keen dog man who raced a number of hounds with the 'Alsucaan' prefix (the two letters from the first names of his four children) at Milton Keynes.

He first arrived at Westmead in 1985 with a pup to be schooled and has been a twice weekly visitor (Wednesdays and Sundays) ever since.

He said: "I would help school pups, let the racing dogs out during the evening, walk dogs, you name it.

"I also helped out on track maintenance, helped with the track fencing, whatever needed doing really.

"Sometimes Nick would ask me to take a dog home if he wanted it kept in isolation, or I'd have the occasional racing dog for him.

"No money has ever changed hands, its not that sort of relationship. Anything I ever wanted, Nick would give me, he is incredibly generous."

There was just one very small downside to the relationship as Bob explains with a smile. . .

"Everybody at Milton Keynes knew about my friendship with Nick and whenever I had a winner, I'd hear, 'that looks like another one that's come out of Westmead.' I never got the credit of having a winner!"

Nick says: "In many ways Paddy, David, Derek and Bob were so similar to me. They were non-gamblers who sought no reward and just took great joy in being involved with these wonderful animals.

"Sadly we lost Paddy several years ago, but David and Derek grew disillusioned with the game because of the way owners are treated by the tracks and the NGRC. I feel privileged to have known them. There must be thousands like them, also lost to the game."

During the 1979 Derby Nick received a desperate phone call from a Northern Irish

STALWART: Bob Lowth, an invaluable member of the Westmead team for more than 25 years.

trainer in a severe jam.

It came from a man widely acknowledged from his successes on Irish tracks and coursing fields, a fine sportsman who would become a close personal friend – Colm McGrath.

Nick recalls: "Colm arrived in England with four dogs for the Derby and was due to stay at a kennel near Dunstable. When he arrived he wasn't happy with the facilities and phoned Paddy McEvoy in a panic. Paddy suggested that I might be able to help.

"I told him that I didn't have any room but I would make some by transferring some young dogs from the kennels back into a paddock so he could stay overnight. By the time he arrived it was 10 o'clock in the evening.

"The next morning he had a look around the place and was so keen to stay that he offered me half the prize money if any of his dogs won the Derby. I couldn't accept that of course, but we managed to find room for him and we became firm friends.

"In the following years, Colm became a frequent visitor and we had a lot of good times.

"I recall one year he wanted to back his dog ante post and he brought over a suitcase stuffed with £100 Northern Irish bank notes. The dog was was 66-1 and Colm wanted about £20,000 on him.

"Three of us set off the next day to place the bets on, but it was a farce. Nobody knew what a Northern Irish £100 note looked like and the bookies laughed at us; we might as well have tried to bet with Monopoly money. In total we got around £1,000 on the dog between the three of us.

"The head line in the Sporting Life the next day was 'COUP!' I don't think the dog survived the first round.

Colm continued to be involved in the kennel including buying two young open

BOND: Colm McGrath remains one of Nick's most trusted friends.

race littermates, Westmeads Kim and Milos."

Conversely, when his young sire Glenroe Hiker – one of the original quartet given overnight refuge at Westmead - was failing to attract the number of bitches that his owner thought he deserved, Colm gave the dog as a gift to Nick.

That inspired move would have a major effect on both the kennel and British breeding during the next decade.

At the time of writing, the two old friends remain in close contact.

Chapter 4

WINNING TIMES

For nine years, the Westmead runners had been trained privately or attached to either Bletchey or Coventry, but in late 1978, Nick was offered the chance of a first training contract.

Suddenly 'Savva – Wembley' started to appear on racecards. But it would prove a short term relationship.

By late1980, Nick had decided to give up his deal at the Empire Stadium to concentrate on breeding.

Nick said: "I ruined two good litters at Wembley. The track was just on the point of transferring over from grass to sand and basically they were racing on pure mud.

"The other problem was that my pups were badly outgraded. I got so fed up that I asked General Manager Peter Shotton for the reason. He replied, 'its because you have a schooling track, it gives you a big advantage.'

"I realised that I was wasting my time and left soon afterwards. It was not a good experience."

But the Westmead pups were about to be hit by something far more dangerous than muddy racing surfaces.

By the early 1980s, a new disease, parvovirus, was striking down litters on either side of the Irish Sea.

Westmead was spared until the Feb '83 litter by Glenroe Hiker out of Westmead Satin. A month later Westmead Seal produced a similarly blighted litter by Special Account.

By the time the pups were two months old, the lounge of Nick and Natalie's home resembled an animal hospital.

Nick said: "Parvo arrived with us quite late. We had tried to prepare for it and our vet recommended that we get the dam inoculated with the cat parvo inoculation, since the dog one still wasn't on the market.

"He inoculated one bitch while she was in whelp, but the entire litter died a few days after they were born.

"When we did finally get parvo in the Satin and Seal litters, it didn't strike until after the pups had finished getting milk from their mothers.

"Then virtually overnight they dropped like flies. We had them all on saline drips."

Typically, Parvo killed entire litters, or ravaged any survivors so badly that they didn't make the track.

As a testament to Nick and Natalie's hard work, they didn't lose a pup and several went on to contest open races.

Nick didn't breed any more litters at Westmead for the next two years. His only litter, by Ks Prince out of Westmead Alva, was whelped down by Mel Bass.

"Basically, we were just waiting for a vaccine to be developed" he recalls.

The early 1980s also saw a big rise in puppy thefts. Prior to the introduction of earmarking in the UK, pups were virtually untraceable.

Some of the thefts were eventually traced back to travellers and, given the proximity of several camps in the area, Nick attempted to prevent theft by training an Alsatian guard dog to run with the pups.

He said: "We knew that thieves would attempt to get the guard dog out of the way by killing him, probably by poisoning, so we trained him not to take food from anyone but us.

"Unfortunately, they threw in poisoned meat and two saplings ate it and died.

A second incident took place in June 1981, when two seven month old litter brothers were taken from the paddocks.

Nick said: "I knew a gypsy quite well and he tipped me off that I would find them on a travellers' camp near Cambridge.

"We found them on the camp, but one of the travellers claimed that he had bought them from another for £60. There was nothing we could do to prove it and I bought them back for £100."

The two Westmead County pups, County Border and County Final both went on to win minor opens.

Incident three took place after Nick returned home from Wembley on a wet and windy night.

He said: "We arrived home to see pups running everywhere and we discovered that two were missing. I was furious and I went down to the local travellers' camp armed with a shotgun.

"I shouted out that they had better let the pups go or they were in for big trouble and I fired a couple of cartridges into the air. The next morning the pups were found running loose near the travellers' site."

Unfortunately, although the thefts slowed up, they weren't eradicated by earmarking.

The next incident took place in 2004. The main gate to the kennel was damaged and a thief drove in on a horse-drawn buggy. He burgled Andy Ioannou's caravan stealing a phone and some money.

He also took off with two pups from the Larkhill Jo and Mega Delight litter (Westmead Billy and Westmead Joy).

Nick says: "Fortunately, we spotted the horse and buggy driving away. We went to a travellers' site and spotted the horse. We went back with a policeman and found the pups.

"They had tried to paint their ears, but thankfully we recovered them."

Two litters later and thieves were back again. This time they stole a sickly blue bitch from the second Droopys Kewell/Mega Delight litter.

Nick said: "They must have realised that she was ill and phoned up to say that they had bought her in innocence and did I want her back.

"I told them that she would probably die anyway and that I was sending the RSPCA around to prosecute them. The whole thing got a bit messy and in the end I think I paid £30 to get her back."

Unsurprisingly, Nick remains wary. Despite improved fencing and installing surveillance cameras, he knows that he could be targeted again.

He said: "I have the best guard dog I have ever had, but after all this time I am always on my guard."

Although Nick loved his time on the flapping traps, he never went back, with one exception.

The scene was Doncaster flapping track in the early 1980s. There was a plunge on one of the runners. The field drifted. Then there was a rush of money for another who was cut to odds-on. The first dog started to drift and connections went in hard again. The second crowd lumped on again.

Punters and bookies realised that his was going to be a serious buckle as both sets of connections then started to hesitate. Who on earth were they taking on?

As is the way on the flaps, they started to check each other out. Who was putting the money on? Who was the 'jockey' who had brought the dog in? Who was trying to hide in the shadows?

"Oh, no" realised one set of connections, "we are taking on Geoffrey De Mulder". Geoffrey's connections also twigged, they would be taking on another leading open race kennel (who still have a licence – hence the anonymity) with one of the top stayers on the NGRC circuit.

The traps opened and the two hotpots bombed away. They cleared the first two bends neck and neck, and crossed the winning line with a circuit to go.

But as they approached the next two bends a big fawn moved up into their slipstream. Going into the backstraight he eased between them and – BANG – he'd gone.

There was no official winning distance, though it would have been well into double figure lengths.

The two sets of connections returned to the carpark to see who took control of the dog. As the figure of 'Big Phil' Bradley emerged, the penny dropped. 'It was a f****** Westmead!'

He said: "It wasn't because it was against the rules. But from the day we took out a licence, I just enjoyed seeing my dogs' names on the racecards and in the newspapers. I was so proud of them, I would have raced for no prize money.

"Doncaster was merely a rehabilitation outing after Special Account had broken his hock. He had been off the track for six months and I wanted to know what condition he was in.

"He had gone okay at home, but basically I wanted a 'private trial'. If the hock hadn't healed properly and he was a shadow of the dog he had been previously, it isn't how I would have wanted him to be remembered; he would have been quietly retired.

"Geoffrey saw me after the race. He'd had a dog called Golden Sand in the race. He said: 'which one was that?'. I told him that he knew all the dogs in my kennel, so who did he think it was?

"He concluded that it must have been Special Account's brother Westmead Gem. I didn't have the heart to tell him that Gem was running at Slough on the same night."

Although the Doncaster outing proved a great gauge for a 640 metre Walthamstow open that Special Account won immediately afterwards, Nick's original caution proved well placed. He broke down again soon afterwards and was retired.

MYSTERY: 'Big Phil' Bradley with the fawn machine that was Special Account.

Special Account f d

(Westmead County-Ka Boom, Jan 80)

Special Account was actually bred by Doreen Cobbold, but his conception, whelping and rearing all took place at Westmead Kennels.

The litter was split, with Joe Cobbold taking away the future 'Decoys' Ranch, Ranger, Diane, Doreen and Dallas. Nick was left with two dogs and two bitches, which included future St Leger third Westmead Ruby and Test winner Westmead Gem.

The litter were 10 months old when Theo persuaded Nick to sell him the athletic-looking fawn dog.

Nick said: "I didn't really want to sell, but I said to Theo, 'you can have him for £1,000, but if you ever decide to sell on, you must give me first option.'"

After qualifying in fast trials, 'Rikasso Special' made his debut for Theo in a puppy open at Cambridge in July 1981. He was beaten, and Theo let Nick know that despite his fast trial times, he was disappointed with his purchase.

Nick said: "I saw the dog at kennelling and he obviously hadn't settled at all well with Theo. He looked depressed and disinterested, not the dog I knew at all. When Theo said he was looking for £2,000 for him, I nearly snapped his hand off."

'Special' rejoined his rearer and instantly began to look a shrewd purchase, winning heats and final of a Cambridge puppy competition by a combined 10 lengths.

Nick said with a smile: "Theo went ballistic- there wasn't a name that he didn't call me!"

The fawn was still only 20 months old when he won a Harringay 475 metre puppy open by 14 lengths in 28.57. It would be his final race under his old name.

By now Nick was convinced that he had a potential superstar and Bob Morton asked to buy him. Nick agreed and at £5,000, Special Account remains, to this day, the most expensive greyhound ever sold at Westmead.

The re-named Account clocked 27.58 (TR 27.45) in the opening round of the Wimbledon Puppy Derby, but found trouble and did well to qualify from the semis.

He came good in the final, though, with a 27.79 length and three quarter win over crack pups Gigolo Diomedes and Kilacca.

The Savva hound rounded off the year by running second to Diomedes in the Anglo-Irish at Shelbourne Park (Duke Of Hazzard was third) as the British breds completed a white-wash.

It was March before Special opened his 1982 account. Contesting his first race of the year, he set a new Cambridge 400 metre track record of 25.53 – 18 spots inside the previous best.

He went straight into the Pall Mall and although only winning one qualifier, he started favourite to win the final. But after being 'impeded run-up & half way' he finished second to 28.58 winner Sugarville Jet.

Four indifferent lines of form followed, but Account showed he was returning to form with a 28.41 win at Harringay (TR 28.37) in a trial stake for the English Derby.

The main event didn't go well for Account in the early stages, but by the semis he found his form and clocked 29.30 for White City's 500 metres, some 25 spots quicker than the other semi winner Lauries Panther.

However, a bad draw on the outside of the wide running Killimy Ivy (T2) saw Panther installed as 6-4f with Account available at 7-2.

The race went as expected. Panther secured a clear run on the rail, Killimy Ivy ran across the field badly baulking Special Account as Supreme Tiger led up.

The Savva runner was fully six adrift of Tiger and Panther by the time he re-found his balance and set off in pursuit. He dragged the margin back to three quarters of length, but failed to catch Panther, who got home in 29.60.

His next outing was the Select where he ran third,

beaten half a length by Brief Candle and litter brother Decoy Ranch, but bounced back to set a new 500 metre track record at Perry Barr.

Next up was a Scottish Derby. Oozing class, Account won his opener in 30.20, set a new Shawfield 500 metre track record in the semis (30.01) and then led home a field that included Duke Of Hazzard, Long Spell and Cooladine Jet to set another record of 29.99 in the final.

He completed the year by finishing second in the Anglo-Irish and third in the Edinburgh Cup.

Nick says: "I would put him in the same top three category as Phantom Flash. He had tremendous pace and was hugely impressive when he won the Scottish Derby.

"I suppose though that the race of his life was in the English Derby Final. Of course he lost his chance at the first bend, but was absolutely outstanding to finish second.

"In terms of his most enjoyable race, the 1982 Scottish Derby victory was memorable. After the race, the crowd gave us a standing ovation. It was better atmosphere than the English Derby and very moving."

Fearless Champ was easily the classiest of Account's offspring. Others included Able Sam (Produce Stakes) and the Pall Mall winner Forest Fawn, who was subsequently disqualified for fighting.

Able Sam's victory saw a clean sweep in the Produce Final for the kennel – all six runners were by Westmead sires, two by Special Account, two by Glenroe Hiker and two by Westmead Milos.

Many Account offspring, including some bred at Westmead, were not totally focused.

Nick says: "I was disappointed that he didn't produce as a sire, but I wasn't totally surprised. He was so much more like his dam, Ka Boom, than his sire, Westmead County.

"I always felt that he had inherited more of her genes. There was a question mark over Ka Boom's sire line which I think came out in Special Account's pups."

Westmead Seal

bk b (Wired To Moon-Westmead Satin, Feb 79)

Westmead Seal was a very lightly raced bitch who much preferred the inside lure. She won heats and final of the Buckinghamshire Cup at Slough, beating kennel-mate Westmead Betty in the 593 decider.

She also won opens at Derby and reached the final of the Midland Oaks.

Nick recalls: "Seal ran too wide on the McKee hare, but ran middle to the inside hare. She wasn't lacking pace."

Her first litter, by Special Account, were struck down by parvovirus, but Westmead Account went on to break the Oxford 250 metre track record as well as making the finals of the Scurry Gold Cup and Silver Collar.

Nick says, "She went to Colm McGrath for a couple of litters (Glenroe Blue and Cooladine Super), but they picked up parvovirus. In the end I gave her to Reading trainer Vera Green."

Seal produced four dogs and five bitches by Glenroe Hiker. Significantly, the only ones who made it, were the pups that had returned to

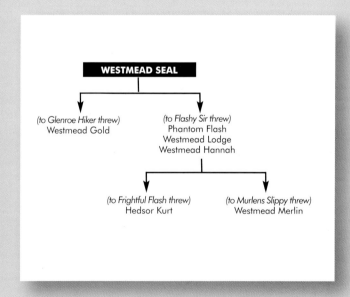

WESTMEAD SEAL

(to Glenroe Hiker threw)
Westmead Gold

(to Flashy Sir threw)
Phantom Flash
Westmead Lodge
Westmead Hannah

(to Frightful Flash threw)
Hedsor Kurt

(to Murlens Slippy threw)
Westmead Merlin

Westmead Kennels for rearing.

Westmead Gold won the Cosmic Sailor Puppy Stakes in 28.96 at Walthamstow and was beaten 1-2 favourite in the 1997 Produce Stakes Final. Litter brother Change was runner-up to Able Sam in the same final. Gold also reached the Eclipse and Arc Finals.

Seal then produced a litter to Fearless Champ. The only one to make it was Westmead Roman who won the Cambridgeshire Cup and finished third in the Arc.

Nick said: "One day Vera said she was packing up and asked if I wanted Seal back. She was nine and a half.

"I put Flashy Sir across her and because of her age she only had small litters. The first included Westmead Lodge who went unbeaten to the semi finals of the Derby.

"We decided to go for a repeat mating and from that litter we got Phantom Flash and Westmead Chloe. I always wondered what she might have thrown had I got her back sooner."

In fact, the line did continue via Lodge's sister, Westmead Hannah, who threw Westmead Merlin and Produce Stakes winner Hedsor Kurt.

Seal was finally put to sleep aged 11 in October 1990 in deteriorating health brought on by a severe mouth ulcer.

Westmead Alva

f b (Glenroe Hiker-Westmead Satin, Apr 81)

Compared to sister Tania, Westmead Alva's introduction to racing was comparatively quiet, with her first two outings in opens at Cambridge and Milton Keynes, both of which she won.

But her low profile wouldn't last long. On Oaks final night, the 18 month old won a Harringay 475 metre supporting open in 28.60. The Oaks final was won by Duchess Of Avon in 28.72 and a £1,000 Select Invitation was won by the £50,000 purchase Long Spell in 28.55.

It was then off to Wimbledon and the light fawn was the fastest of the three semis final winners in the 1982 Puppy Oaks. Alva started as 7-4 favourite for the final but finished fourth behind Contact Breaker.

After a winter break, Alva made her reappearance in the Pall Mall and only missed out on a place in the final in a photo finish.

Next up was the 1983 English Derby at White City. In the qualifying round she beat a young open racer called Whisper Wishes by five lengths in a fast 29.88. Alva survived another round but was then eliminated.

Her next appearance was at

Harringay on the night before the 1983 Derby Final. This time she beat Whisper Wishes by nearly four lengths in a new Harringay 475m track record of 28.34. She was retired soon afterwards with a hind muscle injury.

Alva's first litter were by the American sire Ks Prince and included a talented marathon performer in Westmead Helen.

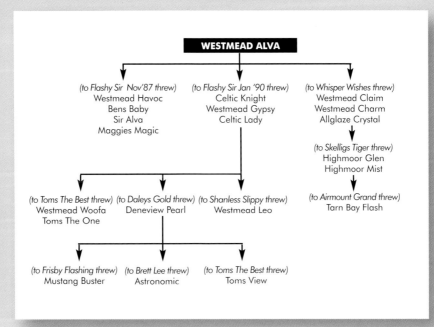

The second litter were also by a sire who would fail to make it at stud – Matthews World, although it did feature Wembley Gold Trophy winner Olivers World.

Alva's third litter was the first by a successful stud dog – old rival Whisper Wishes. The star of the litter was Westmead Claim. With more ability than luck, the early paced white dog was second (1-2f) in the 1988 Produce Stakes Final and was also runner-up in the Anglo-Irish. Four of the litter won opens. Allglaze Crystal eventually made the biggest impression at stud through her grandsons Highmoor Valley, Highmoor Glen (Ebor) and Tarn Bay Flash ('97 Grand National).

Alva's fourth litter, by Flashy Sir, proved to be her best. The two biggest stars were Bens Baby and Westmead Havoc, who finished 1-2 in the away leg of the 1989 Anglo-Irish.

Havoc also finished third in the Wimbledon leg and, like half brother Claim, was beaten favourite in the Produce Stakes.

Brother Maggies Magic won a £1,500 stake at Hove, and another four members of the litter also won opens.

Alva was duly voted the 1989 Dam of the Year.

Alva's fifth litter, by Fearless Champ did little on the track. The sixth litter was a repeat to Flashy Sir.

Blessed with a little more stamina than the first litter, the most successful on the track was Westmead Gypsy (Boxing Day Marathon, RU Greenwich Cup).

Although another three members of the litter won opens, it would be Celtic Lady who would prove the most significant.

When mated to Shanless Slippy she produced Westmead Leo (Greenwich Cup), while to Toms The Best she threw Westmead Woofa (Puppy Classic) and Toms The One (Derby Plate, RU Pall Mall).

From her mating to Daleys Gold, Lady threw Deneview Pearl, dam of Toms View, Astronomic and Mustang Buster.

Alva's final litter to Greenpark Fox were probably her worst, a bunch of massively built, but otherwise untalented, graders.

Westmead Tania

bd b (Glenroe Hiker-Westmead Satin, Apr 81)

Knowing the depth at which you can start a youngster takes good judgement and a degree of bravery.

But it was something of a surprise when Nick entered the 18 month old novice Westmead Tania in the 1982 English Oaks at Harringay.

Tania had been beaten in her first three opens but had trialled well. Nevertheless, her 28.49 run in the first round was a stunner. She was quicker than the eventual winner of the stake, Duchess Of Avon (28.54), and the recent Irish Oaks winner Quick Suzy (28.77). In fact, Tania's time was only 12 spots outside the Harringay 475 metre track record.

She won her second round heat in 28.71, but went out in the semi finals and was put away for the winter.

The brindle made her reappearance in the first round of the Pall Mall and finished a creditable second.

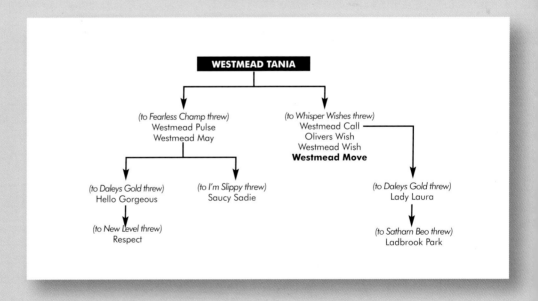

In the second round she collided with another runner at the first bend. He was KO'd and she was eliminated. It would be Tania's last race as a pup.

Her first as an adult was in the heats of the Midland Oaks, which she won in the fastest time of the night.

The 7-4 favourite for the final, the brindle was well placed when she became the first of a long line of fast Westmeads to break a hock at Hall Green. She never raced again.

It was 18 months later that Tania produced her brilliant litter to Whisper Wishes (see Westmead Move). Her second litter by Special Account were very disappointing, though the third, by his son Fearless Champ was better.

The star was the 1988 St Leger runner-up Westmead Pulse. Olivers Question and Westmead Dream won opens while another sister, Westmead May, threw Saucy Sadie (Northumberland Gold Cup).

Litter number four were the 'TV litter', while the

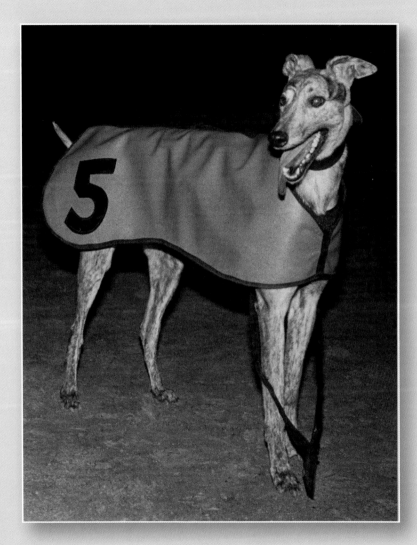

fifth and final litter was a repeat mating whelped so tragically some 14 months later (see page 78).

Most were minor open racers though one of the bitches, Westmead Kara, went on to throw Stones Silver Collar winner Touch Again.

GLENROE HIKER: An act of kindness led to an important friendship and a huge bonus for British breeding.

Glenroe Hiker was a failed stud dog when he arrived at Westmead in the autumn of 1980.

Now four and a half, he had made his name three years earlier when winning the Dunmore Puppy Cup. In 1978, he showed brilliant early pace in the English Derby and was second favourite to Lacca Champion when fifth in the final.

But there had been nothing of note produced in his first year at stud in Ireland. After around a dozen and a half bitches, the phone had stopped ringing.

But Nick saw something in the dog that he liked – and as soon as Colm McGrath realised that fact he gave him Hiker as a gift.

Among the 11 bitches covered by Hiker in his first year in England was Westmead Satin. The haul also included brother Theo's bitch, Lady Myrtown.

Two years on and Nick realised he had stumbled on something special. The Satin litter featured Westmead Dena (GRA Stakes) and Westmead Chase (Autumn Cup), plus the most important litter sisters ever bred at the kennel, Westmeads Alva and Tania.

Theo struck gold too. Rikasso Mick, won the British Breeders Stakes, and the Midland Grand Prix as well as breaking track records at Milton Keynes and Leicester.

Brother Rikasso Hiker won the Circuit and Midland Flat, setting a new 474m clock at Hall Green.

Hiker took off and the winners came from unexpected sources. Owner Mel Bass, put Westmead Rhythm to Hiker and asked Nick to train the best two dogs from the litter.

MODEL MUM: Westmead Tania was a wonderful caring mum who passed on those qualities to her daughters.

Westmead Cannon, who Nick also reared, won the 1986 Produce Stakes, the Breeders Forum Stakes and the Peterborough Cesarewitch.

His brother Cannonroe won the Oxfordshire Stakes.

Mistley Trojan was also a prolific winner for the kennel. By Hiker out of a daughter of Westmead Silver, she won the Classic Select at Harringay and the Wimbledon leg of the Anglo-Irish.

By the mid-1980s, Glenroe Hiker had established himself as the No.1 sire in Britain. He was put to sleep following a short illness in March 1987, having made a significant contribution to the bloodlines, and finances, at Westmead.

'Big Phil' Bradley spent eight and a half years at Westmead in two spells. The first began in the early 1980s and lasted six years and a half years.

He says: "When I first arrived there were only about 20 dogs and I thought it would be easy, but I soon learned that Nick was very demanding.

"I worked six days a week and they were long days, from half six in a morning, and often it would be 2am before you got to bed if you had been open racing.

Westmead Move

bk b (Whisper Wishes-Westmead Tania Nov 84)

Move began her racing career in a Reading puppy open on May 1 2006. Despite being beaten in her first few races, the 19 month old pup was made favourite and easily won the Upton Rocket Stakes in 28.69 for the Stow's 475 metre – just 15 spots outside the track record.

Despite her age, Move was tested over the 'short' six bends at Catford, and had been laid to lose £28,000 in ante post bets when she lined up for the final of the 1986 Gold Collar.

She had failed to win a round, but had shown improvement in every one. Backed from 4-1 to 11-4 on the night, the 22-month-old pup was in second place with a circuit to run, behind Essex Vase winner Rosehip Trish.

But showing great speed around the last two bend Move went on to win by two and a half lengths in the fastest Gold Collar decider ever, 34.80 for the 555 metres.

It was then on to Walthamstow and the Grand Prix. She was beaten once during the qualifiers but started at 10-11f for the £5,000 final.

Clear at the first turn, the pup went on to win by more than five lengths in 39.35 – five spots inside Ballyregan Bob's track record.

She also ran both legs of the Anglo-Irish, finishing second and fourth.

In 1987 she easily won the Midland Oaks and Brighton Belle (29.79) and finished runner-up in the Select Stakes, then produced her first litter later in the year.

At four years old Move returned to the track and won the Midland Oaks, the Stewards Cup at Walthamstow and a semi final of the English Oaks.

Move's first litter, by Fearless Champ, were 11 months old when she retired for the second and final time.

The star would be Westmead Harry though there were five open race winners in the litter.

Westmead Cruise won two £1,000 stakes - beating Chicita Banana in one. Westmead Flow and Mistley Supreme both reached the Produce Stakes final.

Of the bitches, Westmead Wendy finished runner-up in the Brighton Belle. Litter sister Westmead Fairy went on to throw stud dogs Mustang Jack, Shoot To Freedom and the useful American brood Articled Clerk.

Move's next litter, Nick's least favourite, were by Tico. The hyperactive dog and ten bitches included five minor open racers with the dog Phantom Move (29.44 490m - Wembley) the best of them.

Interestingly, a couple of the bitches later appeared on the dam lines of some decent open racers: Westmead Glow (Glue Vixen, Skywalker Ace, Elderberry Vixen) and Westmead Athena (Colourful Champ, Castleboro Katie, Pinewood Blue).

Litter number three were the 'feisty' January '90 lot by Daleys Gold, and arguably the best of all Move's litters.

Eight months after her Daleys litter, Move threw seven dogs and two bitches by his son Airmount Grand.

Once again there were category one winners among them and none better than Westmead Darkie. He won the 1992 Grand Prix and finished third in the same year's St Leger.

Like the Daleys litter, there was great variety among the pups, including the early paced Next Move who won the Henlow Derby and was runner-up in the Produce Stakes.

Litter brother 'Mount' won the Test and the game Westmead Paddy won 31 opens from 440-685 metres.

Litter number five featured four pups by I'm Slippy. They had problems in rearing and only one, Westmead Vicky, made minor open class.

Whether Nick would have used I'm Slippy again had he known how they would turn out is debatable, but they were only eight months old when Move produced a repeat mating of five pups.

The star was of course the great Westmead Chick. Also in the litter was Westmead Hazzard, a big handsome brindle who was injured early in his career and eventually went to stud in the USA, though he wasn't a great success.

One interesting member of the litter was Westmead Odd, who as his name implies was a

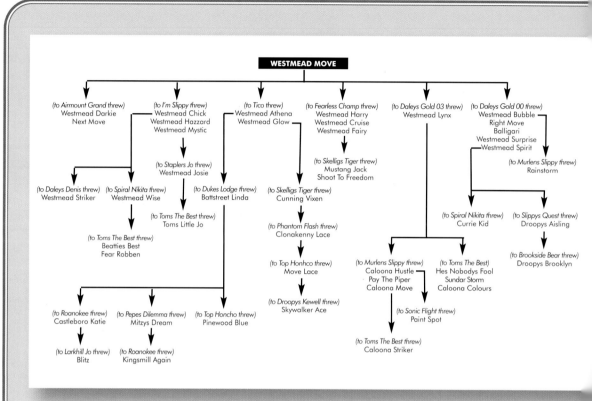

Move Litters

By	Pups in litter	Open winners	Opens
Fearless Champ	8	5	38
Tico	11	4	12
Daleys Gold 1/90	11	10	109
Airmount Grand	9	6	58
I'm Slippy 5/91	4	1	1
I'm Slippy 1/92	5	4	47
Daleys Gold 3/93	7	1	1
Murlens Slippy	7	2	9

strange looking sort. While a big strapping specimen, facially he was as undershot as a Bulldog. He nevertheless went on to win numerous opens, specialising in the Stow's 415 metre trip.

On the track, sister Westmead Mystic was always in Chick's shadow, despite winning a dozen opens including the final of Sheffield's Autumn Puppy Cup. She also reached the finals of the Oaks, Puppy Oaks and Gold Collar.

Mystic only produced one litter before dying prematurely, but it included Westmead Josie, dam of Gold Collar/Sussex Cup winner Toms Little Jo.

Litter number seven was a repeat mating to Daleys Gold and resulted in seven bitch pups.

The best turned out to be the Attwater family's Westmead Lynx, who went on to throw the 2000 Produce Stakes winner He's Nobodys Fool and Golden Jacket winner Sundar Storm.

Two of the bitches went to the USA where they threw some decent grade winners.

Move's final litter were by Murlens Slippy, and fittingly, had the most stamina, with Westmeads Amour and Spur both marathon performers.

Another sister, 'Flirt' was also exported to the USA and threw a string of AA and stake winners.

Westmead Move was put to sleep in February 1996 following a losing battle with cancer of the shoulder.

Twice voted Dam of the Year, she threw 275 open race winners and was the leading dam of the 1990s.

Nick says: "The best bitch that I ever bred. She was so consistent, a tremendous tracker and in my opinion, only ever ran one bad race.

"We received an invitation to run against Ballyregan Bob but I declined it because I honestly thought that we would beat him and I wasn't prepared to do that.

"I often thought that she was retired too early, which is why we brought her back to run in the Oaks."

"Nick would also have me running around like he thought I was some sort of athlete. When we were schooling I'd have to put the dogs in the traps, and then run over to the pick-up before the dogs got there. If I didn't get there in time, he'd go absolutely potty.

"But it was interesting and we had some great dogs, starting with Special Account, going on to Westmead Move; it was a golden era for the kennel.

"I once worked out that during my two spells working with Nick that we won nine classics, including Tralee Crazy's win in the St Leger.

"I'm claiming that one for myself because Nick was away in Australia at the time.

"More than anything, I loved being around the pups and would play with them. Nick used to give me regular bollockings. He'd say, 'stop playing with them, they are not pets!'.

"So I would leave it until he went to London in the afternoons and would sit in the paddocks with the pups. I loved it."

An experienced kennelman who also worked for Adam Jackson at White City and champion trainer Linda Mullins, Phil remembers being instantly impressed by Nick's knowledge and thoroughness.

He says: "I soon realised that he was very capable for things like first aid and injuries. He would put stitches in wounds and knew how to use all the veterinary equipment.

"What did surprise me was that he didn't use any of the muscle men. If any of the dogs had muscle problems, he would just lay them off for a while.

"I suppose the one thing above all others that I will remember about Nick as a trainer was that he was an absolute perfectionist in everything he did."

Flashy Sir

w bk d (Sand Man-Cherry Express, Sep 84)

The Flashy Sir story is simply amazing. His mother died when he was born, leaving 'Flashy' and one surviving litter brother to be nursed by a foster mother.

One morning breeder John Fitzpatrick went into the kennel to find both pups missing. After a lengthy search the pair were presumed dead, but three days later, crying and starving, they were found behind some fencing. A frantic search was made for a replacement mother, but the only suitable candidate was infested with mange.

Sure enough, the two adopted pups both developed the disease and lost all their fur. But despite it all, they survived.

Flashy – named after the great American dog who gives his name to the award for the country's top stayer – had a fairly indifferent start to his race career.

He had raced 15 times when Nick Savva arrived looking for a mating to Sand Man (see page 75).

He had five wins on his card including a 29.31 at Newbridge and a 29.64 at Harolds Cross. He was a decent minor open racer, but there was certainly no clue as to what he would eventually become.

Flashy stayed with his breeder and reached the 1987 Easter Cup semis before making the journey to Edelsborough.

Flashy then reached the Derby semi finals, but Nick had already determined that he struggled to recover quickly from races.

He started favourite for the consolation, but was involved in a no-race, where the dogs ran a complete circuit without a hare, and was unsurprisingly beaten into third in the re-run.

But he bounced back to win the Circuit, finish runner-up in the Midland Flat and land one of the kennel's biggest gambles in the Laurels, where he clocked 27.52.

Flashy ran one of his last races on the night his TV litter made their debut at Milton Keynes. He won a supporting open.

But it was at stud where he made such a massive contribution to the Westmead story.

Flashy would sire a string of quality Westmeads including Bens Baby, Westmead Havoc, Westmead Lodge and Phantom Flash.

Without Flashy there would have been no Westmead Flight, and hence no Sonic Flight or Larkhill Jo.

But there were others too, including Pearls Girl (Oaks/Gold Collar), Galleydown Boy (St Leger) and Sir Grand (Cox Cup). Flashy reached No.8 on the UK sires chart; a great feat for a purely British-based stud dog.

Nick says: "Flashy was 100 per cent genuine in his desire to chase and that came through in his pups. He was an outstanding stud dog for the kennel."

Phil has fond memories of his time at Westmead, a sentiment reciprocated by the family.

Daughter Nicola, still refers to the former kennelman as 'Uncle Phil' and recalls the times that she, sister Lisa, and Phil would barbecue bananas.

Phil says: "They were great kids. It is a shame that they had no real interest in the dogs. Nick tried to get them to help out, but they were more interested in painting their nails and wearing make-up.

"There were some furious rows between Nick and Natalie over the girls not wanting to work in the kennel, which Natalie was against anyway."

Over the years, Westmead bred dogs have won every one of the traditional events designated as 'classics' bar one.

Among those events with at least one tick next to them are the English Derby, the Scottish Derby, the Laurels, the Scurry Gold Cup, the Gold Collar, the Cesarewitch, and the Oaks. Which just leaves... the Grand National.

There have been few Westmead hurdlers over the years, though the remarkable Westmead Prince almost completed the classic set.

The strong running black didn't win his first major flat event until his second season.

Then at almost four years of age, he was switched to jumping. He duly finished runner-up in the 1981 Springbok, before ending up as the bridesmaid in both the English and Scottish Grand Nationals. There was some consolation in beating Wimbledon's best in the Gold Cup.

Even more remarkably, Prince came back

Westmead Kim

bk b (All Wit-Westmead Satin, Mar 82)

Kim and brother Milos were sold to Colm McGrath soon after schooling, and the black soon joined her new owner in Ireland.

At 20 months old Kim won a semi and then ran third to Kerogue Nell in the Sean Graham 700 at Dunmore.

She returned to England, but suffered a freak accident in a trial at Milton Keynes.

Nick says: "It was a windy night and the traps were blown back onto the track. She swerved to avoid them and in doing so broke a wrist."

Sold on to Pat Dalton, Kim threw litters by For Real, Whisper Wishes, Gambling Fever, Sail On II, Ps Riptide and Curryhills Gara.

The best was the Whisper Wishes bunch, which featured American Juvenile Classic winner Whisper Wit. Litter brother Energy Pack came third in the same race.

To Sail On II, Kim threw Rymer, who won the 1989 National Puppy Stakes at Shelbourne Park and proved a decent dam in the USA.

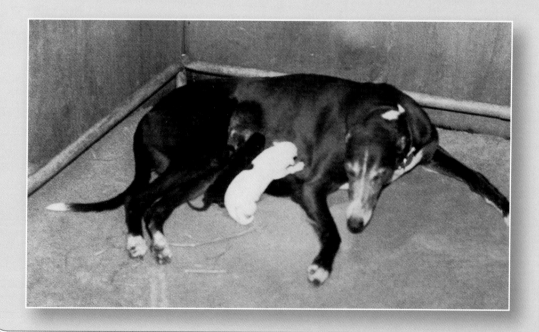

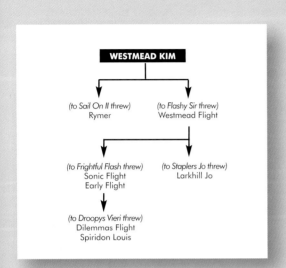

The story might have ended there, but for Nick's chance visit to Pat Dalton's Tipperary Kennels in 1991 where he spotted nine-year-old Kim.

He said: "It was pure luck. I was driving through with Paddy Dunne and had a chance thought to pop in and see Pat.

"I asked about Kim and it turned out she was due to be put down the following day. Pat had originally promised me a pup which I had never taken up and I asked if I could take Kim home instead.

"She had some bad teeth which were removed. I had no plans to breed with her again, but she returned to such good condition that I decided to have a litter out of her."

The dog and two of the three bitches were graders, but the other bitch, Westmead Flight, did just enough to justify a trial litter (see breeding section).

A strange twist of fate had determined that the last roots of remaining original Westmead bloodline were about to burst back into productivity.

as a five year old and finished second in the 1982 Grand National.

After a bad start to the decade due to parvo, the kennel bounced back thanks to two very good litters out of Westmead Satin. But it would be her daughter Westmead Tania who would produce the Westmead litter of the decade in November 1984.

It was among the first litters sired by Derby winner Whisper Wishes. Westmead Tania was a maiden.

Westmead Move was just 19 months old when she landed the Upton Rocket Stakes at Walthamstow with sister Westmead Call back in fourth.

But the event that really brought the litter to the fore was the 1986 Anglo-Irish International.

The Anglo team featured the three littermates, Westmead Move and brothers Olivers Wish and Westmead Wish. Only just two years old, they were given little chance.

The first leg was at Wimbledon. Ireland fielded a very strong team headed by Odell Supreme and it was the Ned Power-trained dog who just held off Olivers Wish by three quarters of a length with Move in fourth and Wish in fifth.

The second leg was at Shelbourne and Nick only just made it to the track after being delayed by fog.

He said: "We were booked to fly out of Luton in a chartered plane, but the fog shut down the airport.

"If it had been a normal race, I would have just withdrawn the dogs, but I felt a lot of responsibility that I would be letting everyone down and I managed to get a last minute flight from Heathrow.

"We had a mad car journey to get there and the dogs travelled as excess baggage. It was very very stressful, but we made it to Shelbourne in time to take part."

Ireland's Odell Supreme completed the double with a trap to line victory, but with the three Westmeads taking the next three places, they won the leg by 15-12 points and the overall contest by 28-26 points.

Although Move was the star (see page 66), Olivers Wish would prove a top class greyhound in his own right.

The following year he won the Grand Prix, Stewards Cup and was runner-up in the Regency.

It was Olivers Wish's love of soft going that resulted in one of the kennel's biggest gambles in the final of the Grand Prix.

Nick said: "A couple of weeks earlier Bob had had a couple of glasses of champagne and had punted two of the bitches for big money, even though I thought they both needed a race.

Bob would later admit that the bet of £30,000 on the 4-6 chance Westmead Move and £20,000 on Westmead Call was his worst ever lapse of judgement in 40 years of punting.

"I was quite angry with him because I thought it reflected on the kennel, that we didn't know what we were doing.

"Fortunately, Grand Prix final night was very wet and the going was soft, which Olivers Wish badly needed. I advised Bob that he could get some of his money back and he duly had a good bet at 7-1. Thankfully he didn't let us down.

"I've had a few dogs who really performed better on soft going. Westmeads Badger and Paddy are the other two who spring to mind."

Brother Westmead Wish went on to finish runner-up in the 1987 Sporting Life Juvenile, Wimbledon and Manchester Puppy Derbys as well as winning the Greyhound Stud Book Trophy at Maidstone.

Another sister, Westmead Call, won the Bedfordshire Derby and Wessex Vase, setting track records at both Henlow and Poole.

Former head man Phil Bradley says: "Call had two styles of running and because I used to enjoy going coursing, Nick would ask me to take her along.

"She wasn't entered in competitions; we would only send her up as a spare dog for a 'bye', but she never got beaten. I could have sold her 100 times over."

Given Westmead's modest kennel size compared to the country's leading open race kennels, it was a surprise to many pundits that Nick agreed to field a team for an extremely competitive Trainers Championship meeting at White City in 1983.

It included the powerful kennels of George Curtis (evens) and reigning champion trainer Adam Jackson (5-4). Team Westmead was eight British bred dogs, half of which were still puppies.

Certainly the bookies gave them no chance with 10-1 readily available before the first heat.

In fact, the team from Edelsborough would win three races, and none more impressively than puppy Westmead Alva, who clocked the fastest time of the night, 29.68 for the 500 metres.

Another three littermates from the Glenroe Hiker/Westmead Satin litter made decent contributions, with sisters Tania and Dena both finishing second. Another sister,

Melinda, was the only Savva runner to finish out of the forecast places all night.

The other victories went to Kris Is Back and Cannondale with Westmead Ruby and Stormy Flight both finishing runners-up.

Others wins on the night included a double for George Curtis (Cashen Son, Sandy Lane), and one win apiece for Jackson (Flying Duke), Terry Duggan (Mountleader Mint) and Joe Cobbold (Echo Spark).

Remarkably, the Savva team, six of them born at Westmead, finished some 15 points clear of closest rival George Curtis.

Final scores: 55-Natalie Savva, 40-George Curtis, 32-Adam Jackson, 31-Joe Cobbold, 28-Terry Duggan, 22-John Coleman

Not bad for a team missing the fastest greyhound in training at the time, Special Account, who was lame.

In late 1986 the Savvas agreed to feature in a Thames TV documentary called 'Greyhound'. The idea was to follow a litter of greyhounds from conception with regular progress reports and footage from key moments including the whelping, earmarking, different periods of growth, leading up to schooling and their first races.

Nick and Natalie thought long and hard before agreeing to take part. The financial gains (£1,500) were inconsequential compared to the aggravation and loss of privacy involved – but they thought it would be good for the greyhound industry.

It was the period midway through the exploits of the brilliant Whisper Wishes/Westmead Tania litter, and Tania was chosen as the intended dam of the 'TV litter'.

She duly came in season in the Spring of 1987 and Nick booked her to the leading Irish based sire, Sand Man, handled by John Fitzpatrick in Portlaoise.

Unfortunately, Sand Man was approaching his 14th birthday and he refused to cover the bitch. Under different circumstances, Nick would probably have returned home and missed the mating, but the film crew were already making plans for the whelping.

Nick said: "I asked Fitzpatrick if he had anything else at stud in the kennel. He said that he didn't. He did have a son of Sand Man, who he thought a bit of, but he was racing the next day, and it all seemed a bit too much hassle.

"I asked to see the dog – who turned out to be Flashy Sir. He was a duplicate of his father, identical size, colouring, everything. I asked Fitzpatrick if I could use him on Tania. He said I would have to buy him first.

"So I asked if he was for sale, and Fitzpatrick said he wanted £5,000 for the dog.

"Flashy had won five of his first 15 races and it seemed a bit steep. I asked Fitzpatrick if the dog was worth it, and he said he didn't know but he thought so.

"I also realised, both looking at the dog and seeing how the kennel operated, that they were so busy they couldn't possibly have trained him to his optimum.

"I didn't look at his card but accepted Fitzpatrick's word. I decided to give him what he wanted, and he gave me £500 back for luck.

"We then had to find out if he could cover a bitch!

"I said to Fitzpatrick, 'You're supposed to be the best at this sort of thing, and I have a lot of experience too. If we can't get him to cover her we should be ashamed of ourselves.'"

Westmead Milos bd d

(All Wit-Westmead Satin, Mar 82)

Milos, who was owned by Colm McGrath, made his mark as a top class pup and landed his first major event, the Northumberland Puppy Cup.

He had set a new track record in the heats and won the decider by seven lengths when only 18 months old.

He returned to Brough Park for the All England, where he beat Squire Cass in the fastest semi. However, the tables were turned in the final,

where he missed out by three quarters of a length as Squire Cass snatched victory and Milos' 500-metre clock.

In October, Milos represented Britain in both legs of the Anglo-Irish, finishing second to Glatton Grange at White City and last at Shelbourne Park.

He finished 1983 as the top pup in training when winning the Sporting Life Juvenile in 27.73.

The brindle returned to Wimbledon to win the International in 27.59 followed by another trip to Plough Lane to set a new 460 metre record of 27.51.

At Harringay, Milos (2-1 second favourite) ran third in the Pall Mall behind Game Ball and Ballyhaden Slave.

At Brighton, he clocked the fastest time in the Olympic when landing his semi final in 29.80. In the final, he caught Amazing Man in the last stride to win by a short head in 30.20.

Milos was ante post favourite for the last Derby to be staged at White City in 1984, and clocked the fastest first round heat in 29.40 (500m). He was then surprisingly eliminated in the quarter finals.

Unfortunately a broken hock sustained at two years and four months old ended a promising career.

Nick says: "Milos showed exceptional promise in a disappointingly short race career. He particularly impressed me when he came from last to first to win the Juvenile. Unfortunately his hock injury was sustained while he was being prepared to run in the Select Stakes.

"He was a 100% genuine, but sadly never had the chance to step up to six bends which is where I thought he would be at his best.

The mating took place and the following night, Flashy Sir set out to win his new owner his money back. He was beaten. It wasn't a great start.

Flashy Sir joined the Westmead team when Nick returned to England the following day.

In hindsight, Flashy Sir was probably the best thing to come out of the whole episode because there were many trying times ahead.

The first came with the whelping of the litter. There were complications and Tania was rushed to the vet for a caesarean – great drama!

Nick said: "Tania had passed the first pup with some difficulty – they were above average size – but then stopped. It might have been the lights, cameras or there being so many people in the kennel that put her off, we will never know.

Six pups were born – Camera Flash, Flashy Madam, Flashy Tania, Just Flash, Sound Man and Yes Sir, and the cameras, sound men, directors and assorted assistants were on hand to witness the event.

Over the following months the cameras appeared on a regular basis to witness the pups being earmarked and then to shadow their progress up to schooling age.

Natalie says: "The crew took over the whole place when they were filming. There were so many of them, it became a real nuisance".

The programme was due to conclude with the first of the pups making his debut in a graded race at Milton Keynes.

The programme was finally aired on December 13 1988 and it was a joy to behold – greyhound racing at its kindest and best. It remains possibly the greatest programme ever about greyhounds. Unfortunately there was a venomous sting in the tale.

The programme concluded with a still shot of Westmead Tania who had died while whelping down her next litter.

Immediately, the atmosphere changed – a documentary about the joys of breeding greyhounds became a story of a greedy breeder exploiting an animal for profit.

The following day's daytime TV programmes were quick to condemn the Savvas, who were distraught.

Nick says: "Tania actually died over a year after the film was made. The director had originally promised me that there would be nothing negative about the industry.

"I pleaded with him not to include the piece about Tania, but he said the decision had been made by his boss to include it. He had no choice, apparently.

"What actually happened is that I had rested her for a season after she had whelped the litter and she was in wonderful condition when she came in season again.

"When she was due to whelp down she showed no sign of wanting to pass the pups. She went past her 'due date' and was very lethargic.

"By the time the vet was able to open her up the womb had already burst open. There was nothing we could have done, or any way that we could have known.

"Had there been the slightest doubt in my mind, I would never have bred with her again and she would have enjoyed a long retirement alongside the other brood bitches.

"Looking back, I am convinced that we made a mistake by allowing the cameras at the vet's for the original caesarean. I think the pressure of being filmed may have affected the vet and he may not have stitched her up correctly. I've had other bitches have caesareans with no problems."

Indeed, of all the brood bitches that have been part of the Westmead story over many years, Tania was the particular favourite of Natalie.

She says: "Losing Tania was very distressing, I had a very close bond with her. She hated being on her own with her pups. She would come to the whelping kennel door and cry so I used to sit for hours talking to her.

"I was away when she had to be rushed in for a caesarian. I was always convinced that it wouldn't have happened if I had been there with her. I was terribly upset when we lost her."

Most of the litter were saved and two dogs and three bitches were registered. They were reared by Alva and Seal who each had small litters whelped the same month.

Over the years there have been tens of thousands of schooling trials at Westmead – including just one for German Shepherd guard dog Rocky.

"I'll never forget it" chuckles Nick. "He started off really well but after 300 yards he started thinking to himself.

"He pulled to a stop, grabbed hold of the hare wire and pulled it off the pulleys bringing the trolley to an immediate stop."

Although the athletic abilities of the kennel's long line of Rottweilers have never been tested, Rocky fully embraced the spirit of Westmead.

Nick said: "One day I found him in the same paddock as a litter of babies and my first thought was panic.

"But he was lying on the ground with the pups crawling all over him and biting him and he never flinched.

"As they got older he used to run around the paddock with them. I'm sure he thought he was their dad."

In 1987, Irishman Tom Prendeville arrived at Westmead at the start of what he would later describe as "five of the best years of my life."

SOLID: Quiet and dependable, head man Tom Prendeville handled some of Westmead's finest.

Tom says: "Although Nick was known as a top breeder, I don't think many people realised what a good trainer he was back then. It only took me a few days to realise that the man was a dedicated genius."

Although he was an experienced dog man, the new head lad was surprised by what he found.

He said: "In Ireland, the dogs had lots of walking. By comparison, Nick seemed to do very little with his dogs, though they had lots of gallops.

"The way he had the place set-up, it could be run by one man, even for exercising the dogs.

"Nick was a great man to work for. He did the same hours as me, he picked up in the paddocks the same as me – and did all the dirty jobs that some trainers would think below them.

"We would go out drinking together or with some of the other lads, particularly Paddy Dunne. Nick was always great company.

"As a trainer, he just had that instinct for getting it right. Sure, I can remember mistakes he made, but there weren't that many.

"Yet the times he would have a dog in a competition, and it would just improve all the way through and peak in the final was just amazing. I could never work out how he did it.

"He would check over his own dogs. He seldom used a vet, but would trust his own judgement.

"I remember we had Balligari in the Laurels and he was walking lame in the car park. Nick was convinced that there was nothing really wrong with the dog and said we would run him. I never found out what the problem was but he went on to win the final anyway.

"Nick was also years ahead of other trainers

in his methods. I remember taking Westmead Claim to Wembley for the Produce Stakes. He won the semi final on the Friday night, but on the Saturday morning he was passing blood in his urine.

"I said to Nick 'well that's him out of the final on Monday', but Nick put him on a drip. I'd never seen anyone do that before and sure enough the dog ran and was desperately unlucky to finish second.

"It was a great period for the kennel. Although Nick had won lots of things already, I don't think he ever had so many good dogs in the kennel at the same time.

"Apart from Claim, there was Alva's other litter that had Bens Baby and Havoc in it. We also had Westmead Harry, and my favourite dog in my time working for Nick, Phantom Flash.

"I remember that when he was being reared he kept going lame on a shoulder. In the end Nick put him in a small paddock to restrict his exercise.

"The owner kept telling me that his pup was going to be a superstar,. but I'd convinced myself that he couldn't possibly make up into a good dog because of all the setbacks. I don't think I could have been more wrong."

Few of Nick's staff have embraced the social life of Edelsborough more than Tom Prendevillle. Such was his capacity to shift a pint that the local landlord challenged him to take on his highest consuming regular.

Pride was at stake and Nick appointed himself as the big Irishman's official trainer.

He said: "I bought in some salted herrings which I told Tom to eat – I even added some more salt when he wasn't looking. In the end he pleaded with me to give him more bacon instead."

The session started in the afternoon on Tom's day off. After a night's racing Nick returned to the pub to see if Westmead honour had been upheld.

Nick says: "By the time that I arrived, Tom had drunk 21 pints and looked in good shape. The other guy had turned yellow and wasn't in a good way at all. It was a walkover."

The consummate pro, Tom was back at work at 7am the following morning. His opponent wasn't seen in public for another fortnight.

Chapter 5

SIMPLY THE BEST

By the early 1990s, Nick was growing utterly frustrated at the volume of injuries to his own and other people's dogs as well as a large number of spoiled races.

He wrote a string of letters to the promoters of various tracks, including those at Oxford, Milton Keynes, Walthamstow and GRA.

Typically, in a May 1990 letter to Charles Chandler at Walthamstow, Nick noted that of his 20 runners at the track in the first five months of the year, no fewer than six had sustained injuries, including muscle pulls, broken hocks, toes and tendons.

A year later, frustrated by the number of letters he was being sent by the tracks offering sympathy without action, he wrote to NGRC boss Archie Newhouse.

The letter, dated March 7 1991,

highlighted nine areas of serious concern:
- Poor surfaces with bad maintenance
- Inconsistency of track banking – many had none at all
- Bad design of starting traps
- Poor track fencing – very often also dangerous
- No consistency in the location of pick-ups
- Racing kennels
- Kenneling times
- Lack of suitable racing jackets at tracks
- Race meetings held in hazardous weather conditions

Nick said: "I gave Newhouse my opinion that a lot of racing dogs were having their careers curtailed due to incorrect, or lack of, maintenance. I could already foresee the growth of welfare issues.

"He invited me to sit on a committee with

PURPOSE BUILT: Monmore's new racing circuit was meticulously researched and prepared by Gordon Bissett.

Bob Rowe and Frank Melville, but there were problems from the start.

"I soon clashed with Melville when I said the NGRC should insist on certain standards. He turned on me and said 'how would you like it if someone came along and said he could improve your place? I replied 'I'd pay him to do it'."

After six months of virtually no progress, Nick decided it wasn't worth continuing.

He said: "It was a pointless exercise and I felt I was being used to make it look as though they were trying, when I knew that the promoters had little intention of spending money on making the tracks safer.

"I suppose I also made a mistake when I stipulated that any work I did should have

been done on behalf of NAGO. I don't think the promoters wanted the owners and trainers association to be seen to be forcing change on them."

It was a wasted opportunity and Nick's original concept was never adequately addressed or understood.

He said: "Over the years, I had observed that although injuries are an inevitable downside of racing, the level is always greatly influenced by other factors.

"To take just one example, when I developed my schooling track, I had to do so with a limited amount of space in a field that wasn't squared.

"I started to experiment with banking. It took me three attempts to get it right but in the end, it made a significant difference. Dogs were able to retain their balance as they strode around the bends.

"The more I thought about it, the more I realised its importance, but the clues are there only if you look for them.

"Look at how the track records improved at Harringay once banking was introduced. More than half a second!

"Now compare the 480 metre track records at banked tracks like Monmore, Hove and Sheffield to un-banked tracks like Sittingbourne and Coventry. There is more than a second difference. Why?

"I formed an opinion, rightly or wrongly, that the dogs were better able to maintain their stride and balance, two major factors in the prevention of injuries.

"Years later, I read an article in the American magazine *Greyhound Review* where scientists had come to the same conclusions, through their research, as I had through observation and experimentation.

"I had similar experiences when experimenting with my sand and watering techniques for example. I managed to get the injury rate down to virtually nil, despite trialling some fast dogs on a very small track.

"I really wanted to see the governing body determine best practice, and then insist that all tracks operate to the same levels of safety and consistency throughout the industry.

"I realised that you couldn't tell the promoter of a badly shaped track to level it and start again. In many cases, they simply don't have the space to create the perfect track.

"But you should be able to demand that

all possible improvements that could be made, should be made."

In November 1992, the NGRC - on behalf of the Track Standards Advisory Committee - produced a fact sheet suggesting a set of guidelines for the staging of greyhound racing.

For anyone who had seen Nick's original letter, it covered a stunningly familiar range of subjects from track design and maintenance, lighting, to the sighting of the pick-up. But instead of placating Nick, it left him dejected.

Despite covering more than two dozen subjects, the whole document was written in large print and covered only five sides of A4 paper.

It was a 'Janet and John' guide to greyhound racing. Starting traps should be positioned on a 'level surface', the hare driver should have an "uninterrupted view of the whole circuit" Track lighting should be 'sufficient' to prevent dark patches.

The entire subject of track maintenance was covered in one paragraph:

The racing surface must be kept constantly worked. It must be kept 'alive'. Rotavating, harrowing, rolling, grading and watering must be applied to consistently produce a surface that safely accommodates the greyhound's galloping action. How this consistent surface is arrived at will vary greatly depending on the materials used and the equipment available to track maintenance staff. With the right equipment and materials, maintenance is a simple task, however the human element always plays an important role in this programme and attitudes on this issue must not be ignored. Track design and correction, selection of track surface materials will be of little value if the

SPECIAL: Paddy Dunne's sense of fun and breezy disposition brought enormous joy to Westmead. "I still miss him sometimes" confesses Nick.

maintenance and preparation programme is wanting.

So that clears that up then! No advice on minimum time and staffing levels, types of equipment, no detailed guidelines or quality control standards. And were we talking about grass or sand tracks?

Banking of bends wasn't considered worthy of mention.

Nick said: "They tried to prove that they had regulations in place, but most people weren't even aware of them. What is unforgivable is that they didn't even attempt to enforce them.

"To give a couple of examples. It says in the guide that racing circuits should be laid on a higher level than the surroundings. Good advice and vital to maintain correct drainage.

"Yet when the new Perry Barr was built, the track was at the same level. Before the place even opened, I warned them that it would be waterlogged. Sure enough, within the first month they had to abandon meetings.

"If the stewards had insisted on an elevated circuit on day one, it would never have happened.

"Then there was the pick-up issue, which was virtually skimmed over in the NGRC report.

"For years we were happy stopping the hare between the first and second bends. Then, during the 1980s, the tracks were putting the 'drop' halfway along the back straight or even, in the case of Walthamstow, at the third bend.

"To ask dogs who are clearly tiring, to run another 200 yards after the race borders on cruelty. These dogs have to be fitter than they would for long distance racing.

"Not only does the extra exertion cause dehydration, but it can also cause sourness, with many dogs becoming jaded and losing interest.

"That extra 200 yards plus also increases the severity of any injury sustained during the race.

"Yet the managements tried to claim it was a 'safety issue'. We raced for 60 years with no one considering the original pick-ups a problem! Also, we now race on sand which is a lot softer and safer than grass when dogs are pulling up.

"The stupid thing is, while the old McKee hare had to be stopped with a break, or freewheeled to a stop, hence the need to use the back straight to slow up, the Swaffham hare could be stopped anywhere, including the ideal position, the second bend after the winning line.

"Why did nobody consult the trainers? Well actually they did. When I complained to Chris Page at Walthamstow about the location of the pick-up at the third bend, he agreed to send a letter to all trainers asking for a vote on where it should be located. They couldn't be bothered to reply.

"Although Walthamstow was the worst of the culprits, Wimbledon wasn't much better. Thankfully, not everyone went down that route; tracks like Catford, Hall Green and Henlow continued to put the dogs welfare first."

What about the actual size of the racing circuits?

Nick said: "It is a fact that greyhounds are bigger and faster than in the early days of the sport when the first tracks were built. But the circuits, on average, have actually been getting smaller. Why not insist on a minimum circumference for any new track licensed?

"I know the NGRC's Frank Melville believed that it could be interpreted as an admission that current tracks weren't safe, but that was just a cop-out in my opinion."

A year after the first draft of the guide was produced, Nick resigned from the Tracks Advisory Committee feeling entirely disillusioned.

He said: "I decided the only course of action was to boycott the tracks that I didn't feel were safe. And that is what I did."

But things would eventually improve, as we shall see later. . .

Nick visited the USA for the first time in the early 1990s. He attended a 'meet' at Abilene in Kansas, which is the home of the National Greyhound Association and the Hall Of Fame.

Nick said: "The meet is really a bit of a mix between a produce stakes and an auction. It is a very good concept and allows breeders to get the market value for their best young dogs.

"I found America very interesting, with different methods of running their industry, and always very professional.

Phantom Flash bk d

(Flashy Sir-Westmead Seal Jul 88)

Phantom Flash was 17 months old when he made his racing debut in an open at Swindon. He started at 6-1 and finished second, to future Derby finalist Burnt Oak Champ.

He broke his duck fourth time out with a seven-length win at Monmore. Flash first showed signs of greatness in the track's Puppy Derby , winning his heats and semis by a combined 15 lengths (best 29.30).

A 1-3f for the final, he missed his break and finished fifth behind 29.97 winner One For Lloyd.

Still only 21 months old, he won his next three opens in 27.78, 27.69 and 27.89 for 460m at Wimbledon, at odds as low as 1-5f. They represented remarkably short odds for a dog who already had a reputation as a notoriously slow starting, wide runner with awesome back-straight pace.

Flash's first major win was the Archie Scott Memorial at Hall Green, where the youngster beat a top-class field, including Linthurst Rita, Murlens Hawk and Galtymore Lad, in 28.75 over 474 metres.

Galtymore and the Savva runner met again the following month, in the first round of the 1990 English Derby. Heavily backed ante post, Flash (2-1f) finished lame with a shoulder injury.

He reappeared as a two-year-old in the Sussex Cup at Hove, and blew away the opposition. Unbeaten, and fastest on the clock throughout, he started at 2-5f in the £3,000 decider where he beat Greenfield Madam.

The Irish Derby was next on the agenda and things didn't start well. Flash finished fourth in the opening round but qualified under the a repercharge system, which determined qualifying places by points.

He made no mistake next time, clocking 30.24 for the 550 yards, and then went to within a length of the track record with a 30.10 first-round win. Flash was then installed as Derby favourite.

The second round was almost a disaster, as he moved wide from the boxes and into trouble. Apparently eliminated, he found half-a-dozen lengths on leaders Concentration and Monaleen Stag to win his heat in 30.84.

Into the semis and Flash was back on song in 30.30. Toss Pit was next quickest in 30.46. The Other Toss landed the other qualifier in 30.62.

The Westmead kennel has probably never produced a wider runner than Phantom Flash.

Unfortunately, the 1990 Irish Derby featured four wide seeds and Flash (11-8f) drew the white jacket.

To say he trapped slowly would be an understatement. He was clear last going into the first bend and forced to run around the outside of the other backmarker.

By the second bend he was 10 adrift of Pets Echo and The Other Toss, but then the outstanding back-straight pace kicked in.

He took four lengths out of his field and was catching the leading pair hand over fist by the third bend. He attempted to take Pets Echo on the outside coming around the last bend, but the fawn drifted off.

By the time he switched to the inside, the race was all over and The Other Toss got home in 30.14. Flash finished third.

It was then back to Britain for the Produce Stakes at Wembley. In a preparatory trial, Flash had clocked 28.61 (TR 28.82) for the 490 metres and he went to traps as a 1-14f for his opening heat.

He duly won in an official record of 28.79, which gave him a 64 spot advantage over closest rival Linthurst Rita. He followed that up with an eight-length 28.95 win, before a surprise defeat (1-7f) in the semis.

For the final, though, he made no mistake with a 28.94 victory.

It was back to Shelbourne for the Anglo-Irish, when Flash was surprisingly beaten into third by kennelmate Westmead Harry, though Flash bounced back to win the Wimbledon version by more than four lengths.

He then rounded off 1990 with a four-length victory in a £1,000 invitation race at Wembley.

At year end, Flash had won 18 of his 24 opens and prize money of £21,385. His Irish record was four wins from six races.

It would also be Phantom Flash's last race for his breeder/trainer. Following a dispute with owner Dave Hawley, Nick asked Hawley to remove the dog from his kennels.

Flash joined Patsy Byrne in early 1991. He won heats and semis of the Blue Riband, but was beaten in the final.

He bounced back to win the Archie Scott Memorial for the second time, clocking 28.60.

Shawfield and the Scottish Derby was next on the agenda and his 14-length win (1-3f) in the first round (29.75) gave him a 71 spot advantage over his closest rival. He won his semi (1-4f) by five in 29.95 (next quickest 30.56), and final (1-4f) by six-and-a-quarter lengths in 29.77.

Just 13 days later he won his qualifying heat of the English Derby in 29.04. He won again in 28.60 and again in 28.80.

A 4-6f in his Derby quarter final, Flash broke his wrist and his racing career was at an end.

As a sire, Flash threw plenty of pace, though never quite achieved the volume of open race winners required to make him a top-three sire.

His greatest son was probably the enigmatic Spiral Nikita, a dog well fancied for two Irish Derby finals, but successful in neither. The first time, of course, he was beaten by sister Tina Marina.

Other Flash progeny included Sure Fantasy, Snow Flash, Spit It Out, Droopys Pacino, Curley Tresa, Gottabegood, Get Connected, Treasury Tag, Tuesdays Davy, Phantom Power, Blonde Returns, Liffey Mills, Dew Reward and Ardcollum Flash.

Flash died of a heart attack, aged 11, at Kerry Hill kennels in Kerry, in August 1999.

Nick says: "He was a brilliant tracker with great back straight pace. I didn't really get the best out of him due to a series of niggling injuries but good dogs run for anyone and he won plenty with Patsy Byrne.

"I thought he was good enough to win the Irish Derby, but the draw in three cost him dearly.

"The highlight of his career with me was probably his performance in the Produce Stakes, where he looked just exceptional.

"I would put Phantom Flash among the fastest three dogs that I've bred."

Westmead Harry bk d

(Fearless Champ-Westmead Move, Nov 87)

The Savvas bred very few faster dogs than Harry, and virtually none with a better strike rate in major events.

He was just 18 months old when he made his open race debut and won a Wembley puppy open in 29.43.

His first big win came in the 1989 Eclipse. The 12-1 shot came from behind to beat odds-on favourite Gulleen Whisper when still only 21 months old. He ran third in the Tennants Ten Thousand and was switched to six bends to win a £1,000 race at Milton Keynes.

His first major success as a two-year-old was in the Blue Riband. Fastest in the entire event with a 29.07 heat win, he came from fifth place to snatch the £6,000 final by a short head in 29.09.

The long, powerful black totally dominated the 1990 Scottish Derby – clocking the fastest heat and semi final.

The 5-4 favourite for the final, he didn't lead until midway along the back straight, but pulled out a near eight-length winning margin to set a new Shawfield 500-metre track record of 29.62.

In September, Harry contested the Irish Derby and only failed to qualify for the final after being drawn in the quickest of the three semis, which was won by kennel mate Phantom Flash. Harry finished third, beaten a neck for second place with only two to qualify.

He returned to England to land the Select Stakes before going back to Shelbourne Park to beat kennelmates Phantom Flash and Bens Baby, plus the best of the locals, in the Anglo-Irish International.

Ante post leader for the St Leger, Harry reached the final unbeaten and started favourite, but finished third to Match

Point. Nevertheless, he had already done enough to be voted 1990 Greyhound of the Year.

Harry was probably the most nervous greyhound who ever came through Westmead Kennels.

Nick says: "Harry was really a bit of a freak. He was a spook – very, very nervous.

"He was like it from the time he was a pup. He was okay around us, but if there was a stranger around he would go to the other end of the paddock.

"Thankfully it didn't really affect his racing and he was 100% genuine.

"I often wondered where Harry's nerves came from. On the sire's side Fearless Champ had no nerves, nor did his father or grandfather, Special Account and Westmead County.

"He was from a Westmead dam line which had never exhibited any behavioural problems. I can only assume that there was something in the Sarahs Bunny line."

"The only time that the nervousness played a part was when we sent him over for the Irish Derby. He never settled and ran below par.

"I decided to run him in the consolation but flew him over on the day of the race.

"He was completely unfancied but because of the change of plan, we decided to gamble him. To memory he was 33-1 and when he won, owner Paul Hoffman won enough to put a deposit on a massive new house in Blackpool.

"Overall, I thought the Scottish Derby Final was his best ever race when he came from last to first to break the track record.

Harry was eventually sold, to continue stud duties for a project that ultimately never got off the ground, for racing in South Africa.

Nick says: "They told me that they were flying him out there and I knew he would go to pieces on the plane. He actually had a heart attack and was dead on arrival."

"The stadiums are huge, impressive places, though they are too big for the size of crowds.

"From what I could see, the American dogs take very little training because they tend to run around three times a week. They are also heavily schooled.

"They are kept in a very different way to ours. All the dogs are kenneled in a big air-conditioned room full of double tier cages – according to the climate. They are muzzled and when their kennels are opened, they all go into the paddock together.

"When they come back, they all know which is their kennel and jump straight into it. The big plus point is that the dogs are allowed to empty on a regular basis through the day. There is no need for them to soil their kennels, which are spotless.

"In some English kennels the dogs are locked up late afternoon and not given the chance to empty themselves until the following day.

"The American system is very streamlined, though many of our dogs would struggle to adapt to it, as I know from personal experience having sent dogs there.

"I found it all a bit impersonal, but the dogs appeared to be in very good physical condition and happy. It is all about what they grow up being used to."

But the biggest single bonus from the trip to the States was a friendship with American breeding legend Herb (Dutch) Koerner, that is still going strong in its third decade.

Nick says: "Dutchy is a proper dog man, very knowledgeable and he genuinely loves greyhounds. His farm is remarkably similar to Westmead, but on a much bigger scale, with probably 200 dogs.

Staplers Jo

(Dempsey Duke-Perfect Rhythm, June 97)

Back in September 1994 local breeder Gerry Beckett began trialling a 15-month-old litter by Dempsey Duke out of former local grader, Perfect Rhythm, at Milton Keynes.

Among them was the leggy 35-kilo white-and-black Staplers Jo. His first solo was clocked at 28.30 but, three trials later, he qualified some 102 spots quicker, a time that would have qualified him into A3.

Instead, Beckett asked Nick to take the dog and qualify to run graded at Walthamstow. He clocked a fastest 29.61 for the 475 metres in trials but was beaten on his debut.

However there was big money for him next time out. Despite missing his break and not leading until the third bend, Jo landed his trainer with a 28.91 time-finding enquiry.

After his following win, he was sold for £7,000 to Harrow builder Pat Whelan, who gave the dog to his wife, Betty, as a Christmas present.

Jo's first big success came in the 1995 Monmore Puppy Derby. Despite repeatedly missing his break, Jo had such incredible early pace that he could lead three to four lengths at the first bend.

It was with precisely that racing style that he won the final in 29.72 (-20) for the 484 metres.

On to Hackney, where the early paced flyer won a heat of the 442 metre Gimcrack by 13 lengths and took over four lengths off the old track record. He won the final at 1-8f.

By May 1995, Jo was ante-post favourite for the English Derby, but missed the event after going lame in a trial.

He returned with a double at the Stow (28.75, 28.66) before heading to Hall Green for the Produce Stakes.

Jo won all four of his Hall Green races – 28.34, 28.44, 28.52 & 28.49. They were won by an accumulated 23 lengths and his biggest price was 1-4f – some performance considering he trapped between third and sixth place in every heat.

But it didn't end there. The sequence continued with another Rye House win (28.80-485) before Jo returned to his beloved Hackney for the Guineas.

Attempting the 484-metre for the first time, the Betty Whelan-owned dog won by just under 10 lengths and sliced 30 spots off Lassa Java's track record.

He would never be headed throughout the entire competition, which end with a flawless trap-to-line win in 28.98.

The winning sequence was taken to 11 when Jo led from box to beam in the Anglo-Irish International.

The Greyhound of the Year title followed, but after a three-month lay-off Jo's career was effectively over when he sustained a serious muscle injury in a trial at Hackney.

Although he returned briefly, the damage proved irreparable.

Jo went to stud in Ireland, where he became the most exciting producer of early pace in the breeding world.

His progeny included Back In Action, El Ronan, Larkhill Bullet, Farloe Hack, Priceless Rebel, Blue Gooner, Kegans Glory and of course his natural heir, the great Larkhill Jo. He also threw more top class bitches than any other dog at stud, including Irish Oaks winners Lifes Beauty Borna Survivor and Marinas Tina (x2), plus Miss Tetley, Hopeful Moment, Cooly Cheetah, Ballymac Minnie, Ballymac Bargain and Tullymurry Tango.

Jo was among the top five stud dogs for four years, twice finishing runner-up to Top Honcho.

Nick says: "In breeding terms, Jo was something of a freak being by a dog who threw virtually nothing else out of a dam who was apparently just about useless on the track.

"Staplers and Westmead Lord were probably the best two early paced dogs that I ever trained. Staplers didn't need to trap because he had such tremendous early pace.

"At his peak, there was no dog in Britain or Ireland that could lead him to the fourth bend.

Like all the great dogs, he didn't have a single fault.

"I really liked Betty Whelan. While her husband Pat was really a horse-racing man, the dogs were Betty's pride and joy.

"Staplers was her 'special dog' but she loved all her dogs, no matter how good or bad they were, with equal enthusiasm.

"I was very sad when she became ill and subsequently died in 1997. Although Pat carried on as an owner, it was never quite the same."

Larkhill Jo

(Staplers Jo-Westmead Flight, Sep 95)

Jo was conceived at Westmead, but was born and reared in Ireland on owner Pat Whelan's farm. He arrived at Westmead at 11 months old and instantly impressed his new trainer.

"There were three bitches and a dog in the litter. They did a very good job of the rearing," recalls Nick.

Jo made his debut on February 15 1997 in a Walthamstow graded puppy event.

The 17-month-old pup finished fifth but was punted next time out (9-4 to 7-4f) winning by eight lengths in the fastest time of the night, 29.07. In almost identical fashion to his father, Larkhill also earned his trainer a 'stewards'.

By his fifth race his personal best was 28.74. Next time out in a puppy open at Monmore, he set a new track record for the 460-metre trip – 27.15.

Larkhill's first major final was the Stylefield Law Puppy Stake at the Stow. A 28.64 semi winner, he was beaten at 2-9f in the final by 29.02 outsider I'm Frankie.

There was more disappointment in the English Derby where he was eliminated in the third round, but he added the Monmore 480-metre clock (27.95) in the Gold Cup. In the final, however, he failed to get a run and was beaten by kennel-mate Toms The Best.

Despite his indifferent Derby form, Nick sent the dog back to Wimbledon for a trial, where he clocked the fastest time ever recorded over the track's 460-metre course – 27.16.

He followed that up with a fine win in the 480-metre Stanton Memorial.

Despite missing his break, he accelerated to lead at the first and clock a stunning 28.41.

Jo picked up a wrist injury in the Coldseal Classic and after failing to find his form was ignored by the press for Nottingham's first staging of the Select Stakes.

But he was drafted in as a reserve for Blue Murlen, was made the 5-4f, and reminded everyone of his ability with a 30.19 win over El Premier.

Three weeks later there was another £7,000 payday as Jo again justified favouritism for a 30.48 win (.50) in the Eclipse Final.

After a winter's break Jo returned to the Stow for the Arc. He qualified for the final with heat wins in 28.51, 28.82, and an incredible 28.56 (-30) in the semis.

Unfortunately, for connections and punters, the 4-9f blew it in the final when third to Ceekay and Greenwood Flyer.

But consolation was just around the corner.

On the big Shawfield circuit, the black set up a series of great runs (29.07, 28.88, 29.40) to see him go unbeaten through to the Scottish Derby Final.

Slow into his stride – he was actually last early on – Larkhill stormed through to win the decider

and take revenge on his great rival and kennel-mate Toms The Best.

Both went on to Plough Lane for the English Derby. Jo won a couple of heats, best 28.53, before finishing lame in the third round and going out.

Next up was an assault on the 1998 Irish Derby.

Jo took to the big Shelbourne circuit like a duck to water.

He went unbeaten through to the final with wins in 30.32, 30.31, 30.10 and 30.18 and was 9-4 second favourite to new record holder Eyeman.

Drawn six in the final, Jo broke reasonably, but was mid divison when forced wide at the first. He came through the field, chased the favourite into the last two, but then checked.

He was half a length adrift at the line with Cool Panther stealing second place by a short head.

Jo never returned to England. He stayed with Seamus Graham, for whom he landed the last major event of his career – the Shelbourne Leger.

Jo sired his first litter in September 1998 but returned for a short third season of racing before being finally retired in July 1999.

Jo was a massive success at stud. Despite a large number of misses, he managed to stay in the top three of the stud table for four years, achieving a highest position of second.

His progeny included two Irish Derby winners, Climate Contol and Like A Shot, plus Fear Haribo, Slip The Lark, Droopys Kewell, Tinys Bud, Hilcroft Josie, Digital, Disguised, and Larking About.

He also sired the outstanding litter out of Mega Delight that featured Westmeads Joe, Olivia, Aoifa, Nicole, Major and Liz.

Nick says: "Joe was an outstanding dog, 100 per cent genuine, a lovely nature with a fantastic running action, very low to the ground.

"There was nothing between Jo and Tom and whenever they ran together I backed the wrong one. I would say his best performance was in the Scottish Derby, but he also ran Monmore very well. He ran most of his career with a minor wrist problem.

"He didn't really have any faults other than he could get a little bit hyper if he was off the track for a while – he was just so genuine. I think that came through from his grandmother Westmead Kim, who was a little bit similar."

"His most impressive win by far was in the final of the Eclipse. It was absolutely pouring down and the track was bottomless, but he showed tremendous tenacity to come through the field. At the pick-up he was absolutely caked in sand."

"Dutchy is also fantastic company. I don't get to speak to him as often as I would like but it is always great fun and I will always treasure his friendship."

In November 1997 Nick made his first visit to Australia and was hugely impressed by what he found.

Though, as Natalie mischievously points out: "He must be the only tourist who ever went to Sydney and didn't see the Harbour Bridge or the Opera House. He did manage to find the dog tracks and dog farms."

He was accompanied by old pal Cecil Law and they drove thousands of miles visiting kennels and tracks in Sydney, Melbourne and Brisbane.

They visited dog farms, racing kennels, country tracks, veterinary facilities, most notably Jim Gannon's Sandown Veterinary clinic, and the biggest and best stadiums in Australia.

Cecil was a huge admirer of Gannon, at that time considered to be the best hands-on greyhound vet in the world, and they spent a considerable time talking to the great man discussing techniques and treatments as well as observing the impressive, well equipped, facilities.

Nick says: "Their tracks don't compare to ours, they are so much better.

"Sandown Park reminded me of Hove. I was stunned by Geelong with its 460 metre sprint. Every track had a huge radius, and they were all immaculately maintained.

"There was virtually nothing about Australian racing that I didn't like."

Indeed, but for the long queues around the Australian embassy, mentioned earlier, and a failed attempt to get a job on a ship heading 'down under', Nick's life could have turned out so differently.

He said "If I had visited Australia earlier in my life, I would definitely have emigrated. By the time I saw how good it was, it was too late."

If the pups by Clonalvy Pride/Cricket Dance were the Westmead litter of the '70s, and the Whisper Wishes/Tania litter were the best bunch produced in the 80s, one litter stood above all the others in the following decade.

The five dogs and six bitches by Daleys Gold out of Westmead Move were born in January 1990. Although they hold an unwanted kennel record for earning the most ASBOs in the rearing paddocks, they could run a bit too!

Over four bends, two dogs dominated – Balligari and Right Move. The former, whose name translates to roughly 'big and tough' was one of the fastest pups of his year, but not the most consistent.

Balligari went to traps as a 13-8 chance for the Wimbledon Puppy Derby, only for his brother (14-1) to take the race. In the Sunderland Puppy Derby, the brindle started at 10-11f, only for history to repeat itself.

Not that Right Move had it all his own way. He was turned over at 1-3f in the Essex Vase, shortly after demolishing the Romford 400m clock.

But old scores were finally settled when Balligari led home his brother for a 1-2 in the 1992 Laurels Final.

Two of the bitches achieved a Classic forecast too as Westmead Surprise led home sister Spirit in the same year's Gold Collar. Surprise also lifted the Champions Stakes and the Gold Cup and set a new six bend track record at Stainforth. Spirit won the Produce Stakes.

In fact, with ten members of the same litter all winning opens, it remains a record holder for Westmead litters.

Interestingly, the 109 open race wins achieved by the 10 litter-mates would be beaten with ease many years later.

The only member of the litter not to put her name in lights was the Dave Hawley-owned Phantom Gold. Only one of her progeny won minor opens in England, but two of her daughters became prolific dams of AA winners in the USA.

Westmead Chick be b b

(I'm Slippy-Westmead Move, Jan 92)

There are very few bitches who can consistently beat the best males in training over the standard distance, but Westmead Chick was one of the very best.

The 34-kilo blue brindle was 18 months old when she won her first open at Milton Keynes. She then dead heated in the 1993 Bazell Puppy Stake.

After a winter break she returned to the Stow in March 1994 for a neck victory in the Arc. A month later she polished off Hove's Olympic.

Chick's English Derby attempt included a 28.57 heat win before she went out in the quarter finals. There was a small consolation with a win in the Brighton Belle.

Chick was runner-up in the Eclipse, but before the

year was out had also landed the Midland Flat and the Oaks, beating Droopys Fergie by five lengths in 28.60 for the Plough Lane 480 metres.

In 1995 she won the Derby invitation in 28.65, one spot quicker than final winner Moaning Lad.

A month later there was another £5,000 pay day with a near seven-length victory in the Monmore Gold Cup

It was back to Wimbledon for the Wey Plastics Invitation. The 4-5f led home a top class field of Pearls Girl, Countrywide Fox, Curryhills Fancy, Moral Standards and Deenside Dean.

She also finished runner-up to Westmead Merlin in the Dundalk International, and equalled the Walthamstow 475-metre track record (28.49) before retiring with a record of 29 open race victories.

She was voted the 1994 Greyhound of the Year, the only middle-distance bitch to have achieved the feat in the last 30 years.

Chick produced seven litters of pups, four of which contained open race winners, though nothing approaching her own calibre.

Nick says: "I would say that Chick was the fastest four-bend bitch that I ever bred. In running style, she could lead but didn't have to.

"On the night she equalled the 475-metre track record at Walthamstow the track was like a ploughed field. I always wondered what she might have done on good going.

"It is also worth remembering that she was a 'six month' bitch, which restricted her racing career. I did try suppressing her, but she was of such a strong constitution that she came in season anyway."

Westmead Surprise's victory in the 1992 Gold Collar was the highlight in the owning career of the kennel's second biggest supporter, Paddy Dunne.

The Irishman, a CID officer from nearby Aylesbury, began appearing at the kennel in the early days ("to see what the mad foreigner was up to" according to the mad foreigner himself).

Gradually he became more hands-on, helping with both the dogs and the maintenance of the kennel.

Nick says: "Paddy would be up here at least three or four days a week for a few hours at a time and was a fantastic help keeping the place in shape.

"But his greatest asset was working with the pups – he absolutely thrived on it, and would take great delight in teaching them anything from basic 'walking on a lead' to one star pupil who Paddy trained to go swimming in the irrigation pool to help him overcome injury.

"But being Paddy, he didn't just encourage him to swim, he taught him how to dive. The pup was eventually taking a 30 yard run and then diving headlong into the pool. It was the funniest thing you had ever seen.

"Paddy wouldn't just teach pups to go into traps, he would train some of them so that you could take their leads off 30 yards away and they would walk to the traps and go in themselves.

"But everybody remembers Paddy for his bubbly personality. He was a celebrity in all the local pubs because of his sense of fun. You never saw him in a bad mood."

There were many funny stories about Paddy Dunne. One of Nick's favourites may

Toms The Best

(Frightful Flash-Ladys Guest, May 95)

Toms The Best made his racing debut at Shelbourne Park on a cold January night in 1997. A 29.58 win was followed by a 'for sale' advert in the Racing Post and 'Tom', was snapped up by luckless owner Eddie Shotton for £10,000.

After two 29.56 trials for his new kennel, the handsome black made his British debut in graded company at Walthamstow.

Heavily gambled, Tom won third time out in 28.71, earning trainer Savva a steward's enquiry.

With a total of eight races so far in his career, Tom was entered in the 1997 English Derby where he gave a first glimpse of greatness – a 28.41 run in the quarter finals.

Unfortunately, he found trouble in the semis and failed to qualify for the final by three quarters of a length. But there was consolation on final night with a 28.42 run.

It was then off to Monmore and Hove for the Gold and Sussex Cups, by the end of which he had his first two competition wins and a seven-race winning sequence.

Tom was in the shadow of English Derby winner Some Picture throughout the 1997 Irish Derby, but he produced his best run to date in the semis, 30.26 for the 550 yards.

On the big night the Savva runner was superbly prepared. Connections were confident that their dog would trap faster than ever, and they were proved correct.

'Tommy' broke in front, surrendered the early lead to Vintage Prince and then hauled in Joe Kenny's gallant white and black for a one-length win in 30.09.

Milton Keynes might not be most people's idea of a track to suit the big striding black but a sub track record 26.34 trial for the 440 metres in early 1998 suggested he had wintered well.

In May, Tom reached the Scottish Derby Final which turned into a fantastic buckle with kennel-mate Larkhill Jo. Tom failed to overcome early crowding and was beaten a length.

Tom warmed up for his second English Derby with a 27.61 460-metre trial before a surprise first round defeat (bump 1 ran on) by Farloe Mac.

It would be his final defeat as Tom finished a truly remarkable career with a five timer, culminating in the 1998 English Derby Final and a Greyhound of the Year title.

No greyhound previously had won both English and Irish Derbies. Toms The Best came to within a length of also landing the Scottish and within three quarters of a length of reaching a fourth Derby Final.

His career record showed 40 races Wins-21, 2nds-7, 3rds-8, 4ths-4. He won over £113,075 in prize money.

Tom enjoyed a successful stud career despite numerous fertility problems. He remained a Top-Three sire from 2001 through to 2005.

His leading progeny included Toms View, Louis Saha, Alibulk Lad, Fear No One, Midway Tomsscout, Fear Robben, Frisby Folly, Caloona Striker and Toms Little Jo.

Tom died in December 2008 and is buried near the first bend of Nick's schooling track.

Nick said: "Toms The Best was a lovely greyhound in both his looks and his nature. He was also an incredibly intelligent dog, and not just in how he pre-empted going racing if he wasn't fed on time.

"If he went to a track on more than one occasion, he worked out the time and 10 minutes before he we were due to arrive in the van he would start barking.

"When he ran in the Derby final at Wimbledon, we were 10 minutes from the track and Tom hadn't murmured. I said to Tom Andy Elias 'what is the matter with Tom?' but within two minutes he started, which was a bit of a relief.

"My biggest regret was that I wasn't able to put Tom over the longer distance. I think he would have been sensational.

"Eddie wouldn't have it. He was convinced it would ruin his stud potential. He wouldn't even let me give the dog a trial over 620 metres at Milton Keynes. I would have loved to have known what he could have done."

SIMPLY THE BEST: After a string of near misses, Toms The Best produced the kennel's first English Derby winner in 1998.

have come about as the result of a story that another kennel stalwart, George Hunter used to tell.

George, a former amateur jockey, once related a tale of giving a whole bottle of whiskey to a hurdler that he was about to ride in a race.

The horse won for the only time in his career – a consequence, in George's view, of his newly-found Dutch courage.

Paddy, obviously impressed, chose to carry out a similar experiment on Westmead Pulse who was running in a stayers open at Wembley.

An unusually tight lipped Paddy Dunne arrived in the paddock and, as he put the racing muzzle on Pulse, squirted a shot of brandy into the dog's mouth. (The ruse may not appear so novel to anyone who has been

involved in coursing)

Nick says: "I knew nothing about it until they got home and Paddy was grinning like a child. He told me what he had done and the dog skated up. Unfortunately for Paddy's great training breakthrough, he tried the same thing the following week and the dog got beat."

When Nick and Natalie first began racing, many tracks staged their own Produce Stakes, including Wimbledon, Catford and Leeds.

By the 1980s, we were left with two – one with its origins at Bristol, before eventually moving to Swindon. The other, the Breeders Forum Produce Stakes, was inaugurated in 1983 at Harringay.

Nick had no appetite for the Bristol race

and didn't bother with Swindon until the 'mid 2000s'.

The first serious Westmead presence was in 2005 where three Westmead kennelmates reached the decider finishing second (Swift), third (Eagle-8-11f) and fourth (Natasia)

A year later they made no mistake with a 1-2-5 thanks to Joe, Olivia and Max.

In 2008, there were five Westmeads in the final, albeit Oriole (6th) was trained by Graham Holford. Osprey, Ace and Zest took the tricast places – in that order.

However, that record pales into insignificance compared to the Breeders Forum backed event. It moved first to Wembley and then on to Hall Green and Nottingham, before the decision to scrap the event was taken in 2011.

Seven greyhounds have made the journey from Cow Lane and returned home with the trophy: Westmead Cannon ('86), Phantom Flash ('90), Westmead Spirit ('92), Westmead Merlin ('94), Staplers Jo ('95), Westmead Hawk (05') and Dilemmas Flight ('06).

There were also a string of near misses, including three consecutive runners-up between 1987-89 thanks to Westmead's Change, Claim and Havoc.

The most notable final was probably the '92 decider where Westmead Move was the mum of four finalists from the kennel's original entry of 23.

Westmead sisters Spirit and Surprise (9-4f) finished first and fourth, half brothers Next Move and Westmead Paddy finished second and fifth.

Although Nick rates many current and former owners among his closest friends, there are inevitably also times when it goes wrong.

One of the most high profile breakdowns was with David Hawley, owner of, most significantly, Phantom Flash.

Even Hawley's closest friends would concede that he was, at best, difficult.

Before Nick agreed to have him as an owner he warned him: 'David, you criticise every trainer that you put dogs with. You are not going to do it to me are you?' Hawley was certain there would be no problems.

But things started going wrong when Hawley was refused free admission to Wembley to see Phantom Flash run.

He vowed that the dog would never run at the track again. Nick decided that the big black would benefit from another run at the Empire Stadium and entered him anyway. Hawley was furious.

Flash was then beaten in a couple of races and the grapevine was yielding stories of Hawley being openly critical of his trainer.

Eventually Nick decided to act. He confronted Hawley and told him he no longer wished to train for him.

The day that Phantom Flash headed out of the yard was distressing for Nick and head man Tom Prendeville, who worshipped one of the finest greyhounds ever to draw breath at Westmead.

Nick says: "Tom even had a go at his close friend Pa Fitzgerald, who would be looking after the dog at Patsy Byrne's kennel. I told him not to be so silly, it certainly wasn't Pa's fault."

Flash's career eventually came to an end and David Hawley was never again seen at Westmead. However, there was another side to David Hawley.

Westmead Merlin bd d

(Murlens Slippy-Westmead Hannah, Sep 92)

Merlin is something of a rarity; a 'Westmead' not actually born at the Cow Lane kennels. He was brought into the world by Reading breeder David Pearl.

At 12 weeks old, Merlin was handed over to Nick, though he entrusted the pup's rearing up to nine months to an old and trusted friend, George Hunter from Woburn Abbey.

Nick said: "I've known George Hunter from the very earliest days at Westmead. He has a 500-acre farm, has reared numerous pups for me and made a great job of it.

"I love George's attitude to the game; he doesn't seek money or success, he just enjoys being involved."

Merlin was beaten on his debut in A2 at Hackney but was elevated into open class for his second outing and won convincingly in 29.31 for the 484 metres.

His first major victory was in the 1994 Produce Stakes at Hall Green. He won the final in 28.33 (8-11f) and reached a string of other finals without winning any.

The most notable was Nottingham's Eclipse. In the heats, Merlin had overcome a field that included Westmead Chick, Moral Standards and Moral Director, to set a new track record of 29.65 for the 500 metres.

1995 would prove more productive as Merlin first landed the Arc at Walthamstow. He recorded the second fastest time ever at Wimbledon (28.22) but went out of the Derby in the semis and won the consolation in 28.67.

In July he went to Romford and won the Champion Stakes, recording 35.20 for the 575 metes. Then in August he led home kennel-mate Westmead Chick in the Dundalk International. It was his last major victory.

He went to stud in Kerry and was a limited success, throwing three Irish Derby finalists and reaching No.10 on the sire's table. His fastest UK runner was probably the disqualified McCarthys Duke.

Nick says: "Merlin's record shows that he was incredibly fast, though he wasn't always completely focused and we had to work on that throughout his career.

"It certainly cost him a place in the Derby Final. He ran an absolute stinker in the semis, for which I blame myself. He also stayed on, of course, and might have gone further had his career not been ended in a race at Rye House.

"In my opinion the performance of his career was in the Dundalk International following the debacle with the plane journey."

Nick said: "Several years later David phoned me up. He said he wanted to apologise for how he had behaved previously and asked if we could turn the clock back.

"I reminded him of our first conversation and said it was in his nature to behave that way. He couldn't help himself and it would happen again. I said, 'just remember the good times and we will remain friends.'"

Sadly, David Hawley died of cancer not long afterwards. Nick can still remember the good times, and the funny times, even if some were at the expense of his trigger-tempered friend.

Nick said: "David owned Westmead Lodge who he sold to a kennel in Kansas. He asked if I would accompany the dog and offered to pay my fare.

"I agreed and took the dog out, along with another friend, Brian 'Shelbourne Stud' King.

"Unfortunately, Hawley was at his worst and I couldn't stand his company any longer. I decided to pay my own way home, which cost £700, just to get away from him. Brian came with me.

"When we arrived at the airport, we were asked whether we wanted the 'smoking' or 'non smoking' section. We are both smokers and asked for the smoking section.

"The booking clerk apologized that the smoking section was full. Would it be okay to be upgraded? You can imagine the answer to that one! We had a luxurious flight home in first class.

"After we got home, Hawley phoned Brian who related the tale of being upgraded. So when he got to the airport, Hawley, who was a fanatical non-smoker, demanded a seat in the smoking section.

"To his horror, they were able to

accommodate him. He then spent an eight-hour flight in a compartment full of smokers. I could just imagine his reaction. He would have gone ballistic! That poor stewardess! I laughed for days when I heard about it."

After more than 25 years of training, four finalists and at least one near miss, the English Derby remained an unfulfilled aspiration at Westmead.

However, Nick was relatively optimistic going into the 1998 William Hill Derby with two of the top three in the betting.

The sponsors had Larkhill Jo at 7-1, Barrie Draper's 1997 runner-up He Knows was one point bigger, and Toms The Best next best at 10-1 (14-1 Ladbrokes).

The first round went to plan. Larkhill clocked the fastest time on the first night from kennel mate Lurig King with Annies Bullet completing a double.

Things didn't go so well for Tom who was beaten at 2-5f by the fastest heat winner to date, Farloe Mac (28.79).

When the draw was made for the second round, Tom's heat could barely have been tougher. Three of the top four in the betting – Tom plus Draper pair He Knows and Farloe Mac – were drawn in the same qualifier.

It would prove a messy race after early trouble, Tom ran on gamely to win in 29.08 with He Knows scraping through in third and Farloe eliminated.

Larkhill Jo, meanwhile, clocked the fastest time of the competition to date with a seven length 28.53 run. He was shortened to 11-4 with Tom second in the betting at 9-2.

Then the bombshell hit. Larkhill went to traps at 1-3f for his third round heat, but ran well below form and was eliminated. Journalist

Peter Meldrum labelled him 'a Jekyll and Hyde Character'.

However, a veterinary examination revealed calf and shoulder injuries that proved serious enough to exclude him from the Select Stakes a month later.

Thankfully, Tom, who trapped in fourth, produced a powerful late run to win his heat in the fastest time of the round, 28.95 on .30 slow going.

With Annies Bullet and Lurig King both lame, all hopes rested on Tom who was now 9-4 favourite to land the prize.

With the quarter finals just 72 hours later, things were starting to drop into place for the powerful black.

Although badly hampered throughout his quarter final, he came from fourth for a four length win in 28.77. However, he still had time to find on Jaspers Boy (28.59) and Greenwood Flyer (28.68).

Rated 'impossible to get a run' by the press for his semi, Tom was two lengths adrift of the field going to the first bend.

He cut across to rail and proceeded to pick off his rivals along the backstraight before surging clear on the run-in to win in 28.74.

In the second semi final Greenwood Flyer, with the race at her mercy, turned on Tullerboy Cash and became the first Derby semi finalist to be disqualified since Lively Band some 13 years earlier.

When the draw for the final was made, the bookies views differed widely. While they all had Tom, the innermost of the three wide runners, as favourite, in the week before the final he was trading at all odds between 4-5 and 11-8.

The biggest danger was Jaspers Boy (7-2), on his outside, 6-1 bar the pair.

The evening had started with a torrential downpour, thunder and lightning, not the ideal preparation for a dog who didn't like wet weather.

But as the night drew on, the clouds cleared to reveal a clear warm summer's evening.

The kennel's fifth English Derby finalist stepped onto the track with Tina Turner appropriately belting out 'Simply The Best'.

As the traps opened, Tom, with an empty box on his inside came away reasonably, but then clipped Jaspers Boy (T5) and the pair arrived at the first bend in joint last place.

The early-paced Tuesdays Davy shot clear, but Tullerboy Cash and Honour And Glory collided at the first bend. Toms seized his chance and dashed through a big gap on the rails.

Off the second turn, Tuesday Davy was clear, but within strides Tom had gone past on the inside. He reached the third bend with three quarters of a length advantage, but the result was, metaphorically, already on the board.

The big black then pulled away for a four length win in 28.75 on going rated .40 slow.

It was a remarkable triumph for the kennel and also for owner Eddie Shotton.

Nick said: "Part of the enjoyment of winning is being able to make other people happy. Eddie Shotton had spent a fortune over the years, without ever achieving the sort of success that he deserved.

"I originally thought he had paid too much for Toms The Best given his limited racing career, but maybe Eddie got the luck he was overdue.

"Eddie is a gentleman, who is a good loser, and his whole family were equally enthusiastic. It was nice that we also achieved some success with Sarah Dee."

Indeed, before the remarkable year was over, Sarah Dee had won the £10,000 Coldseal Puppy Classic, beating odds-on kennel-mate Droopys Merson, the Wimbledon Puppy Derby, and the English Oaks.

Toms The Best began his racing career at Walthamstow. Nick had joined the track in June '94 following a short spell at Hackney.

He said: "I quite liked Hackney, but things finished on a sour note. I was given a time finding inquiry with a dog who had done nothing wrong.

"They cocked up the going allowances at trials and refused to accept it was their fault.

"When Chris Page announced that Walthamstow were about to scrap the grass straights and go all-sanded it was just too tempting to say no."

Nick remained contracted for around four years bringing a string of top class dogs through the grades.

He said: "In the end, it didn't make good financial sense. I didn't want too many dogs and I needed more than I had to justify the costs of extra staff and vehicles. So I resigned."

It would be Nick's final position as a contract trainer.

He said: "I was never really comfortable working under that arrangement, even back as far as Wembley.

"The racing manager had too much power over when he would race your dogs, and against whom. So I went back to Milton Keynes and ran my dogs when I wanted to run them."

Nick's record in the Irish Derby is incredible. Although Toms The Best remains his only winner, Phantom Flash. Larkhill Jo, and Westmead Hawk were all unlucky finalists.

CLASSY LADY: Sarah Dee with her English Oaks win pictured with Neil Shotton, Nick and Andy Ioannou.

Perhaps his least celebrated runner was his 2001 entry, Tinys Bud.

A winner of the consolation Irish Oaks in 28.43 (two lengths quicker than final winner Marinas Tina), the daughter of Larkhill Jo and Perrys Pusher had been beaten a short head by brother Droopys Kewell in the Champion Stakes prior to the □100,000-to-the-winner senior classic.

While most eyes were on Late Late Show in the final, it was Bud who led the field around the first two bends and along the backstraight. She was impeded at the third bend and finished third in a three-way photo behind Cool Performance and the favourite.

Nick said: "I think she could have won it. Droopys Vieri was probably the fastest in the final, but he was a clumsy dog when he was behind. He almost cost Sonic the Scottish Derby final by running into him.

"He clawed Tinys Bud down the back of the legs and cost both of them their chance, allowing Cool Performance to scrape though.

"She was a true Shelbourne specialist, nowhere near as effective anywhere else.

"I thought she would have a chance of making it as a brood. She threw a couple of decent litters – I had Westmead Oak out of her – but she died of cancer while still quite young."

Although the 1990s started badly, Nick believes it is the decade when some of the more enlightened promoters started to realise the significance of adequate track safety. None embraced the subject more passionately than Ladbrokes' Gordon Bissett.

Nick says: "Gordon came to see Westmead and was very interested in how we did things. In fact, he was tireless, traveling to tracks all over the world, as well as reading just about every scientific study that had been written on the subject.

"In all my time in greyhound racing, I have never seen someone learn so much in such a comparatively short time."

Following the complete renovation and upgrade of the Monmore racing circuit, Bissett's efforts were rewarded by the Greyhound Writers Association with the 1998 Services to the Greyhound Industry award.

The significance of the award was not lost on the man who had spent so long trying to convince the racing authorities of the importance of welfare. Like Bissett, Nick Savva tried to learn from the best and worst that the greyhound world could offer.

None of the four major racing nations, Australia, Ireland, the USA or Great Britain have all the answers. But some have more than others!

So, *en route* to reaching his conclusions about the best and safest possible tracks and method of racing – what were his international sources of inspiration?

He said: "I very much liked the Australian tracks for the size of the circuits and radius of their bends. The American tracks are similar and are all built to identical specifications.

"The Irish tracks are generally very decent, though they vary. Although it is good, I don't think Shelbourne is the best running circuit in Ireland by any means. The straights are too long for the radius of the bends.

"I was very impressed with Longford when I visited. It is supposedly a replica of the old White City. I haven't raced dogs around Longford, but I've watched a number of trials and was impressed.

"When it comes to hare systems, I much

PIONEER: *Gordon Bissett whose efforts to improve track safety received industry recognition.*

prefer our style of hare, either the old McKee-Scott, or the newer Swaffham lure, to the inside hare that they use in the USA and Australia.

"Although the inside hare can be driven closer to the leading dogs, it can result in crowding on the inside - though much of that bumping might be attributed to the larger eight-runner fields, a lack of seeding, and automatic grading."

"The Swaffham lure is cheap and efficient. I know why Walthamstow went for the more expensive Seally hare - because certain trainers fell in love with the furry lure and persuaded them to buy it. It was unnecessary in my opinion".

It will be a surprise to many, but when done correctly, Nick also favours the British method of track preparation.

"I have watched them prepare the tracks in Australia. They deep-harrow it and then keep plating it until it is very firm; far harder than we would think acceptable, and then they water it.

"Although the tracks run very fast, and I consider them less safe than ours, they get away with it, to a certain extent, due to the sheer vastness of the bend radius.

"The Irish also run their tracks fast – too fast in my estimation. I think the main reason is because everybody, the breeders and the managements, like to see fast times.

"I think they also all feel that if every track

runs as fast as possible, at least they are consistent when comparing one track with another.

"Yet the tracks, which are generally superior to England, do not have such big radii as the Australian circuits. As a result, I am sure there must be unnecessary injuries.

"I like the way the Australian, Irish and American tracks have such short runs to the pick-up, or catching pen, immediately after the race. They are always between the first and second bends."

Nick is not generally in favour of dogs being strapped up with injury supports as is allowed in Australia and Ireland.

He said: "I think strapping up of hocks and tendons leads to restrictions of movement.

"But I do support the use of the soft rubber pads that some countries allow for the protection of dogs running with a track leg."

However, on just about every other issue, Nick believes Australian racing leads the world.

He said: "Their racing kennels and procedures are infinitely better than ours.

"The Australian racing paddock system is particularly well thought out, with the kennels for each race in its own confined area, like a designated room with no access to the other kennels.

"Not only is security so much simpler, there is less noise and aggravation for the dogs in the neighbouring kennels who may not be due to race for another two hours.

"With bad kennellers, that can be the difference between a dog performing at its best or coming out of his kennel acting as though he has already raced.

"Even the racing muzzles are better. Ours, with straps, can be improperly fitted by inexperienced staff, either too tight or too

loose. I remember having an argument with a track vet who wanted to muzzle far tighter than I thought was in the dog's best interests.

"I threatened to withdraw the dog until the racing manager intervened."

"When I think of the expenses paid trips made over the years by our industry leaders, I wonder why they haven't managed to bring back any ideas for improvements."

For some reason, not only were the British tracks unwilling to copy countries with better systems, they weren't even willing to copy each other's better ideas.

Nick says: "The key to so many of these problems is standardisation. Decide on the best example in all the different areas – and make them widespread.

"Going back all those years in my letters to the track promoters and the NGRC, I urged them to prioritise standardisation – and stick to it.

"As a starting point, the authorities should at least insist on a minimum bend radius for all new tracks, and mandatory banking.

"They should only be allowed to use approved sand that is shown between recognised parameters in terms of its consistency and ability to adapt to weather conditions.

"I would insist on a standard hare system. Thankfully, we have one in the UK with the Swaffham, though that came about as a result of cost, not specifically with the greyhounds in mind.

"I would also want identical starting traps, fencing and racing kennels.

"The hare would always start from an identical distance from the starting traps at all tracks and over all distances. It would always start within a set time of the last trap being

SHEFFIELD: One of the best galloping tracks in Britain and a great favourite with most top trainers including Nick.

shut and pass the traps at the same speed.

"The distance between the leading dog and the hare should be universal. The pick-up should always be in a position just entering the backstraight after the winning line.

"All track staff should be trained to a high, similar standard, working with proven techniques.

"The net result? Injuries would be minimalised. Dogs would be able to adapt to different tracks without a trial – like they do in other countries – and there would be greater consistency of performance.

"All this could have been done so easily years ago, had the NGRC not been in the promoters' pocket."

Unfortunately, even given the best equipment and attitude, track maintenance is an on-going battle with the elements and natural deterioration.

Over the years, Nick has been called in to advise tracks when things have gone wrong. Almost always, his visits have been unpublicised. So what sort of problems has he encountered.

He says: "First of all, I should point out that I am not a civil engineer, nor do I consider myself an 'expert'. My knowledge has simply been built on my observations of my own track, and an interest in the subject in general over many years.

"When I was asked to advise, I encountered different problems at different tracks. For example, I was asked by the Romford management to solve a problems when the track kept running almost a second slow for the 400 metres and half that again for the 575.

"There were two immediate issues. The first was that the racing surface needed to be raised to improve the drainage. Also, the groundsman was harrowing too deep.

"At Nottingham they had problems between the inside and outside of the track. I concluded that it was caused by incorrect watering.

"A powerful hose was pushing the sand up from the inside towards the hare rail. The clue was the amount of small stones being exposed on the inside. It also caused a bowling of the surface.

"Sheffield had been having injury problems and Dave Baldwin asked me if I would check the track over.

"It soon became obvious that the level of sand had dropped on the inside and it was holding too much water. I recommended that they could either raise the level of sand to make it level with the inside drainage wall or they could cut slits in the wall to help the water drain away.

"There was also an issue with the sand being contaminated with the shale from the speedway track. It was all comparatively easy to fix and the injuries soon dropped back.

"The important thing to remember with sand is that it is susceptible to change and must be constantly maintained to an expert level. With weather conditions so variable, you must be flexible in your preparation and avoid complacency slipping in.

"In fairness to many of the tracks, including those that I attended, there was no lack of care from the managements, they were simply out of their depth and had often been given conflicting advice as to how to solve the problem."

So – is there such a thing as a perfect track?

Nick says: "In an ideal world, all tracks would be the size of Sheffield's 435 metre circumference with its 50 metre radius. Injuries and race baulking would be reduced to a minimum."

Unsurprisingly, the Yorkshire venue occupies the joint 'top circuit' award with Hove and Monmore.

Nick says: "It isn't just about the size of the circuits. Banking is key, as I originally pointed out to the NGRC. There is no doubt in my mind that it must be incorporated on every single licensed track.

"I have read a lot of studies from around the world about the optimum use of banking and it seems that they have all come to the same conclusions – it should be no more or less than 10% irrespective of the size of the circuit and it is of greatest benefit on small tracks.

"However, although the track circumference is important, as is banking, there are other factors.

"For example, Romford is a better circuit than many people realise because the radius of the bends, pro rata, is quite large. They just have short straights. Sheffield's straights are very small but they are huge bends."

"I would like to make it clear that I am not opposed to small tracks. Many dogs are ideally suited to them and aren't as effective on larger tracks.

"Romford is a good example. Due to its conformation, it remains suitable for many Derby dogs over 575 metres.

"The proof is in the number of big race events, such as the Essex Vase or Champion Stakes, that have been won by Derby class dogs.

"I have run many dogs there, including Right Move, Westmead Keawn and Westmead Merlin and even used it to bring Sonic Flight back from injury.

"I just wish there were fewer small tracks in proportion to the bigger circuits.

"The loss of circuits like Wembley, Hackney and White City has left us with no stadium fit for champions in the south of England and I wish that could be redressed."

So is it possible to improve an existing racing circuit?

Nick says: "Within reason, you can make decent improvements. Walthamstow was a good example.

"The worst time was when they had grass straights and sanded bends. The track staff would stand there between races having a chat and pulling rakes around. It was a disgrace.

"The combination of grass straights and sand bends was the worst of all options because it was virtually impossible to service the sand with the right equipment.

"Switching to a complete sand track was the first priority, but then they pulled down the old inside fence and reshaped the bends. It made a huge difference and was much easier for the dogs to run.

Old enough to remember the many injuries that occurred on grass tracks, Nick's spectacles remain un-tinted about its suitability for racing.

He says: "It would be impossible to race on grass these days. The tracks couldn't even cope in the winter when we only raced twice a week on them, and only eight races a meeting.

"I ruined three good litters at Wembley running pups on mud. It absolutely pulled the guts out of them.

"Nor do I think that any of the plans to replace sand with an artificial surface will work – at least, not on what I have seen and with current preparation methods.

"There are two major types of sand currently in use, Leighton Buzzard fine washed and Leighton Buzzard 26a.

"At their best, they are both more than adequate, though the 26a contains more clay and requires more maintenance. It can also get very sloppy in very wet conditions.

"In my experience any sand surface will naturally become dangerous over time. It has to be harrowed on a regular basis.

"Once it has been dug up, it needs to be plated immediately and then watered. The big danger is when it gets harrowed, but then the rain gets in before they can plate it.

"At that stage there is nothing you can do. If you put the tractor around, it simply makes things worse. The great example of that was in the 2008 Scottish Derby when it ran around a second and a half slow for the 500 metres."

"However, sand remains the best option I have seen, if it is properly maintained. Overall, thanks to the greater emphasis placed on its preparation, and the fund paying for the additional machinery required to work them, racing surfaces have improved massively over the years.

There is a theory that soft tracks are safe and that fast tracks are dangerous. Nick believes the scenario is a little more complicated than that.

He said: "The most dangerous tracks often look the safest. This occurs when the track has not been harrowed and it has gone hard underneath.

"If they just scuff the top half inch of the surface, it becomes soft, yet just below it the sand is solid. The net result is the dog's foot does not make a solid contact.

"It is the lack of purchase that causes the movement within the foot that leads to injury.

"The clue is in the footprint. Research has

shown that the depth should be one inch on the straights and an inch and a half on the bends.

"Of the four main going variations: fast, normal, slow and very slow, a disproportionate volume of injuries occur on fast going in my experience."

So which track has consistently the best racing surface?

"For most recent years it had to be Wimbledon. John Forster, who has now retired, always did a fantastic job.

"The track was always watered to perfection, which is vital. There was a time when tracks experimented with sprinkler systems, but I have never seen one that works correctly.

"John doused the track with water by hose. Considering the length of the meetings and the excellent drainage, he did well to keep it so consistent.

"I would have liked John to stay in the industry as a track inspector and trainer for track staff. All groundsman should be taught by John and then have to pass an exam.

"No track should be allowed to race without a qualified groundsman. It is a job with a huge responsibility.

"I also have a lot of respect for Mick Large, whose abilities first came to light when he managed to transform Milton Keynes after a huge blunder in their track preparation made the circuit unraceable.

"He has continued to learn and has helped various tracks in difficulties, or in laying improved circuits, including Henlow and Sheffield."

To conclude the 1990s, from a racing perspective, the third decade at Westmead remains the most successful to date.

Technically, the early successes were down to Natalie. It wasn't until January 1, 1997 that her long-standing kennel lad took over the trainer's licence.

Thankfully, the winners continued to flow – and the role of honour bulged with major victories and awards.

Westmead Harry (1990), picked up the first of four Greyhound of the Year titles followed by Westmead Chick (1994), Staplers Jo (1995) and Toms The Best in 1998.

During the 1990s, the kennel picked off an English, an Irish and two Scottish Derbys, four Produce Stakes, two Arcs, two English Oaks and around another 90 decent stakes.

Interestingly, although the decade's early successes were from Nick's own stock, they were strongly supported by non-Westmeads.

While the likes of 'Tom' 'Joe', 'Merlin and 'Staplers' dominated over the standard distance, two bitches, Elbony Rose and Tralee Crazy, were prolific over six and eight bends.

Rose was bought on the North East independents for £50 but went on to win the '96 Cesarewitch, and Boxing Day Marathon. The following year it was the turn of Tralee Crazy, a bitch bought by Nick for owners Mim and Dennis Slark, for a mere £3,000.

Not only did she repeat Rose's successes in the Cesarewitch and Boxing Day Marathon, she also ran away with the 1997 St Leger.

That was going to take some following in the new Millenium.

Chapter 6

POSITIVES AND NEGATIVES

In 30 years of virtually unbroken success, Nick had never had major disciplinary issues with the NGRC. But that was all to change with unusual and far-reaching consequences.

Background: The NGRC rules have never stipulated what a trainer can or cannot give a greyhound. There is no list of banned substances. The relevant rule reminds trainers that they cannot give any substance not attributable to 'normal' feeding.

While the restriction on performance-affecting substances, or drugs designed to mask injury, is only common sense, it has always been unclear as to whether a vitamin supplement, iron tonic or herb might be considered 'normal'.

In September 2000, Nick found himself in front of the stewards following the detection of the drug Heptaminol in five of his runners.

Nick says: "I had started using Caninsulin, which contains Heptaminol, a few months earlier. It came from Australia and was promoted as helping fatigued muscles.

"I had a couple of dogs who were prone to cramp and I thought it might help. It was a welfare thing rather than seeking to gain an advantage.

"Of the five dogs, only one of them actually won, and he just looked a 'good thing' on previous form.

"I was aware that in Australia, Caninsulin was allowed by some state control boards, but not others. It was basically a vitamin and mineral supplement, but one version of it contained a substance that could imitate caffeine. Unfortunately, that was the one I used."

The NGRC stewards formed the view that Caninsulin 'was not attributable to normal feeding'.

Nick said: "I don't suppose I was really surprised, but admitted what I had done straight away and agreed to take whatever punishment was inflicted on me.

"Before the hearing though, I was tipped off by someone in the NGRC that the stewards intended to make an example of me and they fined me £2,000.

"What really annoyed me was that I had been deliberately targeted. My five positives came from dogs running at four different tracks. Yet I knew that there were other dogs tested at the same meetings which were definitely on Caninsulin – it came from the same source as mine. So why were they not given inquiries?

"When the stewards asked me during the enquiry whether anyone else was using Caninsulin, I replied 'many trainers'.

But worse – very much worse – was to follow. The story of the Derby winner who never was really begins in September 2002.

Westmead-based Cill Dubh Turbo was randomly drugs sampled in the semi finals of the Gold Collar. Several weeks later, it was revealed that the dog had tested positive for the drug Felbenac.

Nick was on holiday in Cyprus when the stewards enquiry was due to take place in December. He was convinced that an error had been made.

He said: "I discovered that Felbenac was some form of pain killer, but since I had never had it in the kennel it had to be either a mix-up over the samples, an accidental contamination or someone had deliberately tampered with the sample.

"In a letter to the stewards I explained that I could not explain its presence and asked if they would test other dogs in the kennel or even take samples to help me discover what had gone wrong. They refused.

"I was fined £1,000 and was so outraged that I decided not to renew my training licence and to let Andrew take over.

"But at the back of my mind, I was troubled. If we couldn't explain how Cill

HISTORY? Droopys Hewitt (T3) on his way to apparent victory in the 2003 English Derby Final.

Dubh Turbo had tested positive, how could we be sure that it wouldn't happen again."

(Ironically, Turbo kept his prize money for finishing runner-up in the Gold Collar. The rule change that forfeited prize money following a positive test came into effect the following month)

Andrew Ioannou had been Nick's head lad for seven years when his professional trainer's licence became live in February 2003. With mixed feelings, Nick soon found himself licensed again.

He said: "Without my knowledge, Bob (Morton) paid the fine and just before the Derby got underway, I decided, for Andrew's sake, to take out a kennel hand's licence.

"I had no doubt that the NGRC would continue to target the kennel hoping to find me handling the dogs and Andrew would have been in trouble."

Ioannou did not inherit the kennel at its strongest period. The star was the previous year's Midland Puppy Derby winner Droopys Hewitt.

Hewitt, who also ran third in the Laurels, was not among the leading fancies for the 2003 William Hill Derby.

He was a decent open class dog whose greatest asset was his early pace and consistency.

The fifth fastest heat winner in the first round, he had beaten Top Savings in the quarter finals in 28.80, and then scraped into the final with a short head to spare over Droopys Corleone in the semis.

When they went to traps for the final, the white-jacketed 'Hughie' was rated a 16-1 chance. Had Betfair been in operation at the time, Hewitt's odds would have fallen dramatically "in running".

He burst out of the traps and was clear at the first bend as the inside two collided and favourite Top Savings failed to secure a run.

By the second bend, it was all over, and the steady and consistent Hewitt crossed the line with nearly three lengths to spare over Farloe Verdict in 28.82.

On Tuesday July 8, three weeks after the final, Andy received a phone call from Wimbledon racing manager Simon Harris to say that Hewitt had tested positive, following a test received after the Derby quarter final.

The following day, the headline 'Dope Sensation' appeared as a banner headline on the front page of the greyhound section of the Racing Post.

The national press also had a fantastic opportunity to accuse greyhound racing of what the public always 'knew it to be' – crooked.

For the jealous and twisted within the industry, who had resented the kennel's record over many years, it was the only obvious answer to its success.

Within a couple of days, Nick received a newspaper photo clipping of himself on to which devil's horns had been added and the words 'they've caught you at last."

Later the same week, connections of one of the other finalists shouted obscenities at Andy Ioannou as he paraded dogs at Nottingham. But among the more rational thinkers, doubts were being expressed about the whole business.

The fact that Droopys Hewitt had provided a positive test after winning a Derby heat was not in doubt. The fact that he cleanly passed a similar test in winning the final was also not in dispute.

ROBBED: Andy Ionnou with 'Hughie' (Droopys Hewitt).

But why would such an experienced kennel give anything to a dog in a Derby quarter final knowing full well that he would be tested?

Nick summed it up with the words, "we would have to be either stupid or incompetent, or both."

Nick set about learning all about Felbinac and he enlisted the help of leading greyhound vets. He said: "I discovered that it was a drug, used as a gel, for the relief in the symptoms of arthritis in humans.

"Some people decided that I might have accidentally contaminated the dog by using it myself for my back condition. But I had never even heard of the stuff before, and it would have been no use to me whatsoever.

"My back condition was so chronic that pain killers didn't work; the only way that I was able to relieve the pain was by having the surgeon kill off the sciatic nerve. Felbinac was so mild that it had to be applied four times a day for relief – not cure. What use would it

have been to me?"

The stewards enquiry followed and the stewards duly took away the Derby title and handed it to runner-up Farloe Verdict.

Nick recalls: "I couldn't attend the enquiry and I tried to keep Andrew in a positive frame of mind. The rule that allowed the stewards to take away a victory was still new and was still to be tested. Had anybody thought what would happen with accidental contamination?

"One of the racing managers even suggested that we claim that the contamination must have occurred in the racing kennels with dirty bedding. It might have been, we simply didn't know."

So how did Droopys Hewitt come to fail the test?

Nick said: "As you can imagine, the whole episode gave me sleepless nights and a huge amount of worry.

"But because of the timing, I was able to

piece together the only plausible solution to what had happened.

"Hewitt had been tested in the earlier rounds and had been clear. He was also tested in the final and was clear.

"Logically, he had to have come in contact with the drug after the heats, but before the quarter final. We also knew that the amount must have been quite small so as not to have still been present in the final.

"I checked through all our records and two days before Cill Dubh Turbo had run at Catford he had been to see vet Des Fegan because I wanted him checked for a possible thyroid problem.

"Two days before Hewitt ran, he also went to Fegan. He had picked up a slight graze on a toe. It was really minor, but if you are in the Derby quarter finals, you don't want to leave anything to chance. In every other way he was 100 per cent perfect.

"We know that Felbenac can be passed by touch. Des Fegan told me that himself. He also said that he didn't use Felbenac and so it couldn't have happened in his surgery.

"But I am totally certain that the Felbinac was inadvertently passed on by someone who took dogs to Fegan – it was probably for their own use, but it was too much of a coincidence to be anything else.

"I asked my own doctor whether it was possible. He doubted it because he didn't think that the ointment would transfer through a dog's coat.

"I didn't accept that view because what the doctor didn't understand was that greyhounds do not have thick coats all over. Under their back legs, on their bellies, or even in their ears you would be in contact with virtually bare skin.

"But what really convinced me was information that I was finally able to get out of the NGRC.

"Although he didn't volunteer any information at the time, chief executive Frank Melville eventually admitted that there had been two other positives for Felbenac.

"In both cases the trainers claimed that they were users of the ointment and that there must have been contamination.

"In one case, they didn't accept the trainers' view and fined him £750. In the other case, they did, and let him off with a warning. I assume they must have taken a view on the levels of drug found."

So how much was found in Droopys Hewitt?

Nick replied: "I don't know. They refused to tell us."

To this day, Nick remains bitter over the whole incident, even though he doesn't blame the stewards for disqualifying Hewitt.

He said: "Hewitt tested positive during the Derby and they probably had no option – they had to take it away from him. Those are the rules.

"It was a disproportionate penalty based on an accidental contamination. But this sport must be clean and it must be seen to be clean – though I do have doubts as to whether they had even considered the possibility of accidental contamination.

"However, what was totally and utterly unforgivable, was that the stewards were not vaguely interested in finding out what happened.

"They might not have liked me, but they had a responsibility to the industry to explain what happened.

Sonic Flight BK D

(Frightful Flash-Westmead Flight, Feb 98)

Sonic won his first open race in 26.89 for Milton Keynes' 440 metres when he was only 18 months old.

A very slow breaker blessed with good early pace and excellent track craft, Sonic had already won 10 opens when he went to Hall Green to contest the 2000 Blue Riband.

He clocked 28.38 (-10) in the heats and went to traps as the 5-4f for the final, but finished second, and lame, behind track record-breaker Vintage Cleaner.

The powerful railing black spent nine months on the sidelines with a ruptured main tendon that had to be operated on twice.

He seemed unlikely to race again but returned in early 2001 with an open win at Oxford. Just over a month later he was a six-length winner of a £4,000 invitation at Stainforth.

The following month he headed to Shawfield, where he went unbeaten through the 2001 Scottish Derby, beating Droopys Vieri by three and a half lengths in the final.

He then headed to Wimbledon. By the time he reached the final he had completed an eight-race unbeaten sequence, including the fastest semi (28.61).

He was cramped for room in the decider (10-11f) and was beaten by more than three lengths by 28.71 winner Rapid Ranger.

Two weeks later, and at 4-11f, the big-striding black came from last place to land the £6,000 Select at Nottingham.

Sonic was then dispatched to Ireland and, under the care of Dolores Ruth, he clocked 28.40 at Shelbourne, but went out of the Irish Derby in the third round.

Dolores then targeted the Irish Laurels, which he won in 28.41 from Micks Mystic. Two weeks later he won the Waterford Masters in 28.40.

He was retied from racing at four years and two months of age due a recurrence of the flexor tendon problem.

He was a limited success at stud with many of his progeny showing an inclination to stay.

In Ireland, his big race winners included Green Heat (Produce Stakes) and Satellite Flight (Ladbrokes 600). In Britain there was Ronnies Flight (Grand Prix), Paint Man (Produce Stakes) Westmead Swift (Coventry Leger), plus of course a handy dog called Westmead Hawk!

From a rare frozen semen mating, he also sired a litter out of Paul Wheeler's Rosemary Bale, the star of which was the 2009 Australian National Distance Champion Jarvis Bale.

Nick says: "He didn't race for 10 months after that initial injury. In fact, when he ran in the Derby, he still had the stitches in his wrist. The knot even pierced the skin but he was so genuine it didn't affect him.

"I thought he was unlucky in the English Derby final when the four and two crossed in front of him out of the traps.

"He ran well in Scotland to beat Droopys Vieri on merit, but Dolores also did a very good job with him in Ireland. I think the best race of his career was probably in the Waterford Masters.

"We would have put him over the distance. He would definitely have stayed, but the injury recurred and we didn't get the chance.

"Sonic was as fast as any I have trained and I don't think he ever got the recognition that he deserved. He was incredibly genuine and blessed with amazing track craft.

"Although he wasn't the fastest trapper, he only found trouble in two races, the English Derby and the Blue Riband Final. It was that track craft that he passed on to Hawk."

Sonic returned to Westmead and spent many happy years in retirement. He was put to sleep following a short battle with bone cancer in February 2011.

Westmead Joe

(Larkhill Jo-Mega Delight, Feb 04)

The 38-kilo Joe was unschooled when he arrived at Henlow in late July 2005. He was big and green, just a bit hyper, and clocked 29.42 for the 460 metres after slipping at the traps. Two trials and three weeks later, his personal best was an open class 27.81.

Beaten on his debut in a tough A1, the enormous-striding black then won six consecutive opens, clocking 27.49 (TR 27.28) at Henlow and 29.84 at Hove (515m).

The sequence included an unbeaten run through the Bedfordshire Puppy Derby, with litter-mates Major and Olivia in second and third.

It was a remarkable demonstration of track craft and pure all-round pace. Many minor open class dogs were clocking 3.90 sectionals; Joe's fastest in the entire competition was 4.10.

After a winter lay-off, Joe was packed off to Hall Green, where he won one of his three qualifiers on his way to the Blue Riband Final.

In the £10,000 decider, he trapped last but ran right through the field to beat Kays Quest by half a length in 28.58.

Following a 28.66 trial over the English Derby course, he was workmanlike throughout the heats finishing second, third, third, first (28.60) and second on his way to the £100,000 final.

Of course, all eyes were on little (36kg) half-brother Hawk in the final, but Joe ran well,

coming from last to fourth, beaten by just two and a quarter lengths.

He went unbeaten (29.30, 29.31) to the final of the Coventry Derby but finished third to 29.32 winner Coventry Bees in the decider.

He then contested the first round of the Swindon Produce, without a trial, and reduced the 480 clock to 28.52, before breaking it again (28.50) in the semis. The 4-9f beat sister Olivia in the £15,000 final in 28.59

A month later, Joe landed his third category one event with a 27.89 run in the final of the £10,000 Monmore Gold Cup.

An odds on favourite for the Hall Green Produce Stakes, Joe was injured in the opening round and withdrawn.

His final event of the year was the Eclipse, but after leading in his heat, he cramped and only just qualified. Likewise in the semis, he was challenging for the lead at the last bend, cramped and was beaten a head for second spot. He wouldn't be seen on a track again for another five months.

Joe warmed up for his 2007 Derby campaign with a trial stake win, but he found barrowloads of trouble every time he went to traps. In the third round, he faced one battle too many (Crwd & Fcdtock2) and finished last.

Although he trialled over the 460-metre course in 27.35, Joe never really ran

Wimbledon and he was beaten by a length by 28.48 winner Savanna Highlands in the Derby Invitation.

Joe ran another six opens, winning two, but with winter approaching, and cramping problems inevitable, he was retired with a racing record of 20 wins and 10 seconds in 46 races.

Nick said: "I don't think there was ever more than a length between Joe and Hawk, and I wouldn't want to guess in whose favour.

"Unfortunately for Joe, he suffered throughout his career through cramp and with high anxiety during kennelling."

Joe was very lightly used when he went to stud and following two strokes, he died just short of his seventh birthday.

Westmead Lord

(Droopys Kewell-Mega Delight, Jun 05)

The 37-kilo Westmead Lord arrived at Henlow with no schooling beyond a couple of sessions behind the whirlygig. His debut was in A5, but with three wins and a second in his first four races, he was soon contesting puppy opens and won his first at Romford in a calculated 24.58.

Blessed with exceptional early pace, the youngster was lightly raced during the winter of 2006.

By the time he took his place in the first round of the Paddy Dunne Puppy Cup in late April 2007, his record showed six wins and five seconds from his first 12 races.

He went unbeaten through the juvenile event landing the £4,000 final at 4-9f.

He was still a pup when he contested a Derby trial stake at Wimbledon, winning in 28.77. Into the main event, it looked as though the 480 metres was beyond him. Despite leading in each of his first three rounds, he was "Ld run-up to Rn in" on each occasion. On the plus side, Lord was consistently breaking 29.00 and only being passed by one rival.

In the quarter finals he trapped more slowly, and was well beaten by the fastest dog of the round – Loyal Honcho (28.46).

The big scare came in the semis. Three dogs clocked identical sectionals, and Lord, on the outside, took a first-bend bump. But the 4-5f kept going and qualified in third.

At 6-1, Lord was fourth in the betting in the 2007 Derby final, with the market led by Loyal Honcho (6-4f) with kennel-mate Dilemmas Flight next best at (2-1).

To win the decider Lord would have to produce the performance of his career – and that is exactly what he did.

When the traps opens, he exited like a black missile to clock the fastest sectional of the competition (4.79).

Lord was a length clear at the first bend and extended that lead all the way to the third bend.

By the final turn, the field, headed by the favourite, were gunning him down, and they drew closer with every stride of the long Plough Lane run in.

At the winning line, Lord had just half a length to spare over Loyal Honcho in 28.47 (+20), with Forest Scholes a neck back in third, and Dilemmas Flight a length back in fourth. The form would be franked a year on with Loyal Honcho winning the 2008 Derby Final in 28.60.

Unfortunately, Lord finished lame with a toe injury and he didn't race again for another nine months.

It took a couple of races to lose the ring

WESTMEAD LORD (5) holds a great position on the run up before first bend trouble ended his hopes of retaining the Derby crown. Winner Express Ego (1) is poised to take advantage, to be followed home by 66-1 shot Monis Pet (6), far left. Wimbledon 9.5.08.

rustiness and he went out of the 2008 Derby in the second round. It was the first time in his 27-race career that he hadn't finished in the tricast places.

But the form seemed to be returning with heat and final victories in the Stud Book Trophy at Monmore (28.24, 28.37).

Then, after only one win in seven races, the toe problem recurred and resulted in another nine months off. After another 11 disappointing races, the 2007 Derby winner was retired.

Nick was determined to have a litter by Lord, but arguably the most handsome dog ever to grace Westmead Kennels was sterile. He was retired, and at the time of writing was living out his later years with Henlow trainer Kim Taylor.

Nick said: "Lord picked up the original toe injury when he was being reared and it continued to trouble him. He had three operations on it, but we were never able to get it right, which was a huge disappointment.

"I know that the public never got to see Lord at his peak. He was barely two years old when he won the Derby, but that was just fate I'm afraid. I certainly never bred a faster dog to the third bend."

Spiridon Louis

(Droopys Vieri-Early Flight)

Spiridon Louis, named after the first marathon winner of the modern Olympics (1896), would become the fourth Greyhound of the Year born at Westmead Kennels.

Whelped in Dec 2004, Louis left Westmead to join trainer Mick Puzey soon after he had completed his schooling.

He qualified into P8 company at Walthamstow, making steady, if not spectacular, progress. By his 13th race, he had risen to A3, but was already being tipped as a future staying star.

He made his staying debut at 21 months old, looking several classes better than the opposition when coming from last to first to win the Peterborough Puppy Cesarewitch.

Two races later, and around his own patch, he gave a start and a six-length beating to the Stow's top stayer, January Tiger.

At 1-5f in the heats of the Racing Post Puppy Stayers Louis broke the 640-metre Stow track record (39.19), but found trouble in the final and was beaten at 1-7f.

But after a series of poor runs, Louis was switched to Lorraine Sams' kennel.

The big white-and-black finally showed his old zest in the first round of the 2007 Regency.

Indeed, it was the start of a nine-race winning sequence that saw him go unbeaten though the Hove event, followed by the TV

TEACHERS PET: Spiridon Louis with owner Gail May.

Trophy at Yarmouth, where he set a new 843-metre record, and finally the prestigious Dorando Marathon on Derby Final night.

In October, 'Mike' was again asked to take on the best six benders in the country in the St Leger at Wimbledon.

He reached arguably the best Leger final for a generation and came with a brilliant late run to catch Lenson Joker by three quarters of a length.

Back to eight bends, he won the £4,000 VC Marathon followed by the £1,500 Essex Record Marathon.

In January, Louis duly carried off the Greyhound of the Year title, along with the 'Best British Bred', and the awards as the top stayer, and top marathon greyhound.

Louis appeared briefly for a third season of racing, but recurring injury problems saw him retired in May 2008.

His career record showed 64 races, from 475-880 metres, with 33 wins and 12 seconds.

Born with no testicles, Louis had no stud potential, but spent his retirement with owner Gail May.

Nick said: "At the time that the litter were schooled, I had no space for racing dogs and suggested to the owners that they should be sent away to gain experience.

"Some of the litter went to Puzey, and others, including Dilemmas Flight, went to Spencer Mavrias at Sittingbourne.

"I had no idea that Spiridon Louis would turn out as good as he did. You seldom can, at that early stage, with stayers.

"But he turned out a top-class dog and I couldn't have been more pleased for Gail, who is a real enthusiast.

"Under normal circumstances it is almost impossible for someone in Gail's position, as a school teacher, to own a real champion. However, Spiridon Louis is proof that those sort of dreams can sometimes come true."

"We were dealing with the Greyhound Derby and national headlines. They should have been charged with their own rule of bringing the sport into disrepute.

"Had they taken the time and effort to investigate and look at the evidence, including the levels of drugs found, they would have concluded that nobody was trying to cheat. But they had no appeals procedure. Thank God they were disbanded!

"It is interesting that years later, when the GBGB stewards found drugs in a dog that they believed had been in him before he came into a trainer's care, they issued a statement accordingly.

"The other group I cannot forgive are the Racing Post for portraying the kennel as 'dopers'. I asked various journalists who was responsible for the headline and they all denied knowledge of it.

"Yet a few months later, when the St Leger winner tested positive for a more serious drug, the headline simply said 'Not Again.'

"I love this industry and would never want to harm it. The implication that we had 'doped' a dog was unforgivable."

Despite his own experiences, Nick is utterly convinced that greyhound racing is as clean as it could possibly be.

In 40 years of training, he only recalls one incident when he believes a dog of his was 'got at'.

It was during the running of the 1986 St Leger. He had ante post favourite Westmead Move.

He said: "She ran terribly, the worst race of her career by far, and was very distressed after the race. When I got her home she started to pass blood.

"I had the vet out to her. I already had my own suspicions about what had happened. The vet could find no other cause. I always wished that I had had her tested. Having said that, if she'd have tested positive, the NGRC would probably have accused me.

"There will always be the odd bad apple, but everything I have learned suggests that drugs use is minimal.

"First, look at how many positives are detected. They use probably the most highly respected testing facility in the world. HFL, who carried out Hewitt's test, handle sampling from horse racing all over the world.

"Yet despite the thousands of samples that are taken from greyhound racing every year, a tiny fraction of one per cent come out as positive.

"If you look at what those positives are for, the type of drugs used, very few are for people trying to cheat. Most are down to carelessness or for things like season suppressants.

"I think there did used to be more skulduggery in the game. Many trainers were caught out when they first switched their testing from Glasgow University to Newmarket, but not any more.

"Besides, I don't think that in general, drugs are particularly effective. I have been in paddocks over the years when I have suspected someone has given a dog something, without knowing exactly what it was. But I was never beaten by one of them.

"I have never felt threatened by anything anyone might give. I always expected to win because of how I prepared my dogs.

"If you look around the game, you see that some of the straightest people have been the most successful. Can you honestly imagine George Curtis doping a dog?"

Not only does Nick not dope dogs, he doesn't 'stop' them either – barring the failed amateur attempt with Pincano.

Nick said: "I honestly cannot recall ever stopping a dog. We have had some gambles due to circumstances falling into place. For example, there was the occasion that we fancied Olivers Wish because we knew he would run well on slow going or Flashy Sir because we suspected he would run well after a few days' break.

"There were also the young dogs who we expected to find time as they became fitter and more experienced, but they were never deliberately slowed down in trials or races.

"Overall, I'm not very successful at gambling. I think every time that Larkhill Jo and Toms The Best ran against each other, I backed the wrong one.

"I had a thousand pounds on Chick when Merlin beat her in the Dundalk International. I didn't back Hawk in either Derby and only had a hundred pounds each way on Lord when he won it.

"My biggest ever gamble was on Larkhill Joe at various prices throughout the Irish Derby. I only kept backing him because I thought he was value.

"I must have had £4,000 on him at various stages and would probably have collected between £70-£80,000 if he had won the final."

Brother Theo provides an interesting perspective on Nick's integrity. He said: "Nick has cost me a lot of money over the years by refusing to take the edge off dogs.

"I remember a trial stake for the Guys And

Dolls at Harringay. We both had a runner in the race and they were the best two dogs in it.

"Nick had the favourite Westmead Lacos who was even money. I had the second favourite who was 5-1.

"There wasn't much between them, but I thought if Nick would take a couple of lengths off his dog, mine would be a certainty. He refused. I backed my dog and he beat me by a short head.

"On another occasion at Cambridge I had set up a dog for a gamble in an open race. I had been preparing the dog for three months. When the trap draw was made, Nick had one of his top dogs in the race.

"I pleaded with him to stop his dog, but he wouldn't. I backed my dog anyway and Nick beat me. The bookies had a great time taking the piss out of me afterwards."

The events in the first two or three years of the new millennium left Nick totally disenchanted with the greyhound industry – though never his greyhounds.

In addition to handing in his licence, Nick bred only seven litters in the five years between and including 2000 and 2004 – in the previous five he had bred 16.

The name Savva, which had appeared on the open race winners table continuously since 1969, was missing from December 2002 until February 2005 (see chapter 7).

Ironically, the decade had started off well with victory in the Trainers Championship meeting.

Nick (or Natalie) has never finished champion trainer, which is based on points scored over an entire year, but the kennel invariably qualified for the one-off championship meeting for which the top six

trainers in the table are invited.

Nick says: "We never chased the trainers title. We are only a small kennel and it would be impossible to compete over the whole year.

"We have regularly finished high enough to qualify for the championship meeting, but we have withdrawn from it more times than we have competed.

"I can't justify running a dog for my sake if I think he can win a competition for the owner. Sometimes though, you might have a few young dogs who it suits, in which case we will enter."

The kennel's third success came at Sittingbourne in March 2000. Although there were only 20 dogs in the racing kennel, including pups, Nick fielded a strong team.

He was quoted in the press as having had £200 on himself at 9-4 to win the competition outright and £20 on his first runner of the afternoon. That turned out to be Larkhill Bobby, who duly won at 14-1.

Litter-mates Sonic Flight and Early Flight also made their way to the winners podium; Tessas Dilemma and Westmead Woofa finished second to complete a successful afternoon.

Greyhounds aren't the only animals to have made Westmead their home. There have been a succession of family pets, most notably a goat called Betsy and an African grey parrot called 'Westy'

Natalie recalls: "The goat had been owned by an old man and she couldn't stand women. She used to terrorise me and would sometimes chase me around the garden.

"One day she escaped into the village and we received a phone call from the police.

PERFECT RESULT: Westmead Osprey (above) and brother Diver were only bred by Nick to help prove Westmead Hawk as a sire. They earned their mum, Droopys Jean, a Dam of the Year title.

Betsy had arrived at a factory full of women just as they had gone on their lunch break.

"She had a group of them pinned behind a grid which she kept butting – they were terrified."

Natalie was no luckier with Westy.

She said: "Nick and Paddy Dunne decided to teach him to speak, and needless to say, they taught him all sorts of bad language. They also left the radio on for him and he used to try to imitate it. Then he learned how to sound like the phone ringing, which was a real pain.

"He made such a racket and if you tried to drown him out be turning up the TV, he'd respond by squarking even louder."

Nick's version of events is slightly different. He said: "I tried to teach him two phrases to enamour him to Natalie. He was supposed to say 'Natalie I love you' or 'Natalie I am hungry, in fact I am starving'.

"I thought I had cracked it when I heard him call her name, but it came out as 'Natalie – f*ck off'

Needless to say, Nick and Paddy found the antics of their foul-mouthed feathered friend hugely amusing. Natalie less so.

She said: "If I went to the cage to talk to him, he would say 'What are you looking at? F*ck off!'"

Sadly, Westy's linguistic skills didn't extend to the paranormal, much to the disappointment of Paddy Dunne.

The eccentric Irishman famously wrote numbers on a bowlful of mint imperials. Although Westy dutifully selected six sweets from the bowl, they never did coincide with the week's national lottery draw.

Westy became ill quite suddenly and died. The air around Westmead kennels became less blue for a while – at least until the arrival of assistant trainer Gary Slater!

Nick's reputation as an outstanding trainer has always been enhanced by the non-Westmeads that he turned into champions – the group would include Larkhill Jo, Toms

The Best and Flashy Sir.

With a 'Westmead' champion, the line between Savva the breeder and Savva the trainer, was always a little blurred.

Not dissimilarly, some questioned, could any competent breeder have produced dogs of similar calibre if they had been blessed with brood bitches like Hacksaw or Westmead Move?

Mega Delight should have convinced most of the cynics – though her racing reputation and bloodlines would have made her a decent bet to be a top brood.

More interesting though, was a 17-month-old pup who arrived at Westmead in 2005 – Droopys Jean.

Nick said: "All I was looking for was a litter by Westmead Hawk and all my broods were related to him.

"I asked Sean and Michael Dunphy if they had anything suitable and they offered me this unraced puppy. I later discovered that she had been sent to Ted Soppitt, but was returned because in schooling trials she didn't look capable of staying four bends.

"But I took an instant liking to her and she duly produced a litter of eight pups by Hawk. Although she didn't produce much milk, probably because of her age, she proved a very good mother"

What a litter it proved to be. It was headed by the inseparable Westmead brothers Osprey and Diver.

Osprey won the Ocean Trailers Puppy Stake and the 2008 Swindon Produce Stakes. He was third to Fear Zafonic in the Graphite Puppy Derby (Diver was runner-up), beaten half a length in a £4,000 Puppy Final at Sunderland and just over a length (1-2f) in Nottingham's Puppy Classic.

Following the first of two serious hock injuries, he would start odds-on favourite for the 2010 Arc Final.

Diver, whose early form included a 28.53 run at Walthamstow, broke a hock while still a pup.

Five of the litter went on to win opens, though it could have been better still.

Nick says: "There was another litter brother, Condor, who looked as good as either Osprey or Diver in his schooling trials. Tragically, he was killed when he hit the fence in his qualifying trials at Henlow.

"They were not a lucky litter. We spent £5,000 on Diver's operation, but he came off sore when we re-trialled him.

"There was nothing between Diver and Osprey in my opinion. They even kenneled together. Both had good early pace, but didn't have to lead to win."

The unknown, imported maiden, Droopys Jean, was voted 2008 Dam of the Year.

It was Napoleon who appreciated 'lucky generals'. Nick doesn't underestimate the value of lucky owners.

He inherited Jack Elias, one of the joint owners of Derby winner Moaning Lad, when brother Theo decided to return to Cyprus.

The pair won the '99 St Leger with Dilemmas Lad, and the 2006 Produce Stakes and Oaks with Dilemmas Flight.

Lad was from a litter that Jack had bred himself out of his St Leger winner Kens Dilemma.

Flight was a litter sister to Spiridon Louis, being by Droopys Vieri out of Sonic Flight's litter sister Early Flight.

Like the best partnerships, Nick and Jack are good friends, though Nick was initially reluctant to have Jack Elias as an owner, because of all strange things, he is a Cypriot – albeit one who has lived in Britain since he was a small boy.

He trained as a barber, moved into the property market and through shrewd investments went on to become a multi-millionaire.

Nick said: "I've had bad experiences of Cypriots as owners; they tend to be gamblers and naïve as to the many downsides of owning dogs.

"But Jack's son, Andrew, was very persistent about me taking their dogs, and two things went in Jack's favour. The first was that he was lucky. Any man who wins the Derby with the first dog he owns and the St Leger with the second cannot go far wrong.

"Secondly, I worked out he must have been a decent guy to have stayed with my brother Theo for so many years. Theo could fall out with his own reflection, so Jack could not have been too bad to train for.

"That is how it has turned out. Jack is a very good sport and a realist who doesn't expect to win every time, but has also become a good friend.

"I often meet up with him when we are both taking a break in Cyprus and I am in awe that he achieved so much, despite becoming profoundly deaf following an accident when he was a boy.

"But as husbands all around the world can testify, sometimes a curse can turn out to be a blessing."

Throughout his time in greyhound racing, Nick has retained an interest in industry issues, either through failed official bodies and committees or through action groups.

Nick was one of the 500 or so audience at Paddy Sweeney's inaugural Greyhound Council of Great Britain meetings back in the early 1970s.

He was a founder member of the owners and trainers group NAGO in the early 1990s, and at the time of writing, is an active member of another pressure group, GOBATA.

He says: "I know some people would say, 'he isn't as badly affected as the trainers who rely on graded racing', but I don't approve of the trainers who adopt a 'blow you Jack, I'm alright' attitude.

"The Greyhound Council had very good motives. We could see that the industry was being run for the benefit of the promoters. The behaviour of the NGRC towards owners and trainers, and their dogs, was absolutely scandalous.

"As soon as Paddy set it up, the NGRC set out to break him. I don't know if the Council could have survived if Paddy's tactics had been more subtle. Realistically, I don't think they had any intention of making any changes.

"NAGO had many similar aims because nothing had really moved on. Also, I'm not sure that everyone connected with the organization had the same motives. It certainly didn't help when the chairman Roy Gibbons went on to become a promoter at Brough Park.

"GOBATA was different in that it came into the industry after the break-up of the NGRC and BGRB. The priority was less about change and more about industry survival."

Chapter 7

HAWK FLIES IN

It was Valentines Day 2005, two years into a self-imposed exile, that the name 'Savva' next appeared on a racecard.

A 21 month old youngster called Westmead Hawk was contesting his first race for his breeder, a 460 metre puppy open at Henlow.

A winner of seven of his 14 races for Barry Bakewell at Hall Green, the 35 kilo black overcame a slow break and first bend bumping to win in 28.06.

While it was a decent performance, no one present could possibly have appreciated its significance – including the dog's trainer.

The solidly built youngster then headed for Monmore for the heats of arguably the highest rated puppy event in the Calendar, the Monmore Puppy Derby. He ran third in the final, but his performances had made Nick's pulse quicken.

He said: "It was a very high class competition, but seeing the way Hawk pulled away going to the pick-up, it was the first time I realised that he could be something special."

A month later, he returned to Monmore to win the Stud Book Trophy, a race in which brother Westmead Eagle had started favourite.

It was then back to Monmore for the three-run Summer Classic.

Although he didn't get clear runs, the strong-finishing black went through the event unbeaten and set a new 630 metre track record in the final.

It was now May 2005 and to the surprise of many, Nick decided to put the country's most exciting novice stayer in the English Derby.

Almost unnoticed in the betting, he won his first two heats in 28.91 and 28.71 before coming up against the highly-rated Droopys Marco in the third round.

DAD: This might seem an unusual photo, but Hawk still greets Nick in the same way when he visits him at stud.

Marco took the lead, but the ever-improving Hawk almost reeled him in with a devastating finish to be beaten half a length in 28.60.

The re-match came in the quarter finals with Hawk half a point shorter in the betting than in their previous meeting. This time he made no mistake, catching the Irish dog on the run-in for a one length win in a brilliant 28.57. Game on!

The punters made the Hawk 5-4f to win his semi. But it would be a trouble-strewn race. At one stage, mere qualification looked big odds against, but Hawk rallied strongly to get to within a length and a quarter of the 28.77 winner, Mineola Farloe.

By now, the brave black with the most amazing track craft that many seasoned punters had ever witnessed, was established as the biggest crowd pleaser in racing.

So into the final, sheer weight of money saw the Dunstable-born two year old made the 5-4f. The draw saw Hawk allocated the black jacket.

Few doubted that he was the fastest in the final, but would he get the chance to clear a field littered with early pace?

It was a messy run-up with plenty of crowding, but the favourite reached the bend in third place.

The pace was being set by 33-1 outsider

GET ON: Hawk was a 66-1 chance to win his first Derby and an ante post favourite to win his second.

Blonde Mac, but as Hawk entered the back straight some four lengths in arrears, the result was beginning to look inevitable.

By the third bend, the Savva runner was slip streaming, at the fourth he switched up a gear and pulled away with apparently effortless ease.

The winning distance was a length and three quarters; the winning time was 28.56.

Nick said at the time: "If someone had told me, even four months before, that Hawk would win the Derby I would never have believed them.

"Hawk was entered because he looked like the sort of dog who could keep qualifying. I

had no expectations of him winning it. Bob backed him each way at 66-1.

"Fortunately, he also started to come right in himself during the competition, you could see it in his coat.

"I only really started to believe he could win it after he ran so well against Droopys Marco. He is certainly the best tracker that I can recall.

"I don't like to plan too far ahead because things can go wrong.

"If everything went to plan though, I could see no reason not to put him over the longer distance again at some stage in his career. In my opinion, he will make an exceptional stayer."

MISSION ACCOMPLISHED: 'The Hawk' comes home a length and three quarters clear of Blonde Mac to win a first English Derby by a dog born at Westmead. Mac was trained by the late Arthur Hitch, who would quip that his dog was so far clear at the third bend that he kept replaying the video expecting Mac to hold on at least once.

Away from the reporters and cameras though, this wasn't simply a second Derby win for Nick.

It was the culmination of so much more. It was the fulfillment of a dream that began more than 30 years earlier, when the first litter was born at Westmead.

It was the long overdue win that Nick had so wanted to deliver to his oldest friend and most patient owner, Bob Morton.

It was also the happy end to a fairytale that had gone so horribly wrong at Oval Road, when the stewards almost ended Nick's desire to train greyhounds. And the whole thing had been achieved just seven months after his training licence was returned.

Nick says: "I had never intended to train again. I gave the licence up as a matter of principle, but also had a chronically bad back that seemed unlikely to ever improve.

"But I also felt as though there was some unfinished business. I wanted to make a point after having my reputation savaged in the NGRC inquiries and also by the media.

"I have always believed in there being natural justice. If I ever did anything wrong, I would get punished in another way.

"In greyhound racing, I have seen many people do bad things, such as not keep their word or double-cross other people, and invariably fate has a repayment for them.

"Make no mistake, I had some help from up above."

Among all the highs and lows, the trophies and accolades, July 2, 2005 would rate as a very special day indeed for Nick Savva.

Suddenly the world all wanted a piece of 'The Hawk'. Nick and Bob Morton were happy to oblige – but as is so typical of greyhound racing, it wouldn't be that simple.

AND AGAIN... Westmead Hawk (4) gets up to beat Mineola Farloe (2) with Amarillo Slim (5) third and Westmead Joe (3) in fourth.

After a turbulent flight to Ireland, Hawk became so distressed that he was withdrawn from his next engagement, the Dundalk International. The dog lost a considerable amount of weight and his scratching from the Select Stakes was a formality.

Hawk returned to racing in early August with a 28.61 first look at Shelbourne Park's 525 yard course.

He reached the 2005 Irish Derby Final with a card showing three wins (29.98, 30.02, 29.66) and two seconds.

The 9-4 chance, who had been seeded wide throughout the event, trapped moderately, but found himself smashed sideways in first bend trouble. He Said So skipped clear and went on to win in 29.66.

Hawk finished fifth, the worst result in his 38-race career and only the third time in his career that he had finished out of the trio positions.

Nick said: "The final was dominated by the antics of Droopys Maldini who ran from trap two and went straight on at the bend ruining the race for everyone including himself.

"It was a pity, because I was convinced that Hawk was absolutely spot on for the final.

"We had had a few problems in him settling at Dolores Ruth's kennel. He had become a bit hyper, both at the kennel and travelling.

"In one heat he had failed to go past Droopys Marco in his usual style and some people were suggesting he waited. That was rubbish, he was just too excitable and not able to produce his best form.

"In fact I even considered giving him a trial between rounds just to settle him down a bit. By the final he had settled, but it wasn't meant to be."

The double Derby finalist was welcomed home like a lost son when he returned to Hall

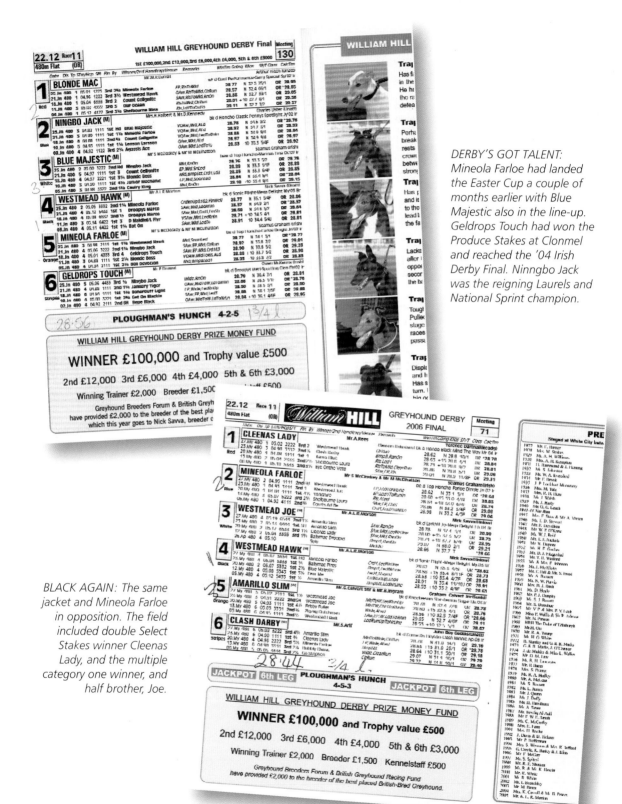

DERBY'S GOT TALENT: Mineola Farloe had landed the Easter Cup a couple of months earlier with Blue Majestic also in the line-up. Geldrops Touch had won the Produce Stakes at Clonmel and reached the '04 Irish Derby Final. Ninngbo Jack was the reigning Laurels and National Sprint champion.

BLACK AGAIN: The same jacket and Mineola Farloe in opposition. The field included double Select Stakes winner Cleenas Lady, and the multiple category one winner, and half brother, Joe.

SIX AND OUT: Hawk, in the stripes, gets a good break in the Irish Derby Quarter Final.

Green for the Produce Stakes later in the month.

He reached the final with one defeat (bdly bmpd run-up) and a best line of 28.24 for the 480 metres. The 4-11f duly dispatched the final by almost seven lengths in 28.44 (-30).

Hall Green reported the biggest crowd for two years had turned up to see the former local hero.

Hawk duly collected the '05 Greyhound of the Year title and went into 2006 as the ante post favourite to retain his Derby title.

First up though was the Scottish equivalent and things didn't go exactly to plan. Hawk looked a bit ring rusty when beaten in both qualifiers of the Shawfield event. But things were starting to come right by the final and he duly ran Fear Me to half a length in the £25K decider.

Nick said: "It was part of Hawk's nature

that he needed a few runs to get to know a track. By the final, he was just getting used to Shawfield."

And so to Wimbledon! A year earlier Nick had forecast that Hawk would be even better as a three year old and that prophecy did not take long to be fulfilled.

Badly bumped at the traps in his opening heat, he provided a glimpse of former glories by rallying to win in 28.53.

In the second round he overcame bad early crowding to come from behind and Fear Me by more than three lengths. The unbeaten run continued with more wins in 28.53 and 28.58 before what many people believe was the race of his career.

The favourite in a top class semi final, The Hawk appeared to be in danger of elimination after trouble around the first two bends.

DOUBLE ACT: Bob and Nick enjoy every moment at the post Derby press conference.

From a seemingly hopeless position, 'the dog with sat nav' began to weave his way through the field.

The race is still remembered fondly by connections for the incredible commentary of SKY's Errol Blythe, who got more and more animated as the people's favourite hound managed to force his way into a qualifying position around the last two bends.

And then, to the astonishment of all watching, and an increasingly agitated race commentator, Hawk loomed up to the apparently invincible Mineola Farloe "Oh my God he is going to win it" screamed Errol. He was right. Hawk prevailed by half a length in 28.62.

Nick says: "In my life, I never saw a better performance from a greyhound, not just among my own dogs, but ever.

"The track craft and determination he showed against top top opposition was just incredible. It still makes me smile whenever I see a replay."

On June 3 2006, Hawk was made a 4-7f to join Mick The Miller, Patricia's Hope and Rapid Ranger as the only three Derby winners to successfully defend their title.

What's more, he was joined in the final by half brother Westmead Joe.

If the semi was dramatic, the final would be clinical.

When the traps opened it was Mineola

Farloe who was the first to show, just in front of Amarillo Slim. Westmead Hawk had got off to a great start for him, clocking his best ever sectional of 5.02, which allowed him to turn the first bend in third.

Down the far side Mineola Farloe was on the bunny, but the Hawk was 'only' five lengths down and he began to pick up approaching the penultimate turn.

As they straightened up for home Westmead Hawk was in overdrive and hit the front in the last thirty metres to score by three quarters of a length in 28.44, the best time of the competition, the fastest final time since Some Picture won in 1997 and a personal best at Wimbledon for the Hawk.

Could Hawk become the first greyhound to win the English Derby three times? Connections allowed themselves to dream for

a couple of weeks until the curse of racing struck again.

The plan had been for Hawk to take on an ambassadorial role with a series of invitation races around the country. The first was to be at his second home Hall Green.

But disaster struck in a preparatory trial and the mighty Hawk smashed a hock. It was plated and opinion was divided as to whether he would race again. In the meantime, he was dispatched to the Droopys kennel in Ireland to commence stud duties. A second Greyhound of the Year title was a formality.

Nick says: "It is a bit annoying because the injury should never have happened. The BGRB wanted him to run in a series of £5,000 invitation races and Hall Green was the first.

"I should have put my foot down. I hadn't intended to run the dog over less than 500

DOUBLE TAKE: Will the real Westmead Hawk step forward. That's him on the left at Madam Tussauds.

metres again, and only on the bigger tracks; Sheffield 500, Hove 515 and so on.

"Then he would have gone six bends properly and run in the top events like the St Leger. He was born to be a stayer, not a Derby dog.

"I remember George Curtis saying that if Hawk ran in staying races he just wouldn't be beaten. I totally agreed."

It would be 10 months before the tentative return to racing began with solo trials. The results were inconclusive. Yes, he was slower than before, but there was no reaction from the injury and it was always going to take time for him to return to racing form.

The comeback actually lasted four races. Nick wanted to give the dog every chance to prove he could do himself justice and

decision day was May 26 2007 – two years and one day after he had announced his arrival with that Monmore track record.

The race was a Derby trial stake, and although Hawk ran to overcome trouble and finish second, Nick and Bob Morton had seen enough. The Hawk was retired after a career of 58 races: 1st-33, 2nd-15, 3rd-6, 4th-2, 5th-2.

Nick says: "We had done everything we could. The operation cost £5,000 and appeared to be a success. But when the time came, he had lost at least five yards of pace and we had to succumb to nature."

Westmead Hawk's Derby win was the culmination of over 40 years and several near misses for the kennel's most loyal owner and supporter Bob Morton.

The pair first met in 1972 when Nick had

Westmead County in training and Bob owned the Tom Johnston-trained Merry Gossip.

Nick says: "I actually recognised Bob from the flaps, but had never spoken to him. To begin with, I didn't know what he did for a living; we just talked dogs.

"Some time later I was having some hassle with the tax man and Bob offered to help me out using his expertise as an accountant."

It was inevitable that the two friends would get involved in greyhounds together and the first was a fawn May '74 bitch pup by Westmead County out of Pallas Melody – Westmead Melody.

A game little stayer, she won the Mercury Trophy at Romford, the Top Dog Stakes at Watford and ran-up to Stormy Spirit in the 1977 St Leger.

(*The beaten favourite in the Watford final, and three places behind her in the Leger was City Salesman, the pride and joy of one White City kennel lad who has since turned his hand to writing.*)

Bob became a regular visitor to the kennel and he would also meet Nick at race meetings.

One night at Wembley, Bob introduced Nick to a stunning blonde air hostess, who he was trying to impress. Being the classy guy he was, he had taken her dog racing on their first date!

It started off so well. One of Bob's runners won the night's big final. The champagne flowed, but there was a little too much of it still in the system when the blue lights started flashing on the journey home.

The conclusion of the first date resulted in a retrieval mission to the police station the following morning to reclaim the trophy.

But Sue, the future Mrs Morton, was not put off, and she was soon accompanying Bob on visits to the kennels.

The next big breakthrough for Bob, as an owner, was his purchase of one of the fastest dogs ever to grace the Westmead range, Special Account.

The fawn's racing career is featured separately, but the highlight, or lowlight, was when he became Bob's first runner to contest an English Derby Final.

The magnificent fawn started favourite to land the 1982 final, but failed in truly heroic circumstances.

"Bob takes defeat in the same spirit as victory" recalls Nick, "with great style"

Bob recalls: "I was absolutely gutted, the dog had to hurdle the Irish dog who fell and made eight lengths on the leader, but just failed.

"I had taken £100,000 to £3,000 with Tom Jenkins at the John Power organisation, though I am not sure that he would have been able to pay out if we had won.

"As it turned out, I laid off some of the bet and actually won money anyway. He then went off to Scotland and went unbeaten through the Scottish Derby which was a fantastic experience."

Over the years, the Morton family grew to include four sons and they too would arrive at the kennel and follow their father's dogs in major races.

It would be another 19 years before Bob would find his name on the owners' list of Derby finalists.

Like Special Account, Sonic Flight had been born and reared at Westmead and went to traps as favourite for the final.

Sonic's chance was over even sooner. Drawn white, he was badly bumped as he left

Mega Delight

bd b (Smooth Rumble-Knockeevan Joy, Jun 99)

Mega Delight made her racing debut in a confined 575 event at Cork in June 2001. Trained by John Kiely, she won her heat by more than 12 lengths, and the final by almost as far.

It was most unusual for Bob Morton to buy a non-Westmead, but stud keeper Richie O'Regan was so convinced of the brindle's potential that he convinced Nick, and Bob Morton, that she was worth buying.

'Meg' joined Westmead and won a 620-metre open, but Nick reckoned "the penny hadn't dropped" in terms of her commitment and he suggested she return to Ireland for more schooling.

She returned to Kiely and soon afterwards reached the Munster Marathon final, but the following month she joined Derby-winning trainer Seamus Graham.

Nick says: "It was John's suggestion to send Meg to Seamus because he realised that she would be running regularly at the top tracks and Seamus was in a better location. It proved to be a good decision."

Within weeks she had landed the Evelyn 750 at Harolds Cross.

A month later, she polished off the Irish Cesarewitch in a new 600-yard track record at Mullingar, swiftly followed by a six-length win in the Corn Cuchulainn.

In May 2002 she won heats and semis of the Barrys Tea 700 by a combined 13 lengths, but was beaten at 1-3f in the final.

A month later, Meg won a semi of the Irish Leger in 29.75 but she finished second to Larking About in the final.

Meg was retired in September 2002 and returned to Westmead soon afterwards. She came into season in the spring of 2003 and was covered by Sonic Flight. It was an interesting mating in that Aussie sire Eaglehawk Star was relatively close in the pedigrees of each parent (a 3 x 4 cross).

The four dogs and four bitches were born on May 2, 2003. The star would be a dog entitled to his own chapter in this book, the great Westmead Hawk, but it was far from being a 'one dog litter'.

Buzzard possibly outshone Hawk in the early days, winning a Hall Green A1 in 28.51 while still only 17 months old. Unfortunately, he had his card marked five races later.

Although he went on to win a string of opens, including a 29.34 for Sittingbourne's 480 metres, he remained 'dubious', and later went on to the independent circuit.

Another brother, Eagle, finished runner-up in the Blue Riband and was beaten odds on

favourite in the 2005 Swindon Produce Stakes. Switched to Ireland, he was beaten a short head by Tyrur Ted in the Ladbrokes 600 and contested the consolation final of the 2005 Irish Derby.

The other brother, Lark, won a couple of opens, including an identical time around Sittingbourne to Buzzard.

Of the four bitches, Swift was head and shoulders the best. She finished runner-up in the 2005 Swindon Produce and Ladbrokes Stayers Final.

The following year she ran third in the Gold Collar, fifth in the Grand Prix, and won the £15,000 Coventry St Leger.

At the time of writing she was also the most successful brood bitch, having thrown Wimbledon Puppy Derby winner Westmead Logan and the Peterborough Derby winner Laindeans Flyer in her first litter, plus Westmeads Guru (Henlow Derby) and Shaw (Henlow Puppy Derby) in subsequent litters.

Swift's three sisters were all top heat graders.

Meg's first litter were nine months old when she produced 4 dogs and 6 bitches by Sonic's half-brother, Larkhill Jo.

They really were a strapping bunch from the 38-kilo Westmead Joe, down to the 34-kilo bitch, Westmead Joy.

The male star was Westmead Joe. Litter-brother Major, who broke 28.00 at Henlow on debut, showed promise of winning stakes before breaking a hock. Another brother, Max, was a prolific minor open winner, and Billy was a grader.

All six of the bitches won open races, two won category ones. The most prolific was the strong-running Aoifa, whose wins included the Coventry Maiden Derby, the Summer Stayers Classic, the Select Stayers and the Gold Cup. She also collected the only Top Dog award ever staged.

Next in line was Olivia, who was runner-up in the 2006 St Leger and Coventry St Leger. Her biggest win came in the 2006 Prestige, and she was runner-up the following year.

Liz finished runner-up in the Coventry Derby and won a string of opens. Nicole won 16 minor opens. Joy had ability, but was injured shortly after winning her third open, while Delight went on to win decent class races at Shelbourne and Harolds Cross.

The third litter produced three dog pups by Droopys Kewell. Whelped in June 2005, the litter featured Westmead Lord, plus brothers Prince and Duke.

They were a litter blessed with great early pace. Prince won the 2005 Peterborough Puppy Derby and finished runner-up in the London Scurry. He went on to win a string of opens, mainly over sprint distances.

Brother Duke was a sprinter who ran A2 at Hall Green before export to Pakistan.

The repeat mating, whelped in January 2006, was two dogs and six bitches, and they showed more versatility than their older half-brothers.

The pick of the boys was Westmead Keawn, winner of the VC Puppy Standard, the '07 Romford Puppy Cup and runner-up in the Sunderland Puppy Derby. Brother Baliff Brian was a minor open race stayer.

Westmead Tina was the fastest of the females with wins in the Totesport Puppy Stakes and runner-up in the 2009 Champion Stakes. Sisters Amy, Class and Debbie were minor open racers.

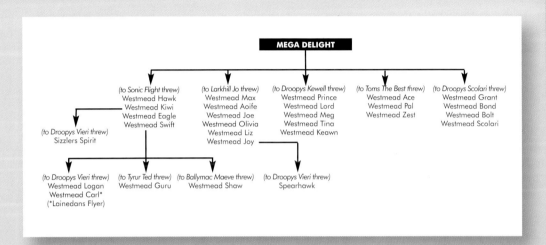

MEGA DELIGHT

(to Sonic Flight threw)
Westmead Hawk
Westmead Kiwi
Westmead Eagle
Westmead Swift

(to Larkhill Jo threw)
Westmead Max
Westmead Aoife
Westmead Joe
Westmead Olivia
Westmead Liz
Westmead Joy

(to Droopys Kewell threw)
Westmead Prince
Westmead Lord
Westmead Meg
Westmead Tina
Westmead Keawn

(to Toms The Best threw)
Westmead Ace
Westmead Pal
Westmead Zest

(to Droopys Scolari threw)
Westmead Grant
Westmead Bond
Westmead Bolt
Westmead Scolari

(to Droopys Vieri threw)
Sizzlers Spirit

(to Droopys Vieri threw)
Westmead Logan
Westmead Carl*
(*Lainedans Flyer)

(to Tyrur Ted threw)
Westmead Guru

(to Ballymac Maeve threw)
Westmead Shaw

(to Droopys Vieri threw)
Spearhawk

Litter number five were by Toms The Best. Though not the quickest overall, with no Category One winner among them, they were extremely genuine, with all nine members of the litter winning open races – mainly over 575 metres or above.

Nick's particular favourite was the giant Westmead Ace, though Pal was the most prolific dog. Zippy and Frisky were the top two bitches.

Westmead Hawk had been at stud for six months by the time Meg's next litter were born.

The seven dogs and two bitches, by Droopys Scolari, included Texacloth Puppy Derby winner and Harold Cross Puppy Derby winner Westmead Grant. Another two brothers, Scolari and Bond, contested the 2010 Scottish Derby Final.

Megs final litter were whelped in December 2008, two of each by Droopys Maldini. The star was Sunderland Puppy Derby winner Westmead Maldini, though two of the quartet were fighters.

Mega Delight died on January 19, 2010 and was buried alongside Toms The Best near the first bend of the schooling track.

Her legacy is a series of achievements that may never be equalled. Her Larkhill Jo progeny won more open races than any other litter in the history of British racing – 140.

Meg is the only brood to have thrown winners of three English Derbies. At the time of writing, her 38 successful progeny had won (UK win prize money only) more than half a million pounds.

Nick says: "Meg was a brilliant mother. She stayed with her pups until they were several months old. She would discipline them but she was also very patient. Several of her daughters seem to have inherited that devoted maternal streak."

the traps with Castlelyons Dani moving wide from trap two and Rapid Ranger (T4) moving to the rail.

Big black Sonic was knocked back to last place. He rallied brilliantly, going past four of the opposition, but couldn't catch eventual winner Rapid Ranger.

The most successful owner/trainer combination in the history of the sport is based on friendship and mutual respect.

While success often brings a divorce between owner and trainer as quickly as failure, Bob and Nick have never had a serious fall-out.

The closest was when Bob changed his mind about purchasing Milton Keynes – something Nick had set his heart on.

But Morton has supported the kennel, not interfered in any decision making and trusted Nick's judgement completely.

Nick says: "Without Bob's support, Westmead would never have progressed in the way that it did, we probably wouldn't have even survived."

On October 18 2007 Westmead Hawk became the first animal athlete to be honoured at Madame Tussaud's wax museum in London.

He was included in a 'Best of British' exhibition alongside the likes of the Queen and David Beckham.

Tussauds staff rated the project one of the most difficult they had ever undertaken.

The fibreglass core was standard, but the eurythane skin and coat, painstakingly applied, one hair at a time, took 20 artists four months to complete.

The net result though was exceptional for the grand opening attended by the Morton family, Nick and the star himself.

The museum were keen to make the most of the photo opportunity and asked Nick if Hawk would stand nose to nose with his lookalike.

Nick said: "I told them that they would just get one opportunity and it worked out brilliantly, as the photos showed, with Hawk with his ears up checking out the model."

With the fomalities out of the way, Nick took off Hawk's collar and lead. The people-loving black was soon mingling with the guests and being totally spoiled, having helped himself to a plate of bacon sandwiches.

The day was a great success, bar one unfortunate incident at the end, when the superstar guest decided to cock his leg on the beautiful white dress worn by one of the other exhibits. Nick was hugely embarrassed.

To this day he won't reveal the identity of the desecrated model – but whenever he licks a stamp he invariably apologises.

Chapter 8

MY WAYS

There is a small cabin in the main yard at Westmead. It is where owners and visitors meet up, enjoy a coffee or something stronger, and talk all things doggie.

The walls of the cabin are plastered with dozens and dozens of presentation jackets, dating back to the 1970s. Trophies fill every available space – and they are just the ones that the owners didn't take home!

Since 1969, literally thousands of winners have made their way home along Cow Lane. Yet the subject of training has been by far the hardest section of the book to complete.

The problem is certainly not down to a lack of transparency. Just as he was helped and advised when he was a novice trainer, Nick gives advice freely and openly.

There are really two main issues that make this section particularly difficult to convey.

The first problem relates to diversity in greyhounds and methods. Nick doesn't train all his greyhounds in the same way.

There is surprising variety in how he does things, or used to do things. Throughout the chapter the reader will be given alternative options for feeding, exercising and handling. Certain aspects of Nick's methods are set in stone, many others can be adapted.

The second major difficulty, that cannot be understated (and a frequent source of frustration for the author), is Nick's overwhelming modesty.

Any line that suggested 'this is how to do it" was thrown out. Any hint that another method was wrong or inferior, went the same way.

We were left with a methodology based on 'it works for me' and hopefully it would work for anyone who cares to emulate it.

FIRST PHASE: The start of the gallop.

RACING KENNELS

The main racing kennel at Westmead is far less salubrious than many people might imagine. The kennels are over 40 years old, and there aren't many of them, 14 to be exact.

Nick says: "We have some additional kennels on the other side of the property, where I tend to put pups when they first come in from the paddocks.

"I also used them for graders when I was contracted at Wembley and Walthamstow. At that stage we had around 50 on the strength.

"Now it would be rare for us to have more than about 16 racing dogs, plus pups, being schooled.

"The kennels were meant to be temporary, but I never updated them because I was never convinced we would last.

"They are fairly basic, but they are clean, dry and spacious. Every one is bigger than the GBGB minimum specifications, some considerably so.

"They face south to give the best light throughout the day and they are all heated in the winter.

"We don't put down sawdust anymore because it is very rare for the kennels to be soiled. Besides, it causes a lot of dust for the dogs to breathe in, and it blocks the drains.

"In the winter, if it is damp outside, we may put newspapers on the floor.

"In summer we use carpets and fleeces on the beds. In winter, the best paper that I can lay my hands on."

Had Nick been building his kennels today, he would have made one significant change.

He said: "They would all have been singles instead of doubles. The downside is that they take up more space, but there are many more positives.

"It is simpler to feed, less hassle when you are trying to put excited dogs on leads, and immediately obvious where the problem lies if one of the dogs has a health issue such as a stomach upset.

"Last, but not least, you greatly reduce the chances of kennel fights."

ROUTINE

The working day gets underway at 6.30am in the summer and half an hour later in the winter.

All the dogs are paddocked and any soiled kennels are cleaned. Since most of the racers are let out late in the evening there is seldom any cleaning out required.

Paddocking, like most procedures at Westmead Kennels, is a slick operation. The dogs do not have to be put on leads. The kennels and paddocks are all interconnected and the dogs can be directed to the individual paddocks by a combination of open or closed gates.

The dogs are then taken for a 15 minute walk.

Nick says: "Years ago, I could take them further, but there are now so many pet dogs loose in the village that it became dangerous, so they would generally just be taken down the lane.

"Or as a change, we might put them in the van, or even walk them muzzled, to the four acre field at the end of the lane.

"Apart from breaking up the routine for the dogs, this is an ideal time to check out what condition they are in.

"I'll be looking to see how the dogs are behaving. Do the racing dogs seem tired? How are they emptying out? Are there any obvious injuries? You can learn a lot about the wellbeing of the dogs if you are observant."

Following the walk, and a quick check on

SECOND PHASE: A left turn at the top of the gallop and the dogs race along the backstraight.

HALFWAY THERE: Pups midway along the backstraight at full speed.

STILL PUSHING: The pups have just one more bend to go.

HEAD FOR HOME: The pups leave the track and head back across the main paddock.

GASP: It's further than you think.

HOME: The course completed – and a photo finish for bragging rights.

the scales, all the dogs who have raced or trialled the previous evening, are checked over for knocks or bruises.

Following a cup of tea for the staff, it is grooming time.

Nick says: "I don't suppose our routine varies greatly from other kennels. The dogs are lightly brushed over. If the coats are a bit scurfy, I use a linament to clean them up. In warmer weather we shampoo the dogs if necessary.

"But I am not a big fan of strenuous massage. I used to massage all their muscles with linament but with my own back giving me problems bending over, I stopped doing it as an experiment and could see no difference in terms of performance or condition.

"We also check ears and teeth. We give the dogs bones about once every fortnight, but I still like to have their teeth brushed regularly too. I used to use a hydrogen peroxide solution, but recently switched to mouthwash. Nails are trimmed every two weeks.

"Sore quicks are also important and can soon lead to bigger problems, so they are regularly treated with antiseptic creams.

"We don't have many race dogs, so grooming doesn't take long, but there are always plenty of other jobs including cleaning the paddocks, which are done every day, and other odds and ends involving the pups."

Interestingly, Nick allows the small group of dogs to wander around the kennel off a lead during grooming for 'socialising' with each other.

After a lunch break for the staff, the whole kennel is fed the main meal of the day.

After feeding, all dogs are paddocked again and any that are off racing are readied for the journey.

At 8pm, all the adult dogs are given another 15 minutes in the paddocks and are then put away for the evening.

However, on race nights, the whole kennel will be given a final outing in the paddocks, while the racers are eating their late meal.

Apart from that final late night paddocking, there are no major variations between race days and non-race days.

ACHIEVING FITNESS

There are many aspects to training a greyhound, though few can matter more than the monitoring and achievement of race fitness.

Nick says: "Although the people reading this book would probably want a foolproof method of getting a dog 100% fit, I do not believe that is achievable.

"The problem is, dogs vary so much. How can I say 'give a dog X number of gallops or trials' when it might prove ideal for one dog, but totally unsuitable for another? Apart from anything else, one might be a sprinter and the other a stayer.

"Greyhounds vary so much in terms of their ability to respond to work, it is impossible to produce a 'one size fits all' approach to reaching racing fitness.

"Secondly, training methods vary considerably. Other trainers may use methods quite different to mine, but still get to the same position as me at the end.

"Thirdly, the way I train has changed many times over the years. Some of the changes came because of changes in circumstances, where I had no choice.

"I can't say that my methods today are better than those I was using 30 years ago. I had a fair amount of success for an amateur trainer and my dogs were pretty fit."

Nick's first attempts at training were from the back of a small house in Collindale, North London.

He said: "We had a small converted shed with a concrete run and two dogs, Pincano and David.

"I used to walk the dogs every day, but most of their exercise came when I took them to a disused private airfield nearby. I would let them loose and just call them back after they had run around for a while.

"I didn't have any major plans, but would do things on instinct.

"Overall, I don't think I made too bad a job of it. David never won a race, but never ran a bad one. Pincano was seldom beaten on the inside hare and although I was only a novice, I don't think many professional trainers would have done much better.

"When I first started at Westmead, I would walk the dogs probably four or five miles a day – one main walk early in the morning and another shorter walk in the evening.

"I would walk up to 10 at a time, which was risky looking back, though I never thought so at the time.

"I would let the dogs off in the 20 acre field, two at a time and allow them to exercise until they had had enough. Sometimes, if I had someone with me, we would gallop them between each other.

"If there were cattle in fields, we might go to Ashridge where we would gallop them over 500-600 yards.

"Sometimes we would take them in the van to George Hunter's farm just to give them a change of scenery. I also had my track operating and would gallop them around it without the hare.

"As I said earlier, it was due to the increase in pet dogs that I realised that I had to change my methods, not only for walking, but galloping too.

"It was for this reason, and also because I was struggling to find staff, that I built my gallop. It enabled me to single-handedly exercise a large number of dogs."

Many trainers use straight gallops for exercising; but Nick relies on a form of free galloping that is tailor-made to the available land and manpower.

He said: "Most professional trainers tend to use a straight gallop of around 300-400 yards. They might whistle them or use a skin or drag hare to encourage them to chase. I don't have this option.

"My dogs gallop on the basis of their natural enthusiasm and that can vary quite considerably. You can gallop them behind an apparently keener dog, though even then they seldom give 100 per cent."

The start of the gallop is situated at the right hand edge of the property. It comprises a 300 yard straight gallop, before turning left onto the back straight of the schooling track.

After clearing the third and fourth bends of the track, the dogs then set off, across the main paddock and on the third leg of the 500 yard triangle, finishing within around 20 yards from where they set out.

The system can be operated by one person, and unlike other gallops, there is no requirement for either a drag hare, skin, or second person encouraging the dog to gallop.

Nick said: "On our gallop, the dogs are not going full speed, but I estimate that a 500 yard gallop here, is the equivalent of a 300 yard gallop at 100% effort.

"Apart from a titbit at the end, the only encouragement they need is their own enthusiasm. New dogs follow one of the more experienced dogs for their first time, but they soon pick it up.

"They love to run. In fact, Westmead Chick would try to go a second time if I didn't catch her. On one occasion she got away from me and ended up dehydrated."

Nick would never trial an unfit dog without a string of gallops.

He said: "Typically, after a long lay-off, I would start them off with gallops every second or third day, and incorporate a walking machine.

"The machine can be particularly useful in the winter if we can't gallop the dogs because the ground isn't suitable.

"I would also use it to take the edge off a few hotheads before I put them on the gallop. A couple of minutes at a slow trot calms them down a bit and also enables them to loosen up."

In fact, no dog goes on the gallop 'cold'. If he doesn't go on the walking machine he will be given a few minutes in a paddock to warm up and encouraged to run around if he is a bit reluctant to move.

Nick says: "If there was a decent walk between the kennel and the gallop I wouldn't bother, but it is only ten or twelve yards."

"On average, it would take about two weeks of intensive galloping before I would even consider trialling a dog."

The balance between galloping and trialling a dog in an attempt to achieve race fitness varies from trainer to trainer.

Given the unusual nature of Nick's gallop, it is possible that he gallops more, and trials less, than some trainers.

He said: "I don't know in detail how they do things, but I think the amateur could learn from top trainers like Charlie Lister and the late Geoff De Mulder.

"Before they raced their dogs, they would usually start with a sprint, and then perhaps another three trials over the standard distance.

"It would be unusual for me to trial dogs that often, but clearly they have been getting excellent results over many years with a slightly different approach."

"There was a time that I used my schooling track, but it isn't necessary."

Sometimes, Nick will allow racing dogs the freedom of the big paddock just to top up their fitness, and they thoroughly enjoy it.

He said: "If you get a high-spirited dog who is inclined to build up a bit too much speed, then you might put him in a smaller paddock to reduce the risk of injury."

On average, Nick believes that following a long lay-off for lameness or a winter rest, it would take six to eight weeks to bring a dog back to sufficient fitness to contest a major competition like the Derby.

The is more than one aspect to fitness, and it is something that this particular writer has never seen discussed in a training book. It is the *mental aspect* of fitness.

Nick has no doubt that some greyhounds need a number of races or trials to overcome 'freshness'.

He says: "No matter how physically fit you produce a dog in home gallops, the excitement of returning can affect the performance, with the most genuine dogs particularly vulnerable.

"The dogs simply get too hyper at the thought of being back racing. They put too much effort into the early part of the race and simply blow up. But its not a physical thing, its purely mental.

"I first came across the problem years ago with Westmead County. He had been off for the winter, but I was determined to bring him back 100 percent fit to win first time out.

"I did everything that I thought was necessary. He was fast walked for miles and had several hard gallops, much tougher than I would use on my dogs now.

"Yet in his first race back, after one satisfactory trial, he led up, but faded in the latter stages. I couldn't believe it, he had never been caught once in front over 525 yards. Yet three or four nights later he romped up in another open at Wembley.

"I racked my brains to work out what had gone wrong in his first race and I came to the conclusion that he was simply 'over keen'.

"He had got himself into such a state of excitement that he had gone too fast too early and his body went into overload.

"His stamina never had the chance to kick in. What I should have done is given him another couple of trials.

"I have seen this many times since. Hawk was very similar. He was so keen that it took three or four races before he settled into his best form.

ASSESSING FITNESS

The process of assessing fitness, is on-going throughout training and is the interpretation of a combination of various signs.

Nick says: "The starting point is a mental check list that most experienced trainers will run through automatically.

"How did the dog perform in its last trial or race - which certainly isn't the same as saying 'did he win or not?'

"Did he perform to the level expected, after balancing out all the factors, the track, the distance, the going, the standard of opposition and any trouble in running?

"Be brutally honest, but don't be afraid to give the dog the benefit of any doubt.

"How did he come off the track? After the trial or race, watch the dog to see when he starts to labour. Does he drive all the way to the pick-up? Clearly, there is a balancing act to consider if the distance is beyond the dog, even if he were fully fit.

"These are all fairly basic questions, but that doesn't make them any less relevant for a grader or a Derby dog."

Many novice trainers will try to form an opinion of a dog's fitness by how heavily he is panting when he returns to the paddock. Some may form an opinion based on how much water he drinks.

Nick says: "Personally, I don't think either behaviour says much. Many genuine dogs come off the track panting like steam engines whether they are fit or not.

"The amount of water consumed varies from dog to dog, and it can also be affected by the weather.

"A better guide is to see how the greyhound behaves the next day. Is he or she lethargic? A bit slow to get off their bed or eat their meal, maybe.

"The ultimate proof that the dog was not fit enough for the work you asked him to do is dehydration. This may onset within hours, or may not be obvious until the following morning.

"It is certainly not a common occurrence,

but even after many years of training, I can still get it wrong."

"There are various levels of dehydration and the book *Care of the Racing and Retired Greyhound* describes them better in pictures than I can in words.

"Basically, the dog experiences significant weight loss and extreme thirst. The symptoms should be obvious even to the amateur trainer.

"Minor cases can be treated by adding electrolytes to water and leaving them with the dog for a few hours after he returns to his kennel.

"For more serious incidents, you might have to put the dog on an intravenous drip into the vein on the foreleg. It is simple enough if you know what you are doing, but I would not advise anyone to try it unless they have been trained.

"At the lower end of the scale I would use Duphelyte around 100-150ccs.

"In severe cases, I would also give saline solution intravenously. I would usually give the whole sack of one litre, and sometimes include some Duphelyte.

"It takes between an hour and ninety minutes to assimilate into the dog's system, but it can be incredibly effective and bring about a very quick recovery.

"But it has to be done correctly and as soon as possible. In severe cases, you may have to repeat it.

"Many years ago, I took Delroney Leader and litter brother Westmead Valley coursing. Although they were very fit, my inexperience showed through – quite simply they weren't bred for coursing.

"Basically, I saw a hare 400 yards away, and when the dogs saw it too, I set them off after it.

"It was a poor decision. The hare was too far away and the field wasn't fenced. The dogs and hare soon disappeared from sight.

"When we eventually caught them, they were exhausted. I realised I'd had no control over where they could run and they could easily have found themselves heading towards the road.

"Although they weren't seriously injured, they became badly dehydrated.

"I don't know what procedure the vet used to re-hydrate the dogs, but it wasn't very effective and they took three months to recover. Thankfully there were no long term effects and Valley eventually went on to win the Scurry Gold Cup."

"I certainly learned my lesson. Never again would I even consider letting a dog loose in an unenclosed area."

So should a dog be brought to peak fitness during a competition?

Nick says: "In my opinion, anybody would be ill-advised to attempt it. My dogs should be near enough 100 per cent fit going into the first round. Experience has taught me that it is simply not worth taking the risk."

Despite the fact that Westmeads Hawk and Lord produced their best performances at the 'business' end of their respective Derbys, Nick refuses to take any credit for what many judges consider to be two great training feats.

He says: "It is likely that the five runs during the space of the competition brought them to their peak.

"My dogs naturally improve throughout the event because they learn to run the track better and mentally adapt to the competition, rather than because of anything I do.

"In the case of Lord winning his Derby, he

picked up a split web in the semi finals and even if I had wanted to gallop him during the week before the final it would have been impossible to do so.

"Yet with Hawk, I allowed him to exercise himself between the semis and finals. I took him into the big paddock and let him off. He galloped around a few big circles as he has always done and got it out of his system.

"I certainly didn't encourage him to run, he just did what he felt like doing.

"It was a chance that I had to take though the paddock was big and safe. If I was concerned that he was a bit too full of himself, I might let him loose in a slightly smaller paddock to restrict his speed."

So how long can a dog be kept at peak fitness?

Nick says: "In most cases, probably for a whole season, around eight or nine months, before they train off.

"Dogs like Special Account and Toms The Best eventually became so musclebound by the end of the season that they started to cramp up; always an indicator that a dog needs a lay-off.

"In my experience, one race a week is ample for most dogs to maintain their fitness, providing that they are already fully fit.

"But I must stress, every dog is different. At the two ends of the scale you have a dogs like Flashy Sir and Special Account.

"In the case of Flashy, I already knew that he didn't cope well with quick runs and I was very aware of it when he was due to contest the Laurels. He had to run Saturday, Thursday and then Saturday in the semis.

"He finished very tired in the quarter finals and really struggled to get through the semis just holding on for third.

"But I was confident that with a week's complete rest he would fly in the final. Bob had a decent gamble on him, and he didn't let us down."

"There was a similar timescale for the Derby with Special Account, but he absolutely loved the quick runs and took off in the semis, only two days after the quarter finals. It was for that reason that I trialled him on my schooling track in the week before the final."

So what could Nick Savva of 40 years experience have taught the young novice who handled David and Pincano about racing fitness?

Nick says: "Probably not a lot. I think they ran pretty fit.

"I would possibly know a bit more now about injuries than in the early days – though I still learn something nearly every day. I also probably place the dogs a bit better than I did. I was a bit indiscriminate on where I raced them, inside or outside hare and without trials.

"There is no substitute for experience, though the biggest difference between then and now is probably just better dogs and being more conscious of safety."

RACING WEIGHT

The inclusion of a greyhound's weight on a race card was the brainchild, many years ago, of former Wimbledon general manager Con Stevens.

Punters have been known to change their betting plans based on a quick glimpse of a pre-race weight sheet.

Nick says: "I am not too concerned about racing weights in most cases After all, we used to flap dogs who were never weighed.

"I think you form an idea of a dog's correct racing weight according to how they look, but after a while it tends to settle at its own level.

"We do have regular weighing, though that is just a simple safeguard for the kennel staff to keep track of things. It can certainly raise the alarm if any of the dogs have dehydrated and they haven't noticed.

"Under normal circumstances dogs should not be underweight unless there is a reason.

"I would normally be happy for competition dogs to put on a bit of weight, rather than losing it. When Hawk won his first Derby he gained a whole kilo between the start of the competition and the finish. Lord gained half a kilo between the semis and the final.

FEEDING

Nick believes that correct feeding is equally as important as training in getting the best out of his canine athletes.

There are no shortcuts in terms of quality of food, but beyond that, the options are many.

Most racing kennels in Britain feed two meals per day. In general, Nick does not feed breakfasts to racing dogs.

However, if the scales show that a dog in work is struggling to maintain weight, then he would rather feed it breakfast, than load up its stomach with a larger main meal. So what's on the menu?

Nick says: "There is no set breakfast. It might be scrambled eggs and toast, or fish, with a few vitamins and additives. Or it might be Wheatabix with honey and in all cases with olive oil".

The main feed of the day takes place at 2.30 in the afternoon. It will surprise many people to learn that the pups, their mums, every sapling in the paddocks and all racing dogs

are fed from the same huge tub of feed.

Nick says: "I know that many successful kennels make up individual feeds for race dogs. My dogs are fed the same food, just in different quantities.

"I have changed the way I feed many times over the years. We originally used to feed a rusk with cooked vegetables plus meat.

"It was based on the 'Northaw' style of feeding, which I had seen and thought would be a good starting point. Basically, they fed a 'slop' kind of feed.

"I wasn't convinced that it was necessary to feed so much liquid because the dogs always have fresh water in the kennels so I started to experiment. You name it, I've tried it."

Former head man Phil Bradley said: "When it came to feeding, the dogs ate like kings and queens. All the food was fit for human consumption, I would sometimes eat a mouthful myself.

"The chicken was from the same supplier as for the supermarkets. Even the vegetables were top quality. One of my jobs was to collect the veg from a wholesaler in Luton who also supplied the local greengrocers."

Despite the kennel success, Nick continued to experiment.

He said: "In recent years I have switched to a high quality all-in-one food which I feed in equal proportions with fresh meat.

"We then add a little bran, some sunflower or cod liver oil, some garlic powder and some cider vinegar.

"You cannot cut corners on feeding. It is vitally important that you keep their stomachs in good order, because when they go wrong it is impossible to train them to their potential.

"But there is some scope for manoeuvre. For example, we sent Westmead Harry to

CAUTIOUS: Westmead Harry's nerves were a complete mystery to Nick. "Nothing ever happened to him in his rearing" said Nick, "he was just born very cautious of people. He was okay with us but didn't like strangers.

"It was interesting because I knew the dam line inside out and there were no temperament problems anywhere. Fearless Champ, who I stood at stud wasn't like it, nor was his sire (Special Account) and I trained both his parents. I always assumed there must have been something in Sarahs Bunny's breeding, but it was a real mystery. Thankfully it didn't affect his racing."

Scotland for the Scottish Derby with a bag of complete feed and vitamins and I told the head lad to buy half a pound of mince from the local butcher every day. The dog went on to win the final and break the track record."

Overall, it is rare for processed feeds to fail. It has only happened to Nick once.

He said: "The dogs started to look poor in their coats. These things happen from time to time and I thought it might be a virus or some form of infection that we could treat with antibiotics.

"I had the dogs blood tested but learned nothing. No matter what I tried – the dogs didn't improve. They weren't ill, they just weren't gaining any condition.

"The next likely scenario was that we had been sent bad meat. The problem was, you may get the odd bad batch, but not one bad batch after another.

"The only remaining possibility was the dry meal. I found it hard to believe it was to blame because of the modern manufacturing process.

"But I started phoning other trainers who used the same meal and discovered they were getting similar symptoms.

"I questioned the manufacturers, but they assured me there was no problem.

"In the end, with all the other options used up, I changed feeds and everything started to drop into place. There was a noticeable difference in the dogs within a fortnight.

"When I looked back afterwards, I realised how much it had affected my judgement. Young dogs hadn't progressed as much as I would have expected, and I had blamed other factors.

"I can never prove how much the dogs were

affected, but I am certain it cost us a lot of winners.

"For example, we had one dog in the kennel, whose best time at Henlow for the 460 metres was around 27.80.

"After we changed the feed, he recorded 27.40. This was a dog who was completely exposed at three and a half years of age.

"I can't prove that feed was a factor, but we also had the highest level of injuries that I had experienced in many years during that period."

Under normal circumstances, substandard meat is very much more likely to be the cause of upset tummies and dips in form.

Nick says: "I only feed meat fit for human consumption and even then you have to be so careful. Problems can still occur if it isn't correctly handled.

"Years ago I used to feed knacker meat and it was a recipe for disaster.

"The dogs would regularly get the runs and when you think of the chemicals and medicines that were probably fed to the beast, plus the conditions that the meat has probably been kept under, its no surprise that things go wrong. And of course the implications for the pups are even greater."

However, it isn't just the quality of the ingredients that is important. The slightest change in ingredients, their storage or preparation, can also have far reaching consequences.

For example, at one stage Nick noticed that several dogs were experiencing an allergic reaction, with the skin becoming red and inflamed.

He said: "I racked my brain as to what had gone wrong. It finally occurred to me. I had started buying organic bran because I thought it would be better for the dogs than the original. As soon as I switched back, the problem went away."

On another occasion, when Nick was away, one of the staff forgot to remove the frozen meat from the freezer and leave it to thaw out overnight.

It was cooked from frozen the next day, and while that shouldn't present a problem, it seems likely that it wasn't cooked thoroughly and many of the younger dogs developed upset stomachs.

Always keen to learn, Nick has discovered a surprisingly wide variation in feeding methods as he has travelled the world.

He said: "I was very interested to see how Australian trainers fed their racing dogs.

"The majority of trainers tend to feed kibble and raw meat. But one of the most successful trainers in Australia feeds coarsely minced chicken carcasses, bread and water.

"The American feeding regime is completely different again. American trainers feed a lot of raw meat, up to two and a half pounds per dog, supplemented originally by kibble, but more recently by a complete feed. No food is ever cooked under the American system from what I saw.

"Looking at both America and Australia racing, I came to the obvious conclusion, that there are many ways to feed greyhounds and be successful.

Former head girl Kelly Findlay said: "I learned so much during my time working for Nick, but the single most valuable lesson was his view on feeding – 'get the stomachs right and everything else will fall into place'."

CONDITIONING/ PREPARATION

"In the early days, I used to go to look at the dogs in the stadium racing paddocks as the trainers prepared their dogs before going on race parade.

"Looking through the fence I would study their condition and see how they were prepared for racing. I soon found that I was watching the dogs of two trainers in particular, Geoff De Mulder and George Curtis.

"I admired George for his meticulous preparation before the race and how he behaved afterwards, win or lose. His dogs were always immaculate. I was a little bit in awe of George and didn't really get the chance to learn from him.

"It was different with Geoffrey. His dogs always sparkled, but when it came to preparing a dog for a specific event, he really came into his own. The coats gleamed and the veins bulged out of the muscles.

"We started to send some of our pups to him when he was at Hall Green and it gave me the chance to ask him about his dogs.

"He was always very kind with his advice, telling you how he trained and fed his dogs. Geoffrey was always a bit eccentric in some of his ways, but in my view he was as good as anyone at 'doing' a dog."

The process of a dog 'coming right' is the point where the trainer's work ends and nature takes over. In most cases this is in the summer after the dogs have grown a thinner summer coat and are clearly just feeling good about themselves.

Nick says: "The coat is the obvious sign that a dog is blooming, I like mine to shine, but there are other signs in their behaviour if you know your dogs well.

"But you can still have a dog in peak form, even if it isn't visibly outstanding. Since the

TEAM WORK: Sometimes you can see a bond between dog and handler. "Ballyregan Bob and George Curtis were a real team" said Nick.

Derby has been run slightly earlier in the year, many dogs still haven't fully cast their winter coats. Both Hawk and Lord were still quite woolly when they won their Derbies.

"Although they looked like sheep, I knew that they were both actually in good physical shape, as they then proved.

"Westmead Move was very different in terms of appearance. She always had bare hind legs when she was racing, though it all grew back when she retired. It might have been something to do with race stress. She was like it when she was at the peak of her performances.

"For many years there was a theory that bald legs were a sign of a thyroid deficiency. Personally, I have had very few problems with thyroids. I believe some of the original thoughts about what was a natural level for a greyhound have since been discredited.

"The best example I can think of for a dog running despite his apparent condition was Linacre many years ago. His coat was always a bit moth-eaten even when he was breaking track records and winning competitions.

"Dogs naturally vary in terms of the quality and thickness of their coat, but don't underestimate the part played by kennel conditions and environment.

"For several years now I have had heated kennels and keep the temperature at around 16 degrees all year round.

"Before that, the dogs would have deep straw beds, and/or kennel coats to keep them warm. It is one of the reasons that so many flapping dogs, who live in the house have coats like glass.

"A dog cannot thrive if he is outside his temperature comfort zone. Not only do they lose energy keeping warm, in some cases they will pass loose motions if their accommodation isn't warm enough."

However, no matter how warm and cosy the dog's living conditions might be, if there is any significant problem with the long term diet, it also reflects in the dog's coat.

It was the failure, over many months, of any of the kennel stars to exhibit a beautiful glossy coat, that first alerted Nick to the problems with the processed feed described earlier.

Parasitic infection will also take the edge off the best fed and groomed dog and it is an on-going battle given that open racers can come into contact with fleas in unclean racing kennels.

As a precaution, all the dogs are treated with Stronghold or Advocate every two months during the summer.

Fleas inevitably lead to worms and worming is also carried out on the whole racing kennel every two months.

Nick says: "We alternate between Drontal Plus, Milbamax and Panacur, which are all effective. Stronghold is also effective against worms.

"Obviously we wouldn't worm a dog if he was due to race within the following couple of days."

Of course, the surest indicator of a dog's wellbeing is his attitude.

Nick says: "How can you describe it in words? They come out of the kennel first thing in the morning with that extra pep in their stride.

"They might be keener when they go out, they might want to tear around the paddock. Sometimes you detect it when they are on parade.

"But every dog is different and you have to know your dogs. Some dogs would exhibit outgoing behaviour irrespective of their overall condition.

"The greatest example I had was Special Account who would go ballistic at the slightest hint it might be a race day."

It was due to Account's hyperactivity, that we referred to earlier, that Nick devised an unusual preparation for the 1982 English Derby Final.

Nick said: "He had 30 spots in hand on semi final form and was in fantastic condition. He was beaming!

"In fact, he was a bit too full of himself and I was worried that he would become too hyper before the final, so I gave him a private trial around my schooling track and he smashed the clock to pieces.

"I was so confident that he would win the final that I watched the race from near the pick-up ready to collect him after the race for the presentations."

The history books show us that Nick's confidence in a big performance was spot on. Unfortunately... Special Account trapped well, but was wiped out at the first bend by Killimy Ivy who ran straight across the track from trap two leaving the race at the mercy of Lauries Panther in red.

The Savva runner rallied brilliantly and made fully eight lengths on the leader before failing by a rapidly reducing three quarters of a length.

If the reader ever gets a chance to see the video, this writer defies them to nominate a more unlucky Derby finalist – ever.

Sometimes, excess enthusiasm needs to be curbed, both in terms of races and exercise. If Nick feels a dog will benefit from it, he will send it up the gallop on the day of a race.

That burst of latent energy just takes the edge off their anxiety and they perform better in the race, though he is keen to stress, only a small percentage of dogs require it.

Cramping is another issue likely to affect performance. In mild form it may result in a runner fading in the latter part of a race or trial. When severe, greyhounds can experience almost total paralysis of limbs as muscles appear to become frozen solid.

Nick says: "Cramp is bought on by a mixture of factors which include a lack of fitness, racing in cold weather, and racing over an extended distance

"Some dogs are just born prone to cramp. Westmead Joe was one of the worst sufferers. Others never show signs of cramping. The only solution for the cold weather crampers is to lay them off for the winter

"As I mentioned earlier, both Tom and Special Account suffered from a different type of cramp, brought on by their being muscle-bound. This can just as easily occur in mild weather and is brought on by extreme fitness, not lack of it.

"I have tried just about every known substance to try to offset it, with limited success, and I am still trying to find something that cures it."

PRE-RACE

Although Nick might be unfazed by a dog's weight, there are occasions where energy loss is definitely a factor, and that is when it comes as a result of dogs being bad kennellers.

In many cases, the problems start before the dog even gets to the track. Because the kennel routine changes little, receipt of a race feed is a sure sign that it is a race day. Cue lots of agitated barking, often accompanied by jumping around in the kennel – and it might still be eight or nine hours before they are due to race.

Nick says: "One solution that works with some dogs is to gradually push back the time that we feed them by around 15 minutes per day.

"Eventually the time that they expect to be fed coincides with the time that they will leave for racing and therefore they don't have the opportunity to fret.

"It isn't too bad if you are lodging somewhere else, for example, when I go to Ireland. But when it happens at home, the whole kennel timetable has to be changed to suit the particular dog.

"The worst culprits are usually the keenest and most intelligent dogs in the kennel. As examples, Sonic Flight and Toms The Best would start fretting unless we changed the feeding routine."

Some kennels are rumoured to give their dogs exotic pre-race feeds including eggs, glucose, sherry and a variety of other goodies.

They may be of benefit, though Westmead success has been achieved without them. Nick's race feed is identical to the full meal, just in smaller quantities.

However. . .is it possible that he once stumbled across some amazing pre-race rocket fuel? Nick says: "Many years ago I took Countville to Yarmouth for an open. I was absolutely shattered when we set off and bought a couple of packs of Dextrose cubes. I thought they might help my energy levels.

"The dog decided that he liked them too, and we shared them on the journey, one for me, one for him. He won by 17 lengths that night.

"To be honest, I was never convinced that

the sweets made the slightest bit of difference and I haven't tried them since."

For a certain section of excitable dogs though, the problems only really become apparent at pre-race kennelling – an ordeal that can, at worst, drag out for more than four hours.

Nick says: "Westmead Joe was probably the worst I have trained for losing weight during kennelling. He would drool very heavily for three or four hours. We have weighed him between kennelling and racing and he would often lose a whole kilo.

"If you trialled him before racing, he was just as likely to break the track record, no matter what the distance, and he often did.

"With bad kennelers it is worse at some tracks than others. For example, at Hall Green, the kennels for any individual race were allocated all over the paddock, which was an NGRC directive.

"But on top of that, the vet would trot dogs up outside the kennels and the runners would be washed down in the same area. If you had a bad kenneler he had one distraction after another.

"I wrote to the general manager Stephen Rea and he made several changes, including having the dogs checked outside the paddock, and having them washed down away from the racing kennels.

"The system in Britain is an absolute shambles and there should be a full investigation to alleviate the problem. The Australian and American systems are vastly superior.

"We are still restricted by the old NGRC rules that insist on scattering the runners around the paddock in an apparent attempt to prevent doping. The Austalians and Americans make a much better job of it. Not only is their security better than ours, they don't upset the dogs.

"Anything you can do to reduce the stress on the dogs has to be in everyone's interest, including the punters. I have no doubt that many races are lost due to bad pre-race kennelling every year."

Even the most important races can be affected by kennelling issues. In the 1997 English Derby Final Nick had future Oaks winner Annies Bullet drawn in five.

He said: "There was two-tier kennelling and I can't remember which was which, but Annie used to freak out if she was in the wrong tier.

"She got herself into a right state and lost her race in the kennels. I'm not sure she could have beaten Some Picture, but I was convinced she could have been runner-up."

Sometimes, though, a more 'radical' solution can be found.

The scene was Milton Keynes. Some months earlier Nick had sold brother Theo a young dog called Westmead Aim for a couple of thousand pounds.

The dog had failed to live up to expectations and Theo demanded his money back. Nick agreed.

A couple of weeks later, Nick entered the rejected dog in a Milton Keynes 620 open only to find that Theo had the favourite and intended to back the dog.

Nick said: "The only problem with Aim was that he was a bad kenneler, which I wasn't aware of when he was sold because he had only been schooled. But when I realised, I came up with a plan to get around it.

"I had a small kennel lad working for me at the time and I asked him to come to kennelling. When nobody was looking, I pushed him in the kennel with the dog and shut the door.

"Instead of fretting up, Aim came out of the kennel as fresh as a daisy and duly romped up at 12-1 beating Theo's dog."

So how did Theo take the result.

"He went potty and called me a f***ing crooked b*****d" replied Nick, bursting into uncontrollable laughter.

"I really didn't set out to do anything other than teach Theo a lesson about observing his dog's behaviour. But I have to admit, it was funny."

Westmead Aim was then sold on to the flapping circuit, where his kennelling antics were not an issue.

Nervy greyhounds seldom present a major problem – as Westmead Harry amply demonstrated (see Breeding chapter).

Occasionally, extreme nervousness can be used to advantage. The best example was Eureka who joined the kennel in the mid 1970s.

Nick says: "When she first arrived in the kennel she was so frightened that I asked her breeder to take her back. She only cost £1,000, but I was prepared to take a loss on her.

"He wasn't having any of it. But my brother Theo heard about her and offered to give me what I had paid for her, providing I would train her. It seemed to be the only solution so I agreed.

"She was a decent staying open racer, not top class, but good enough against decent company.

"But we soon discovered that her nervousness had an effect on her racing. She wouldn't run well first time around a track but, when she knew the place, she would run much better.

"I can remember running her at Walthamstow and she was beaten. But I knew there was a competition the following week. We entered her and she was drawn in a poor heat.

"I said to Theo 'you can have what you want on' and they did. They took probably seven or eight thousand pounds off the track, which was good money back then."

The only time that Eureka won first time out was in an open at one of the Welsh flapping tracks.

Nick said: "I knew that a lot of the flaps were very open and I feared that she would panic. I warned Theo that I wasn't expecting him to bring her home – and he didn't.

"At the end of the race, which she had won, Eureka disappeared into some nearby woods and they couldn't catch her. They had to go back the next morning when they were able to recapture her."

Theo eventually decided to breed with the well-bred daughter of Spectre, who was also a litter sister to St Leger winner Stormy Spirit and top stayer Black Legend.

She turned out to be a cracking dam and threw a string of open racers, including Rikasso Pancho.

Sometimes, the best planned pre-race preparation goes so horribly wrong that the trainer is left wishing he had never left home.

The journey to Ireland for the 1995 Dundalk International provides one of the most interesting lessons in 'race preparation' though Nick still has nightmare about it.

He said: "I had been invited to run (Westmeads) Chick and Merlin and decided

to do the job properly by giving them each a trial and chartering a plane to fly them over on the day, at a cost of £3,000.

"Because of the complications involved, I used the trial session to check that the travelling method would work, flying on a private plane out of Luton Airport. It all went well.

"However, on the day of the actual race, I arrived at the airport with the two dogs in plenty of time and we set off. But after a few minutes we noticed oil streaming across one of the wings. The pilot immediately turned back to Luton.

"The mechanics set about fixing the problem but it took ages. It was a boiling hot day and the dogs were panting heavily. I did the best I could by hosing them down but time was running out and I realised that we had a disaster on our hands.

"Eventually, we got underway and I pleaded with the pilot to make up as much time as he could. He radioed ahead, but with little hope of being in time. We arrived with 45 minutes before the deadline for kenneling and an hour long journey in front of us.

"Michael Keaney had arranged our transport from the airport to the track with his driver, called John, who drove like a rally driver to make up time. We kept the track informed and they just said 'keep coming'.

"We arrived at 10 minutes past the deadline. It seemed we wouldn't be able to run, which I wasn't too worried about, given what the dogs had been through.

"But somebody – I think it was journalist Jason Craddock who had previously worked in the Nottingham racing office – came up with a solution.

"He suggested that the track delay the start

of the meeting by 10 minutes which would keep us within the rules.

"Despite the very forceful objections of one Irish journalist, the race went ahead, and much to my amazement, we finished first and second."

For the 1986 Anglo-Irish race involving Westmeads Move, Wish and Olivers Wish, the charter flight from Luton was cancelled due to bad weather.

Nick hastily arranged a flight from Heathrow and took the dogs over as excess baggage. Despite all the turmoil, the trio finished second, third and fourth making the race a tie.

On yet another trip to Ireland for the heats of the Derby, the road that runs alongside the canal leading to Shelbourne Park was blocked with roadworks. Nick was caught in a traffic jam in the middle of Dublin.

He said: "We were in a car behind John McGee who said, 'Don't worry just follow me!'. I have never been on a journey like it in my life!

"We went through red lights, drove over pavements, went around corners on the wrong side of the road, and broke just about every rule of the road.

"We got to Shelbourne late, but the track were sensible in delaying the start of the meeting. Larkhill Jo got himself into a bit of a state with all the hassle, but still won his heat in a slow time.

"What does that tell you about race preparation? In each case it couldn't have gone any worse, but the dogs still performed."

The same couldn't be said for Westmead Hawk, who became so agitated when flown over for the Dundalk International that he had to be withdrawn, distressed and overheated.

Perhaps the most unusual pre-race preparation concerned Westmead Power, who was due to contest an open race final. She had been booked in for mating the previous day, but hadn't been quite ready. Instead she needed to be mated on the day of the final.

Nick weighed up the options, and rather than let down the breeder, he let the mating take place. Later the same day Power duly won her final!

But if you are looking for the ultimate example of keeping your nerve when preparations go wrong there is nowhere better to look than Derby semi finals.

Nick says: "On the Thursday before the 2006 semi finals, we went racing and left one of the lads to let the dogs out, including 'Hawk' and 'Joe'. But, because it was raining, he decided not to put them out. Both were very clean dogs and held themselves rather than dirtying the kennel.

"By the next morning, Hawk couldn't pass water and I had to catheterise him. Joe developed diarrhoea and everything just passed straight through him. Thankfully we managed to nurse them through, and they both qualified."

POST RACE CARE

Occasionally problems arise with inflammation of the urinary tract, which results in dogs retaining water. Droopys Merson had problems passing water, as did Westmead Hawk, though the worst was probably Toms The Best.

In fact, Nick had been aware of the problem with several sons of Frightful Flash, including Droopys Merson,, though fortunately, not with Sonic Flight.

In most cases, water retention is set off by

the stress of a race or trial. So how did he tackle the problem?

Nick says: "All my dogs have access to fresh water in their kennel. Years ago many trainers fed sloppy foods and didn't think it was necessary to have drinking water readily available, but I think it is vital. For a time we also had water in the small paddocks, but it doesn't stay fresh so we don't bother any more.

"It is important to keep the dogs' kidneys flushed and we give electrolytes before and after racing.

"Of course, one of the biggest problems is that the best dogs are always very clean and don't like to soil their kennel.

"So those that struggle to empty their systems after racing are kennelled for that night in a kennel with access to an outside run. I would also reduce the size of the feed when they get home and make up for it the next day.

"If things get really bad then I would catheterise them. We also use an injectable drug called Bascoban that helps relax the bladder muscles."

INJURIES

Every trainer has faced the dilemma of a dog not running well. There is always a reason for it. The difficulty is pin-pointing it.

Even before he has had the chance to lay hands on the dog, Nick will have considered some of the common factors associated with the race itself.

Nick says: "There are at least a couple of dozen possible reasons for a disappointing performance. Some of them will naturally relate to your assessment of a dog's fitness, as mentioned earlier.

"But you might also question whether the track suits him? Does he run the hare? Does the going suit him? Is there variation between the rails and wide? Is he an 'in and out' performer, or a confirmed front runner?

"If none of those queries provide a satisfactory answer, the most likely reason for a disappointing performance will be an injury.

"We check our dogs the morning after every race or trial, irrespective of whether they appear lame or not, and whether they have won or not.

"Many injuries occur after the race, though obviously you tend to be less concerned about a dog who has run well than one who has underperformed for no obvious reason.

"Nor is it unusual to find injuries on dogs which are apparently walking sound.

"To check the dog over we use the technique developed by Jim Gannon. It was taught to us by Plunket Devlin, who trained with Gannon. We have adapted it only slightly over the years. I can see no point in trying to describe it in this book since I wouldn't do it any better than Jim Gannon in the book 'Care of the Racing and Retired Greyhound.'"

Nick takes around five minutes to check a dog and works in meticulous and methodical fashion. Nails, toes, pads, tendons, joints, muscles and bones are examined for irregularities and flexibility, while looking for any signs of discomfort.

So what goes through Nick's mind at each stage of the examination?

Feet: "Things like web damage and bruised and broken toes should be obvious. In general, toe injuries are less of a problem than when we raced on grass.

"We sometimes get strained ligaments on

either side of the toe. Either injury would probably mean a two to three week lay-off. Depending on the severity, I would also cut back the nail to take pressure off that toe. It is very rare for toe problems to develop into something much more complicated, though it can happen as we discovered to our cost with Westmead Lord.

"The initial injury occurred when he was a pup. The end joint was damaged and never fully recovered. We managed to get through the first Derby, but eventually we had to have the joint taken off because it was still giving him some discomfort.

"In hindsight, his career was already over. We eventually had another joint removed, but that also failed to heal to a point where it didn't irritate him, and eventually it cost him his career."

Wrists: "If I get any reaction to flexing the wrist I always fear the worst. There are two major types of wrist injury, sprains and breaks. In the case of a sprain, it is inevitably many weeks off racing. The only real treatment is rest and daily massage with a good liniment.

"In severe cases, I will sometimes have the wrist injected and have found Carpofen to be the best I have used.

"Bone damage, including the detaching of tendons within the wrist, are just about as bad as it gets. The only option is surgery by a top class veterinary surgeon. These sort of operations are notoriously difficult. Realistically, the odds are massively against you.

"Yet I can also recall wrist injuries that just defy logic. Many years ago Frank Baldwin trained a dog called Say Little who walked off lame on either a wrist or shoulder after every time he raced.

"Yet a few days later he would be back sound and ready to go again. He went on to finish third in the Derby final. How do you explain that?"

Tendons: "When we raced on grass, the dogs often strained the small tendons behind the wrist. You just have to manage them. Dogs like Drynham Star and Ivy Hall Jewel raced for much of their careers with thickened tendons. In severe cases, we may still have them taken out.

"Sonic Flight, ruptured his flexor tendon (the big tendon above the stopper pad) while still a puppy in the final of the Blue Riband.

"I had the two sections sewn back together by a top vet, but the dog still seemed to be in great discomfort. I took the dog back to him but he said, 'don't worry its perfectly normal'

"But I wasn't convinced and asked Allesandro Piras to take a second look. He discovered that the knot in the stitches had become so tight that it was cutting through the tendon.

"He re-sewed the tendon and after a long lay-off, it eventually saw the dog through the rest of his career. It was superb skill by Allesandro and undoubtedly saved Sonic's career. Thankfully it isn't a common injury"

Shoulders: "All shoulder muscles are liable to injury, but the large monkey muscle tends to be the one most likely to be injured. The worst case I ever had was with Staplers Jo.

"His muscle ruptured so badly it virtually exploded and instantly finished his racing career."

When a muscle injury is first detected, the

priority is the ice pack and the first treatment may take place on the night of the injury, as soon as he arrives back at the kennel.

Nick says: "It would be applied for 10 minutes. We would resume treatment the following morning at two hourly intervals, the treatment time being dependent on the severity of the problem.

"If it is bad, I would seek professional help, which might include injecting with an anti-inflammatory. In more minor cases I might just decide on a six week lay-off, supported by treatment from the ultrasound and Magnetopulse machines and massage with a good liniment.

"Throughout the time, I wouldn't attempt to restrict the dog. He would be allowed access to a big paddock where he could exercise as best he felt able."

Back problems: "I check the back for injuries, though I cannot recall ever finding anything significant.

"Why this is, I don't know. Some of the quacks seem to find back problems on a regular basis, but I never have.

"The only time that you do get some reaction is if the dog has developed acidosis, but then it is a more widespread discomfort."

Hocks: "Hock injuries come in a variety of forms, from mild sprains, to stress fractures, to bad breaks. In my experience, I have never had a dog come back as good if there has been a need to operate. But you have a very good chance if you are only dealing with sprains or minor fractures.

"I have changed my view about badly broken hocks in recent years. There was a time when I would have them plated, but the results were disappointing, even though they looked good, the dogs didn't perform to the previous standard.

"Hawk was a good example. The hock looked perfect, but he lost half a second when he came back. If you are dealing with a grader, it might not be an issue if he comes back a couple of grades lower than he once was. But you might think differently if you have a top class dog.

"So in the case of bad breaks, I now have them put in plaster the old fashioned way and hope for the best. I have had some dogs come back far better than I'd dared hope.

"Of course if it is a very bad break you may have to get the hock screwed and plated just to save the dog's leg. But those injuries are write-offs in terms of racing anyway."

One particularly interesting case was Westmead Osprey. He sustained a hairline fracture of a hock at Hall Green. After five months off, he came back quite well, but then seemed to go backwards.

Finally, the hock went again with a full fracture. While it may have seemed to signal the end of his career, Nick gave Osprey another five month break.

Incredibly, he went on to produce some of the fastest times of his career, quicker than before the first injury.

Nick says: The first time the bone didn't callus correctly. It was almost like a bad piece of welding. When it fully fractured the healing process was much stronger with a good callus that made it stronger than before."

Hind leg muscles: "One of the most common muscle injuries is a ruptured gracilis – the plump muscle on the inside of the hind leg. It is also one of the more serious muscle injuries, though it is possible to get the dog back after a decent lay-off.

"I have also seen the muscle sewn back successfully by Plunket Devlin and the dog return to good racing form. The other common hind muscle injury seems to be a torn TFL, though thankfully not with us."

Nick says: "I cannot emphasise enough that injury problems vary so much from the obvious to the obscure. If you cannot find the problem, then call in the professionals.

"These days, we tend to see mainly wrist and hock injuries. Years ago, on the grass tracks, we would get similar injuries, plus a lot more toe and tendon problems.

"I don't care how experienced you are, when you get wrists or hock injuries you must get them x-rayed. No amount of experience can see what is going on under the skin. You will always be reliant on the skill and judgement of a top class vet."

Nick has little faith in the self taught 'muscle men' but has a healthy respect for the opinion of former trainer and long term friend Cecil Law.

Nick says: "If I am in any doubt, I will usually ask Cecil Law to check the dog over for me. I don't tell him what I suspect and if he comes to the same conclusion, it is a great help.

"Cecil spent time working for Jim Gannon, Plunket, and Denis Beary and has learned a lot. I will often ask Cecil for a second opinion on a dog and over the years he has shown himself to be very capable."

Nick has used a variety of vets over the years, and had mixed results.

He said: "I would say that Plunket Devlin

was as good as any I used. Paddy Sweeney was also extremely capable. Although I haven't been able to use him very often, Allesandro Piras appears to be a top class surgeon.

"Over the years I can recall cases where top vets appear to have found injuries that I couldn't find. On occasions, I have disagreed with their diagnosis and have won races with apparently lame dogs.

"In other cases, there has clearly been an injury, but nobody has been able to detect it. Injuries high in the groin can be particularly difficult to locate.

"In cases like this, all you can do is lay the dog off and wait for nature to take its course. Thankfully those type of obscure injuries are very rare."

Finally, if the dog has been thoroughly checked and no problems found, you may even consider blood and urine tests.

Nick says: "At one stage I used to regularly blood test, but decided that they usually proved inconclusive. The urine tests can be of some benefit.

"We use dip sticks, which can detect a multitude of metabolic disorders. These would include detecting some infections, dehydration, traces of blood, or protein loss following a hard race."

Of course, not all injuries are serious and some can even be kept at bay with careful nursing.

For example, Westmead Power won the St Leger, despite going through the event with a severe track leg.

On the day before the 1974 TV Trophy Final, the Savva-trained Stage Box got something trapped in his pad.

Nick said: "I asked David Poulter to come

over. He took one look at it and said 'you are wasting your time.' I wasn't convinced. I thought he would be okay if we could only get him past the vet walking on the concrete. On the track the problem wouldn't affect him.

"I asked David to try to get out whatever was in the wound, but he made it far worse, and I told him so.

"I dressed the wound with Elastoplast and decided to take our chance. Bruce Prole was the vet on duty at the track and we hated each other. Paddy O'Shaugnessy refused to take the dog in.

"I trotted the dog up in front of Prole and deliberately kept stumbling around and nudging into the dog, as though it was an accident.

"He made me trot him up about four times before he waved him through. I then warned Paddy that when they went on parade he had to keep leaning on the dog as they walked, to cause him to lose his balance.

"We had tested him walking at home and sure enough, when he eventually got onto the grass, he was fine and walked normally."

When the traps opened, the 16-1 chance soon took up the running and was never headed.

Nick said: "According to the rules the dog should not have run. I've had to withdraw many dogs from races over the years, but I knew that Stage Box was perfectly fit and that no harm would come to him.

"Basically, if the dogs had been trotted up in front of the vet on the same surface that they were going to race on – sand – there would never have been an issue."

Sand burns can be an ongoing nuisance for kennels, but they are not directly caused by sand.

Nick says: "They are actually caused in starting traps, usually if they are kept dirty and are fitted with poor quality rubber mats. My dogs, including the pups, never get sand burns at home.

"I remember one night at Coventry, where the vet was so concerned at the number that they were getting that he ordered racing to be stopped while they cleaned out the traps.

"I made a special effort to commend him for his observations and for doing something about it."

Nick says: "Not all injuries are obvious, even if you watch the dog closely when he is walking.

"To complicate it further, some dogs have an unusual style of walking; Hawk was one of them. He could look lame if you didn't know him. We had one dog, Westmead Hall, who had such an uneven action when walking that the vet at Hove withdrew him from an open race. I told him that the dog was sound and he wouldn't even let me trial him to prove it."

Nick and GRA vet Bruce Prole had numerous run-ins over the years. Nick says: "There was something very arrogant and superior about many GRA employees in those days and Prole was just typical.

"When you presented a dog to him at kennelling, he would lean over and take a big sniff, then he would reach out and shake the dog, before making you trot it away from him and back.

"Westmead Myra was very nervous and when I presented her, I warned him. 'You can sniff as much as you want, and I will trot her backwards and forwards 100 times, but DO NOT shake her'

"He just glared at me, and I glared back at him. But he didn't shake her."

SUPPRESSION

The vast majority of Nick's bitches are taken off the racing strength as soon as they come into season.

He says: "In most cases they benefit from the rest and they lose form if you try to race them during their season anyway.

"It doesn't matter so much with graded bitches who are just downgraded until their form returns. But I would rather run bitches through a season than put them on the pill."

It wasn't always so. During the 1980s, Nick was using the male hormone to suppress the bitches, firstly through Nandrolane tablets. He then switched to the injectable form in Laurabolin.

When the NGRC started to crack down on the use of Laurabolin, he switched to the human pill, Primulat.

But when they then cracked down on that too, he gave up trying to suppress bitches.

He said: "I have never suppressed one since. The only substances that the NGRC allowed acted as natural stoppers.

"They claim that Laurabolin improved performances, but that is rubbish in my opinion. Provided it was used sensibly and under veterinary supervision, it was perfectly safe.

"Mega Delight was injected with Laurabolin throughout her time in Ireland and it certainly didn't affect her breeding career, nor did it for thousands of other brood bitches."

It is often said that a bitch will run the race of her life immediately prior to coming into season. Nick has mixed views.

He said: "It is sometimes true. I have seen many cases where bitches have run well in the early stages of season. Over the years I have had several bitches who might have been withdrawn by the vet, but have performed brilliantly. I wouldn't have run them otherwise.

"In other cases, bitches lose form even a fortnight or so before they come into season. We had exactly that experience in recent years with Dilemmas Flight".

But even when bitches are in season, Nick does not like them to lose all their condition.

He said: "They are not in training, but you still like bitches to use themselves by being allowed the freedom to gallop and keep themselves in shape.

"The key is usually when they come into milk, though some bitches don't lactate and it is even easier to maintain their fitness, which can be a big advantage.

"I think The Other Toss was supposed to be around 12 weeks in season when she beat us in the Irish Derby Final.

"Other bitches produce lots of milk and you can't do anything with them. I really don't know if it would do them any harm to race, but I cannot believe that they would perform well, and some bitches continue to produce milk for three to four weeks."

"When Westmead Chick was running, the available suppressants simply weren't strong enough – at the levels they prescribed – to prevent her coming into season and I had no choice other than to let her have a season, even though she came in season every six months."

MENTAL ASPECT

If there are no obvious racing reasons for a poor performance, and no injuries can be found, attention turns to the psychological aspect

Is the dog trying his hardest? In Nick's

opinion, there are many levels of 'ungenuiness'.

Westmead Special, was a great money spinner because he would always produce his best performance first time around a track.

The son of Mels Pupil and Cricket Dance reached a string of major finals, including the Scottish Derby, was favourite for several, but usually ran second or third.

Nick says: "He was a Derby class dog who beat Pat Seamur on merit on one night. He would run either hare, inside or outside, but he would only perform at his best first time around.

"Thankfully, we landed quite a number of gambles with him, once we worked him out. We feared nothing, in fact we hoped for top class opposition to get a better price."

But what about aggression? In the early days, Nick forgave Westmead Silver's red card by labelling it as a one-off piece of retaliation by a pup who had been attacked earlier in the race.

Years later, the kennel's highly able star, Westmead Tina, had her card marked after fighting in an open at Sunderland (the daughter of Droopys Kewell was the second Westmead given the name 'Tina'. The first, whelped in 1977, won two major marathon competitions.).

Nick says: "I blame myself for that. Most of Mega Delight's pups have a very jealous streak at the pick-up, including Hawk, who would attack other dogs who tried to take the lure off him.

"In Tina's case, she was returning after a seasonal break and had been running over four bends. We ran her in a race at Sunderland without a six bend trial, and the incident occurred when she was expecting the hare to come off. I can't condemn her for that."

Then there are the dogs who simply become jaded. They may benefit from a 'bit of inspiration' – a walk in the countryside to catch an up-close and personal glimpse of some wildlife.

While it did the trick to motivate the likes of Westmead Merlin, and on occasion, Westmead Chick, Nick believes the concept is over rated by some handlers.

He said: "I can only speak from personal experience, but all the totally genuine dogs didn't need 'motivation' and never got it.

"I remember Toms The Best saw a hare on the week before the Irish Derby Final, but he never chased it, and he certainly didn't need it.

"I remember one occasion when Staplers Jo found himself in a field right next to a rabbit, and he just ignored it. Yet you couldn't get a more genuine dog, and his pups were the same."

"It was the same with Westmead County. He never saw 'anything' in his entire career.

"Flashy Sir was so genuine that he cut his mouth open trying to get to the box containing the lure. He was a fanatic. Westmead Cannon was another who would go absolutely beserk for the lure, yet he would walk past a 'myxie' rabbit by the roadside and not bat an eyelid."

Nick believes that "villains are born" and it is virtually impossible to turn a bad dog into a genuine racer.

5 training theories that I wish I'd known when I started out

1. Whatever you decide to do, do it for the dog's sake and not your own insecurities.

Nick says: "When I was a novice trainer with a dog in a big race, I sometimes felt the temptation to do something extra when the pressure was on. That might be to give it some extra tonic, or to take the dog somewhere where it could see wildlife, or give it an extra massage or an extra walk. Today, I might change something if I thought it would help, but change for its own sake is just as likely to be detrimental.

Sometimes, it is the opposite, being scared to do something for fear of changing a routine. Whichever I choose, I always try to put the dog's requirements first. If he is running well leave him alone!

2. Don't enter a competition expecting a dog to run himself into full fitness. Nick says: "This applies to any competition, whether it is the Derby or a smaller event. In the case of the English Derby, it is not too difficult to see why. In the early stages, you may have to contest very tough qualifiers. By the time they get to the semi finals, they have run three times in a week and need the last week to recover. Whatever the competition, I would not anticipate having to improve a dog's fitness between semis and final."

3. Don't take chances leading up to the final. Nick says: "I remember Geoff De Mulder once saying that he galloped his dogs on the day of the Derby Final, though I'm not sure if he was serious. It certainly isn't anything I would do. In fact, I try to eliminate any chance of injury by carefully choosing where I will let the dogs exercise."

4. Be flexible in everything but routine. Nick says: "Dogs have an internal clock which is incredibly accurate and they thrive on routine. They want to know when they will be let out, when they will be fed, and when to relax."

The problem was highlighted when Nick decided to stay with Ian Greaves during his tilt at the Irish Derby.

Nick said: "Ian could not have tried harder to be hospitable, but there was no routine. Dogs were being fed and exercised at all different times of the day, kennel doors opening and closing.

"Even though Tom had been reared by Ian, he couldn't settle. I soon had to tell Ian that unless he was able to operate in a more organised way, I would have to move somewhere else. Thankfully he took it on board and things settled down."

Kelly Findlay said: "I remember thinking I would get a lie-in when the clocks go back in the autumn. No chance. We had to start at the usual time on the first day and Nick would gradually bring the kennel times back a few minutes each day."

However, beyond the constraints of the clock, Nick is happy to bring some variety into the dogs' lives.

It was this aspect that surprised former assistant trainer Gary Slater when he first started working for Nick. Gary had previously worked for Tom Foster and Terry Dartnall, two kennels steeped in countless category one successes over several decades.

While all three kennels share very similar kennel routines, some of Nick's training methods are quite different.

Gary said: "Take exercise. Terry in particular is very keen on walking. All the dogs are walked religiously at the same time of day.

"Nick works more on instinct. For a start, we do very little walking. We rely mainly on galloping. But for no apparent reason Nick might get up one day and say, 'We're not galloping today. Put the dogs in the van and take them to such and such field for a change of scenery.'

"It's the same with feeding. He'll basically feed the same all the time, but then he might feed some fish, or some chicken to give the dogs a change.

"You never quite know what he will do next, but obviously it works."

5. Prepare your dogs well and you are less likely to get injuries. Nick says: "Injuries are always possible, but I think some are less likely if your dogs are well prepared.

"For example, although we have had our share of hock and wrist injuries, we have not had a serious muscle injury in the kennel since Staplers Jo damaged his shoulder at Hackney – and even then I suspect it was because he was unable to be trotted round before the race (the traps were very close to the paddock).

"I don't know why this is, but I suspect that it is because we try to get our dogs as fit as possible on the gallop, before we take them to the track. I also insist that the dogs are kept warm by moving around before they trial, race, or even go on the gallop."

AND FINALLY THE 'X' FACTOR

Over the years Nick has studied his dogs and inadvertently become a expert on basic canine behaviour.

For example, from just a few weeks old, Westmead pups are taken on leads and given a few sharp tugs, with a quick telling off, if they fight the lead or refuse to walk sensibly. They learn incredibly quickly.

'Dog Whisperer' Cesar Millan trains owners of badly behaved dogs in the same way. (He claims to 'train the owners and rehabilitate their dogs').

This is not violent treatment, or even primarily about how to behave on a lead – it is about dogs learning their position in the pack.

Nick had heard of the behaviour expert, but was totally unaware of Millan's methods, including 'submission' strategy for even tougher behavioural problems.

Without harming the dog, Milan will force a dog to lie on its back, physically wrestling it and holding in down if necessary, while 'the pack' are allowed to sniff it.

When Nick was first told about the technique, he realized he was already doing something similar.

He said: "Sometimes when we are going racing, a young dog, or a new dog to the kennel, will start to cause trouble in the back of the vehicle.

"My first option is a water spray (something behaviourists call 'distraction technique').

"If that fails, and there is someone else to drive, I will sit in the back of the van with the dogs and when the restless or anxious one starts, I will hold him down on his back for a few minutes until he gets the message who is in charge"

The vast majority of dogs do not need to have 'pack order' forced on them, but it is widely recognised that even domestic dogs retain behavioural patterns based on pack protocol.

And, finally, books on greyhound training seldom talk about the understanding between greyhound and trainer. Some readers may even consider it 'mumbo jumbo'

Most top trainers don't talk about it publicly. But privately ask Linda Mullins, Mark Wallis, Linda Jones or Charlie Lister whether they form special bonds with their dogs and they will concede that they do.

Who couldn't see the special relationship that George Curtis had with Ballyregan Bob? They were a team.

Nick's modesty prevents him claiming any special gifts or abilities, though he does acknowledge that bonding does exist.

Others gladly give testimony to this 'X factor'. Shelbourne Stud's Brian King said: "There is no doubt whatsoever that dogs respond to Nick in a very unusual way.

"Some time ago Nick came to visit and was asking about a litter of pups who were eight months old. He asked if they'd been trained to lead. When I told him I hadn't had the time, he said 'got any wellies to fit me?'

"Within an hour he not only had the whole litter trained to lead, they had also had their first look at the whirly and all of them chased. They just seemed to understand what he wanted. It was incredible to witness."

Is it possible that some would-be trainers fail because they never establish that rapport with their dogs?

Nick says: "There may be all sorts of reasons, but I think that a failure to bond with the dogs could be a significant factor.

"In my opinion you need to form a relationship with a dog to get the best out of him. You need to understand what he is feeling.

"Never forget that dogs can only exhibit their true feelings. They never lie to you. It's true I have had staff work for me who say, 'Nick the dogs behave differently when you are around. But why it is I have no idea."

If the concept holds true, it might explain the reasons behind some of Nick's famous 'instinct' decisions.

For no apparent reason, and often to the bewilderment of the staff, he may decide that a particular dog would benefit from a change in food, environment or scenery.

Do top trainers pick up some form of vibe from their dogs and then respond to it?

The concept would come as no surprise to Millan.

Millan believes that owners transmit 'energy' to their dogs which affects their behaviour.

Years ago, Nick formed a very similar opinion. He became convinced that certain people are able to transmit attributes such as confidence and determination to the dog. He believes this can prove an important factor, particularly prior to a race.

He said: "When I take a dog to traps, I'm convinced that he will give his very best. I've had people work for me who feel the same way. Does it make any difference? I really don't know – but I believe it does."

If so, then someone who had the ability to understand and interpret behaviour would presumably influence the mood and character of the pack members.

Owner Gail May said: "There is a bond of trust between Nick and his dogs. They know what Nick expects of them.

"The first time I came to Westmead was in the week between the semis and final of

Hawk's first Derby.

"I know some trainers could get a bit paranoid at that stage so I originally asked if I should leave it until after the final. Nick told me to turn up anyway, it wouldn't make any difference.

"When I arrived, there were a litter of adult dogs in the paddocks together, all unmuzzled and wagging their tails. It turned out that it was Hawk and the rest of his litter.

"I couldn't believe it. I've been to kennels where there wouldn't even put two graded dogs in a paddock together without muzzling them."

The Henlow racing office staff witnessed something similar when arriving at the kennel to mark up pups.

Much to their amazement, they found half a dozen dogs all lying in the same paddock. Each was happily chewing on a bone. Not a sign of trouble.

If the handler can bring serenity, it seems likely that the opposite is true. Could a handler subconsciously handicap his or her dog?

Former head girl Kelly Findlay said: "I remember the night of the Derby semi finals and I was due to lead Hawk as usual.

"After we had kennelled the dog, we went to the snack bar, but I didn't fancy the meal. Nick saw I wasn't eating, pulled me to one side and asked why.

I said, 'I'm not hungry'.

He replied: "You're not nervous are you? If you are, I'll lead the dog around. He was convinced that any nerves could have been transmitted to Hawk.

This writer saw something very similar seven years earlier.

It was Derby final night 1998 and Nick had the favourite Toms The Best. Nick had never won the Derby and pressure must have been intense.

I stood next to him as the dogs went on parade and with more than a few butterflies, asked: 'Are you nervous?'

Nick could not have been calmer if it had been a grading trial. He replied: "No, why should I be? I've done everything I possibly can. It's down to him now."

Chapter 9

THE MATING GAME

Westmead Kennels is comfortably the most successful British greyhound breeding kennel of all time. It's reputation is world-wide, yet the most common reaction from first-time visitors is surprise at the comparatively modest size of the place.

In the 40-plus years since the Pincano's pups drew their first Westmead breath, the kennel has never produced more than five litters in a year. The average is between three and four.

By Irish and Australian standards, that would make Nick a medium sized breeder. To the Americans, he would be one of the 'small guys'.

Westmead success is built on quality over quantity and a consistent strike rate that few breeders in the world could hope to emulate.

The winning formula is an understanding of breeding and bloodlines, combined with a system for producing and rearing pups to the highest possible standard.

STUD DOGS

Nick says: "Looking back, the biggest mistakes I made over the years were in my choice of stud dogs. Cricket Dance went to Clonalvy Pride, who was a good proven sire, but he was the only one. I used many inferior sires in the early days, and poor old Westmead Satin never went to a top class dog.

"Of course I didn't deliberately choose bad sires. It came about because when we first started out, we couldn't make the kennel pay on its own. I decided to stand a few stud dogs to help pay the bills and felt morally obliged to use them on my own bitches."

Although they all produced 'Westmead' open race winners (and at least one Greyhound of the Year), with the benefit of hindsight, the likes of Prince Champion, Mels Pupil, Fionntra Frolic, Fearless Champ and Special Account could not be considered great successes at stud.

"I often wondered what I might have bred if I had used dogs like Prairie Flash, Monalee Champion and Spectre. I only went to Sand Man at the end, and was too late, with Tania.

"In fact, after Clonalvy Pride, I didn't use a top class proven dog until I went to I'm Slippy. Even Whisper Wishes was unproven when I put Tania to him.

"Of course I regret that some of the dogs mentioned never made it. But there is no way of telling with an unproven dog, and nobody suffered more from the failures than myself.

"I had six litters by Fionntra Frolic, a pile more by Mels Pupil and Prince Champion. I can also honestly say that as soon as I concluded that they weren't good enough, I stopped other people from using them too."

Conversely of course, British breeding benefited from some of the more inspired Savva stud dog selections. The industry would have been infinitely poorer without the likes of Westmead County, Westmead Lane, Glenroe Hiker and Flashy Sir to name but four!

So – older and wiser – what does Nick look for in an unproven stud dog?

He said: "I can think of very few pure two-bend sprinters who made it at stud, nor any out-and-out marathon dogs.

"In general though, the better stud dogs have been those who stayed on well, including a few who went on to run six bends, or would have done if they had stayed in training.

"From my own experience I had Westmead County and in more recent times Toms The Best, Phantom Flash and The Hawk. But there are many other examples of dogs who stayed at least 550 yards including Monalee Champion, Spectre, Easy And Slow, Droopys Vieri, and Clonalvy Pride.

"I have also noticed that dogs who seem to be specialists on just one track seldom seem to make it.

"Everybody can think of some; and the list would include Derby winners. I think the

MISTAKES: In hindsight Nick believes he should have used more proven sires like Monalee Champion (right).

same rule applies to potential brood bitches too.

"If you think about it - how can a greyhound that refuses to give his or her best on all tracks be completely honest? In my opinion, the best sires are those with a strong natural instinct to chase."

Other poor sires may produce honest offspring who are simply not fast enough – Nick would include dogs like Prince Champion and Fionntra Frolic in the latter category.

Nick says: "I also try to avoid dogs from inconsistent lines. There are many examples, but two that recently spring to mind are The Stranger and the Greenpark Fox lines.

"So, as good as dogs like Tico and Tapwatcher (both sons of The Stranger) were on the track, they failed to make the breakthrough. The Greenpark Fox line goes back to Bright Lad and was a line that never did well with my breeding.

"Although Citizen Supreme (a son of Bright Lad) and Greenpark Fox (a son of Citizen Supreme) had some success, they never dominated in the way that the Monalee Champion, Sand Man or Head Honcho lines have done since."

In recent years, no kennel, British or Irish, has produced more top class sires than Westmead. Starting off with Westmead County, it went on to include Flashy Sir, Toms The Best, Phantom Flash, Staplers Jo, Larkhill Jo and Westmead Hawk. Ask Nick why and you get the single most interesting insight into his view on stud dogs.

He says: "There are two reasons. One, my dogs are not given any substance to help enhance their performance. I do not believe that the use of drugs is widespread, but the rules are more flexible in some places than others.

"Two, I am not interested in training any dog that needs 'incentives' to keep it chasing.

"In other words, the dogs mentioned were true champions who were able to transmit their genes onto their offspring.

"I believe that there have been many dogs who failed at stud, not because they didn't throw speed. They failed because their offspring weren't genuine enough to utilise that speed to the best of their ability.

"The same theory also applies to the stayers versus sprinters argument. Clearly some sprinters are 100 per cent genuine. Others are dogs with early pace who don't have the commitment to win if they don't lead.

"Give me a dog who is prepared to battle even if he is behind other dogs. That is the determination that I want to see in my pups. Yet invariably it is the early paced dogs who are in the most demand at stud.

"It also tends to be the early paced dogs who produce 'one season' dogs. I've used a couple in recent years. They start off genuine, but lose interest after about 20 races.

"Among my own dogs, who I handled myself during their racing careers, I don't think I made too many mistakes when choosing them as sires.

"The exception might be Special Account, but I always had reservations about him. In his behaviour he was very hyper. He showed no sign of Westmead County and I feared he would breed to the Right O'Myross (Account's maternal grandsire) side of the family. I always had reservations about Westmead Merlin and never used him."

The debate over the importance of a stud dog compared to the dam is one of the oldest in breeding. Given the 150 or so litters bred at Westmead, each under the same rearing conditions, and with many opportunities to compare five or six litters out of the same dam, how much does the sire matter?

Nick says: "Some people try to suggest that breeding is all about the brood bitch. If that were true, how do the legendary sires emerge?

"I have seen great variation in litters, both in temperament and speed, to which the only variable factor was the sire.

"Even my very best broods have failed if the sire was bad enough. The Cricket Dance litter by Faithful Hope is just one example. Physically they appeared fine, they were just slow.

"A good sire is vital. It is a lesson that I wish I had learned years ago"

BROOD BITCHES

There can't be anyone better qualified to discuss the merits of brood bitches than Nick. His Dam of the Year credits read: Hacksaw ('76), Cricket Dance ('77), Westmead Damson ('78), Westmead Satin ('84), Westmead Tania ('87) Westmead Alva ('89), Westmead Move ('91, '92), Celtic Lady ('80), Mega Delight ('05, '06, '07) Droopys Jean ('08) and Westmead Swift (2010).

Nick says: "With stud dogs, if you don't handle them yourself, you don't know anything about their habits and behaviour. That isn't the case with the brood bitches. I wouldn't consider using a brood if I didn't like her temperament.

"In most cases though the broods have virtually picked themselves. I can't breed with all the bitches that I would like to, so I tend to stick to those who have shown the most ability on the track."

But there were failures in the early days, many of them. The likes of Ardagh Star, Claremont Betty, Houghton Tara, Fevata Flash all produced moderately, though none of them were handled by Nick during their racing careers, so he knew little about their character.

He says: "I was very lucky with Pincano, Hacksaw and Cricket Dance, but the others, who I mainly leased, only produced graders.

"You only find that out the hard way. In some instances I am to blame for using bad stud dogs. But in other cases, I am horrified that I continued to persevere with a second or third litter with the same brood when the first litter were clearly nowhere near good enough."

It wasn't necessarily that the bitches lacked racing ability. Nick experienced failure with at least three English Oaks winners, including Miss Ross and Lucky Empress. But the one that really saddened him was Westmead Chick (see chapter 5).

To this day, no finer bitch has been born at Westmead. Indeed, if you could choose a 'nailed on' racer to become a champion brood, you could have found none better.

At her peak, faster than any male greyhound in training, she was by the best sire at stud, out of the best brood bitch in England. She was 34 kilos of blue brindle athlete. Yet as a brood, she threw Midland Flat winner Westmead Striker, a dog who had more ability than competitive edge, and a string of minor open racers.

By most standards, a bitch that throws open racers in four of her seven litters would not be a failure – but this was Westmead Chick!

Nick concedes his disappointment. An unbroken chain of great daughters matching

DAM SHAME: In terms of all known rules on breeding, Westmead Chick (T2) should have been an outstanding dam. Yet she failed.

and surpassing their own dams over four generations had been broken.

So what went wrong? It is like asking a father to criticise his favourite daughter! Nick says: "I couldn't accept that she wouldn't make it. If I try to find a reason for her falling short of what I expected I can only come up with one realistic explanation.

"Although Chick was 100% genuine on everything she did, there were a couple of times when I sensed she was going stale and we had to take her into the country to see some wildlife to motivate her.

"Apart from that one very minor fault, I think she was very unfortunate in the choice of sires. Her father I'm Slippy and her grandfather Whisper Wishes were head and shoulders the best dogs at stud.

"We ended up using a variety of dogs who, looking back, didn't amount to great sires including Daleys Denis and Deenside Spark, though I would have hoped for better from Staplers Jo and Toms The Best.

"The only other theory that I have heard is that she might have been too big to make a brood. Apparently big bitches don't have great records as broods, though since there aren't so many of them, it's a difficult one to prove.

"Cricket Dance was only around 56 pounds racing weight, so any doubts about using small broods disappeared pretty quickly."

To emphasise the importance of honesty, Nick recalls his former minor open racer Westmead Flight.

Nick said: "Although Flight did not have top class pace, she was 100% genuine – absolutely fanatical.

"I remember that on one occasion when she was about six months old, she was watching other pups schooling. She became so obsessed that she cleared a six foot fence and joined in.

"The only other time that I had seen that was with Jazz Hurricane, who I reared here from a few months old. Of course she went on to become a top class open racer and a very good dam."

Indeed at the time of writing, Jazz Hurricane stood a very strong chance of being voted the 2011 Dam of the Year thanks to a litter by Westmead Hawk. The Dave Wood bred litter included Jazz Apollo and Mark My Words. The former won the Kent Derby and set a new track record for 480 metres at Sittingbourne. 'Words' won the Stud Book Trophy and was runner-up in the Swindon Produce Stakes having set a new track record for the track's 480 metres.

BREEDING THEORIES

Maidens

"As a starting point I would certainly not recommend using an unproven stud dog on a maiden bitch. There are too many unknowns.

"I know young dogs have to start somewhere, but use them on proven bitches so you can determine if they are worth persevering with.

"A good example of this can be seen with

Ian Greaves and Michael Dunne. If Ian had a young unproven bitch, Michael would ususally offer him one of the better dogs. Basically, if she couldn't throw to Top Honcho or Frightful Flash, she probably wasn't going to make it. Once she was proven as being decent, Ian would then use one of Michael's unproven sires. It was a perfect arrangement.

Pedigrees

"Although I don't like to see the parents of any litter too closely bred, certainly no closer than 3 x 4, I'm not a big believer in clever pedigree analysis. Just give me a good brood and a quality stud dog.

"That isn't too say that I don't appreciate the importance of bloodlines. You can see the good and bad traits of sires and dams, and their parents, coming through in pups. But until unproven parents produce their pups, you can't predict it and you don't have any control over it.

"I think Special Account was a good example of that. He was a great dog, but until he sired his first pups, we didn't know whether he would produce like his sire Westmead County, or like his dam – or more specifically her sire, Right O'Myross, who was an ungenuine hurdler. Unfortunately it was the latter."

However, there is a danger of discarding a potentially good stud dog, simply on the basis of a minor indiscretion. Take a dog such as the most infamous of all fighters, Lively Band, barred from an English Derby final after a much debated indiscretion in the semis.

Nick says: "I liked him and bid £5,000 for him after he fought. The way I looked at it,

DRIVE: Nick noticed Jazz Hurricane's incredible will to win when she was a puppy. It shone through her track career and then was transmitted on to her pups.

any dog who can run around 80 races, including many after he had been retired to stud, could not have been ungenuine.

"It is a shame that he was so badly wasted as a sire by sending him to Australia and then him dying early on the return flight. If you look at what he threw from so few matings (Yellow Band, Balliniska Band, Linacre) I have no doubt he could have become a great sire."

Gene traits

"I sometimes wonder whether some form of weakness in genes can be of benefit. Take Mega Delight as an example.

"Now I accept that she put some very fast genes into nearly all her offspring. But what is interesting is that in certain aspects some

of the genes were weak.

"For example, look at the sort of dogs she threw to different sires, Westmead Lord at one end of the scale, and then Hawk at the other. Clearly the sires must have dominated in terms of racing distance.

"If a bitch's genes were all very weak, and the pups took everything from the sire of the litter, wouldn't you expect to produce good pups?"

Repeat matings

"I have no problems with repeat matings. I have done it several times and had more good results than bad. The second I'm Slippy/Westmead Move mating was better than the first. Phantom Flash was from a repeat mating.

"It didn't work so well with the repeat of the Daleys Gold/Move litter, but it was a smaller litter, and all bitches."

British breeding

"Many people in Britain tend to breed on sentiment, I know I've made that mistake many times. Most of the best bitches go back to Ireland, because the owners at the big tracks tend not to be 'hands on'.

"So a large number of British litters are out of bitches who ran graded on the provincial tracks. The other major factor that tends to work against British breeders is a lack of facilities.

"Not many breeders have enough space to

rear adequately. If you give them the space, and equal quality brood bitches, there is no difference between the two countries."

Who Knows?

There are really only two sets of breeding theories in the world – those developed by people who study bloodlines and rear pups, and those developed by people who only study bloodlines. The second group are usually more sure of their facts.

Despite rearing around 120 litters in almost identical conditions, Nick still encounters behaviour and temperament that can't be explained.

Why is one litter destructive? Why do they

Ka Boom, who was owned by Joe Cobbold, threw two outstanding litters by Westmead County, both earning her a Dam of the Year title. The first included 1981 Greyhound of the Year Decoy Boom. The second included half a dozen good quality open racers, but the star was Special Account.

Interestingly, there was also a Derby class fighter in the litter, Decoy Ranger. Unfortunately, as honest as Special Account was on the track, many of his progeny were also fighters (like uncle Ranger!).

In Nick's mind, the villain of the piece was Ka Boom's sire, a dog called Right O'Myross. He won the 1969 Produce Stakes at Clonmel but on arrival in England turned so sour that he was eventually put over hurdles.

To add a further interesting twist to the breeding conundrum, Right O'Myross had a litter brother called Skipping Tim, who went on to sire one of the greatest broods of all time – Skipping Chick.

soil their beds, spend hours barking and are difficult to train to lead? The litter that occupied the same paddock six months earlier had none of those faults.

The non-rearing expert will naturally attribute the behaviour to the parents. Many of Nick's broods have produced six or seven litters with a wide variety of habits and idiosyncrasies.

"Aoifa's latest litter by Vieri are much braver than her previous litter," says Nick, "but for some reason, they play up when they are having their nails cut".

Surely the difference between the two litters must be the sire? No, that isn't necessarily true either.

Nick says: "I have had several repeat matings and the second litter are nothing like the first in terms of behaviour and ability, and, as we discovered earlier, the first litter aren't necessarily the best."

Perhaps the most interesting opportunity to put the theory into perspective comes via Ian Greaves, who sent his brood First To Return to Top Honcho seven times. With over 40 pups to compare, there were huge variation in ability, looks and distance preference between all the full brothers and sisters.

Nick says: "To be honest that comes as no surprise to me. There is much more variation than you might expect. So while at one level you can have a dog like Westmead County, who transmitted great honesty and determination to almost all his pups, there will always be diversity. Its unavoidable."

Nick's secret

"It is the question that I get asked the most often – 'what is your secret?' I wish there was one, I would get it right every time.

"To do what I have been doing for 40 years

requires 100% commitment and devotion. If you are not prepared to give that you cannot succeed.

"You have to put the dogs' wellbeing first, with no thought of the expense. The vast majority of people who have been successful in this industry have been so because they have private means. Quite simply, you need to put in more than you will ever be able to take out.

"You need attention to detail and must always be open minded to learn something new. I am always suspicious of any trainer or breeder who claims to know all the answers.

"There are sacrifices that you have to make in your lifestyle, quite often even when it is in opposition to what your family might want and expect from you.

"I defy anybody to always get it right in their selection of stud dogs and brood bitches. I hope to get it right nine times in ten, but nature always has the upper hand. You can never second guess her.

"There have always been 'freaks' who come out of nowhere to surprise you. But once they happen – accept them. It doesn't matter if they are badly bred, or had no ability on the track. If they breed on, accept it.

"No matter how hard you work, or how much you learn, you will always need a bit of luck. Without your fair share of it, you don't have a prayer."

The relationship between luck and fate in breeding was never better emphasised than in the case of Westmead Flight, winner of a couple of Catford 555 metre open races for Wimbledon trainer Tom Foster. Nick was unsure what to do with her when she reached the end of her racing days.

He said: "I liked her and would have bred

with her, but I only have so much space and I had Westmead Chick. At that time Vince Berland was buying a few British and Irish bitches for breeding in America.

"Brian King found most of them for him and when he asked if I had anything available I offered him Westmead Flight for £600.

"Vince apparently replied: 'No I'm looking for something better than that'. If I had asked for £5,000 she would probably have been sold!

"In the end I gave her to Pat and Betty Whelan with the agreement that I could have her back for one litter.

"I mated her to Staplers Jo, which would produce Larkhill Jo, and Pat sent her to Ireland. Later I had her back as agreed and put her to Frightful Flash."

It was from that mating that Sonic Flight and Early Flight were produced; the latter of course threw Spiridon Louis and Dilemmas Flight.

"With the benefit of hindsight, what single piece of advice would have been most beneficial to me when I started out as a breeder? Probably not to use unproven stud dogs. I got away with it a few times, but I ruined many more litters along the way.

"We know from the few good dogs that come through at any one time, the likelihood of a new dog becoming a top sire are thousands to one."

And the best bitches on the tracks don't always make the best broods.

Nick says: "I have won the Oaks with Sarah Dee, Westmead Chick, Annies Bullet, and Dilemmas Flight. I also produced litters out of another three Oaks winners. Not one of them went on to become a top class dam. How do you explain that?

"The only conclusion that I could come to is that none of them would have made stayers. My best brood bitches either stayed six bends or would have done if they had not been hampered by injury."

PRODUCING PUPS

Preparing The Brood
While some breeders embark on special preparations for brood bitches, Nick expects his greyhounds to be in top class condition, including parasite-free at all times. He does not, therefore, introduce a specific worming programme for bitches prior to mating.

The first indication of a bitch being in whelp is when she goes off her food three to four weeks after being mating– though it is not a foolproof method. Some broods never lose their appetite.

Nick says: "By six weeks the belly is growing. If she only has a couple, you can sometimes not see anything and assume that she has missed. You can get them scanned, but I seldom bother."

The bitch's preparation is not so different from racing dogs in terms of feeding, particularly in the early stages.

But from the 40th day after mating, she is given a daily 10ml dose of the wormer Panacur. This continues until two weeks after the whelping.

The bitch's feeding regime changes as she approaches the whelping date and is unable to hold a full stomach of food.

Nick says: "She will be fed a minimum of three times a day, including a breakfast and as much as she can manage. If she is struggling, we may leave the food in with her."

Whelping Facilities

Nick has three whelping kennels. They are approximately six feet by ten feet in total to include a main bed for whelping, plus a separate smaller bed for the dam (approx three feet square), a ramp to enable the pups to get off the bed and a small floor area. The separate bed is to allow the bitch to be on her own when she needs a break from the pups.

Every kennel has permanent access to its own small concrete and grass paddock with the door just big enough to facilitate the bitch going in and out at will. Each doorway is fitted with a curtain to prevent draughts.

All kennels are heated during the winter. In addition, each has its own heat lamp.

Nick says: "I keep a thermometer in the kennel and try to keep the kennels at 16C. The heat lamps bring some extra concentrated heat, though they aren't always necessary in the summer."

The whelping beds are the size of wooden pallets, roughly 40 inches by 48 inches. On top of the wood there are newspapers and on top of that a carpet that is fixed, so that it doesn't get rucked up when the bitch moves around.

Nick says: "I always put some newspapers on top of the carpet for the bitch to tear up if she gets agitated and tries to nest before whelping down.

"The rest of the newspaper is for soaking up the fluid. We also put newspaper on the floor of the kennel after the pups are born. For years we used sawdust, but we find newspaper more hygienic.

Giving Birth

Whelping can often vary between three and four days either side of the generally accepted gestation period of 63 days. Bigger litters are more likely to be early and small litters late, though this does vary.

As the bitch approaches whelping time, it is quite common for them to stop eating up to 12 hours before.

Nick says: "As the time approaches, they tend to get a bit anxious and start to pant, showing signs of distress. They will start to scratch at their bedding to make a nest.

"Eventually, the contractions start and they may continue for several hours before the first pup is passed.

"If the bitch appears distressed, I might start to think about calling the vet, though in most cases we get through the stage with no real problems.

"If the bitch produces the first pup okay, then she starts to settle. But if the first pup is breeched or dead, it can produce difficulties, though thankfully, problems are rare. If they are going to occur, most of the problems will tend to come with the first pup.

"But the majority of litters go without any major problems. There have been several occasions when the bitch has whelped unexpectedly and I have found mother and pups in perfect condition, without any help from anyone.

"If the contractions are weak or prolonged, a quarter of a millilitre of Oxytocin will often help the contractions. If that hasn't produced any results, then she may need another, but always in consultation with the vet.

"After all the years we have been doing this, I have no hesitation about getting a vet out of bed. I would strongly advise against using a drug to induce contractions unless you are very experienced. You create much bigger problems if she isn't ready.

WHELPING PEN: Designed to be spacious and can be easily cleaned. Note the piping around the outside which is fitted to avoid pups being crushed in corners.

"Experienced bitches are normally better able to cope with whelping. But with maidens, it is sometimes helpful to pass the pup to the bitch if she is slow to clean it when it is first born – particularly if she is still full of pups and struggling to turn around. Very occasionally, apparently dead pups can be resuscitated by being rubbed with a towel or paper.

"Eventually, it will appear that the bitch has produced the last of her pups. The contractions will stop and it is impossible to feel any more movement in her abdomen.

"She is then given a full 1 millilitre dose of Oxytocin, which should encourage the bitch to pass any remaining afterbirth.

"By this stage, the paper bedding will have been changed several times and the bitch is now able to suckle her pups on the carpet.

During the whelping we will make fluids available for the brood, either tea with honey, or whey protein plus fresh water."

The First Few Days

"After the bitch has whelped, she is washed down and the bedding is replaced. Any soiled paper is replaced at least twice a day in the first two weeks, when the mother is cleaning up after the pups and to remove any discharge from the dam.

"After that, when the pups start to soil the paper themselves, it is changed as many times as is necessary. Sometimes maiden bitches will not produce sufficient milk and the pups will have to be fed by syringes before eventually moving onto baby bottles."

Although not ideal, Nick has brought many successful open racers into the world this way. If a brood fails to produce ample

TOLERANCE: *Westmead Alva bearing an expression familiar to mums of all species.*

milk for her second litter, it is unlikely that she will be mated again.

Nick said: "That would be rare though. In most cases the bitch can cope unless the litter is particularly large.

"However, you also need to be wary of mastitis. The teats swell up and you can detect a sour smell. The pups also stop suckling. It needs to be treated with antibiotics as soon as possible."

Within two weeks, the puppies should be able to lap, and they will be fed their Whelpi in a shallow dish. By one month, they would be able to take solids, a puppy meal supplemented with a small quantity of meat

or chicken.

By this stage, 'mum' will probably require several breaks from the demanding litter and will take full advantage of the separate bed where the pups cannot reach her. And even though the pups nails will be regularly clipped from two weeks, they can make her belly sore.

Good mothers often continue to produce milk for their pups for up to eight weeks. Nick says: "Even after Mega Delight dried up, she was happy to remain constantly with her pups until they were around seven or eight months old. I would always try to leave the pups with the dam for as long as she is able to tolerate them."

It isn't long – dependent on weather – before the pups are following their dam out of the whelping kennel and into the paddock. It is cleared of faeces on a daily basis.

Worming & Inoculations

Nick says: "The pups are wormed at two weeks and every two weeks from then on up to 12 weeks. They are then wormed every six to eight weeks at a rate of 1 ml per kilo body-weight. We alternate the Drontal worm treatment with Melbamax.

"In the early days, we followed the vet's advice and started to worm at six weeks, but the pups were full of round worm. We rarely see worms now; this is a much better start to life."

The first inoculations are given at around six to seven weeks of age with a repeat four weeks later.

REARING

The whole Westmead rearing process has changed considerably from the early days, when Nick and Natalie would take the pups to the Downs for early morning exercise.

Back in the mid 1960s, Edelsborough was a fraction of the size that it is today and Nick took full advantage of the neighbouring countryside.

He said: "I would take them up to Ashridge and they would just follow me. There wasn't a great deal of wildlife for them to chase, but they would run miles.

"I would also take them to a big field, open the van door and watch them take off."

The current rearing process is more about controlled exercise, with little chance of pups running on to roads or coming into contact with pet dogs. You also reduce the risk of injury.

After the inoculations have been given, the pups are ready to be transferred into a rearing paddock.

There are seven rearing paddocks, surrounding and with access to the main part of the property, a two-acre field that also incorporates the schooling track and sand gallop.

Each paddock contains a shed and all bar one has natural shelter against the sun.

Once a day, twice in the summer, each litter is let out to gallop around the property, which includes access to the main paddock, the gallop, the infield of the schooling track plus the track itself.

Nick says: "They make me laugh just to watch them. When they go out for the first time, the mother always shows them around. They soon pick it up for themselves and they go from one thing to the next.

"They might start off by chasing each other around in the paddock. Then one will take it into his head to gallop around the schooling track. Another will jump in the pool for a swim and then they will end up finding their way to the whirlygig where they will play for another 10 minutes.

"When they've finished playing we let them back into their own paddock and put another litter out.

"Occasionally, we might take them down the four acre field for a change of scenery and to get used to travelling in a vehicle.

"In my opinion, pups should run until they get tired – that is all they need. It doesn't do any harm for them to spend their whole lives in a 10-acre field, though I don't think it is necessary."

Nick strongly believes that pups must be handled throughout their lives. Westmead pups are fitted with collars and trained to lead from around three months of age.

They are also 'formally' introduced to the whirlygig with short sessions when they will chase a dummy on the arm.

To prevent boredom, the litters are often given rags, plastic bottles and toys to play with, and sterilised knuckle bones to gnaw.

They will normally run riot for half an hour or so before they naturally congregate by the gate to indicate that they have had enough.

Some people believe that pups cannot overcome a bad start. While that may be true if they are badly fed, Nick has seen good recoveries from 'ordinary' rearing.

He said: "Many years ago I had an owner buy a pup from a breeder in Cambridgeshire and he asked me for an opinion on how the dog was being reared.

"The litter was nine months old and didn't look bad, but I advised him to move the pup as soon as possible. There was simply not enough space and they weren't getting enough exercise for the size of the litter.

"He pleaded with me to take the pup. I wasn't keen, but he was a son of Westmead County who looked just like his father and I gave in.

"I didn't have any pups to put him with, but had an old retired bitch who was very active.

"She liked to play 'chase me' games and the pup joined in. On the first day, she ran him so ragged that he had to lay down to rest. But gradually he grew fitter.

"As far as I am aware, Countville was the only member of the litter to make it. In fact, he went on to run third in the St Leger."

Nick does not believe there is 'one way' to rear pups, having seen many successful methods.

He said: "A few years ago I let a guy have two Westmead Milos pups. He didn't have any land, but he lived next to a golf course and gave the pups a gallop every day.

"The dog was eventually sold to race in America for £10,000 and the bitch was worth more, though he didn't sell her.

"I think the traditional Irish method, when pups would live around the farm, seemed to work, though I think it is probably a thing of the past.

"Most pups are reared in paddocks these days. I'm not a big fan of the American style where you get long narrow runs side by side.

"I am not convinced that the pups learn all the skills that they will need when they reach the tracks."

REARING PROBLEMS

Aggression: The size of paddock chosen for any litter will depend on the number of pups that Nick feels he can keep together. In general, litters are kept together whenever possible, at least during the early stages.

In most cases, some splitting up inevitably takes place due to squabbles as the pups grow older.

In severe cases, this can be as early as four months, though it is not uncommon for an entire group to go all the way through to 12 months without needing to be parted.

How the groups are split depends on the level of aggression. Typically, a group of the more aggressive types may be kept together.

Nick believes that aggressive behaviour, in the rearing paddocks or on the track, is

REARING PADDOCKS: These are the basic rearing paddocks from which all the great Westmeads have emerged. All have a gate leading on to the main open paddock area (to the left) and schooling track (top left) where they can have a daily burn up. Simple but effective.

something transmitted by one or other of the parents.

The most aggressive saplings he has handled were two litters by a dog with a notorious reputation for throwing short-tempered offspring – Daleys Gold.

Once again though, there appears to be no link between aggression in the paddocks and any tendency to do wrong on the track. Indeed, the first Daleys Gold/Westmead Move litter produced ten different open race winners and not a fighter among them.

As any trainer or rearer knows, when dogs 'kick off' even a well mannered dog can quickly turn.

Nick can easily recall an incident involving one of the kennel's top open racers of the mid-1970s, Drynham Star.

He said: "I was out with a bunch of dogs and we saw a cat. I was badly prepared, a handful of dogs and no muzzles. I tried to get the cat to move and the dogs got agitated.

"Drynham Star realised that I was stopping him getting the cat, and out of pent up frustration he went for me. I had to hold him by the collar to stop him attacking me.

"Yet he wasn't a naturally vicious dog. I don't recall any problems in his rearing and on the track he was as genuine as they come. Basically, the whole incident was my fault for not having him muzzled."

Aggression is not inevitable in rearing, even among some of the most competitive, successful greyhounds. Nick recalls an incident when the kennel had three of its best mothers all with young litters of virtually identical ages.

Nick says: "I think it was Westmeads Kim, Seal and Tania. At some stage the door must have been left open and all three litters ended up wandering around and intermingling. The dams were so good that they fed each other's litters. There was no friction between them at all.

In more recent times, sisters Olivia and Aoife shared neighbouring rearing kennels. When the pups managed to get through the fence into each others kennels, the mums were happy to play aunt to each other's family.

Non-chasers: When asked to name their last non-chaser, Nick says: "I can't remember, but I think it was one of the Newdown Heather pups in what was otherwise a decent litter". In other words, the kennel has produced one non-chaser in the last 30 years.

So what is the secret?

Nick says: "I don't really know. I can tell you what we do, but unless you compared it with breeders who produce non-chasers, it would be hard to pinpoint why all our pups chase.

"I am a strong believer in handling the puppies and getting them used to people. I have seen some litters in Ireland where the pups have very little contact with people and that cannot be a good thing for when they grow up.

"We have always encouraged pups to play in the paddock with a rag or a skin. I also have a piece of wire suspended over the paddock that we hang things onto, usually strips of material and the pups have great fun holding onto it and dragging it around. Maybe this plays its part.

"When the pups are around five or six months old, I put them on the whirlygig. The 'Whirly' is an American idea that we only started to use over here a few years ago. But it is a great way of getting pups to chase in a safe environment. It has been a fantastic addition to the property.

"Because the pups have regular access to the whole property, we sometimes find they have made their own way to the whirly and are chasing it just for the fun of it."

"Pups are like children. The younger they are, the more inquisitive they are. By showing them the whirly up to half a dozen times during their rearing it seems to have a very positive effect on their keenness to chase.

"They also become familiar with the traps, which means they won't be fazed by them later on.

"You don't want to overdo it, but if you get them interested early on, they never forget.

"I have even had pups arrive here at around seven or eight months old who hadn't been handled and were very shy with people. Initially they refused to chase the whirly, but with a bit of perseverance we've got them to chase it and they turned out the best in the litter."

"By the time they are ready to be schooled, you should have already stimulated their chasing instinct. In the old days, when I could gallop them in open fields, they saw plenty of live stuff. That is no longer possible, yet we still get the same results.

"I know some breeders, particularly in Ireland, wouldn't consider bringing a pup to the track without 'a hunt'. But in my opinion it is not necessary for the vast majority of dogs to be shown any wild life. Very occasionally we might have to, but very rarely.

"Overall, I can't say that all the pups that we produce are good. We have the occasional ungenuine ones, and some who might not be fast enough, but they always chase.

Illness/Injuries: There is a school of thought that says 'when it comes to rearing pups, just let them get on with it'. That is not the Savva way. Litters are permanently monitored; the devil is in the detail.

Just about every boundary is fitted with home made crash barriers. Accidents aren't 'just one of those things' – they are a failure to prevent an injury.

By the time that Nick slit and fitted a plastic bin as a safety skirt around a telegraph pole, it had already cost a young bitch pup her racing career.

Nick says: "It has been a while since we lost any pups in rearing. There was a stage when we seemed to get a few stifle problems in pups aged between five and seven months old.

"We will never know the cause, but personally I think there may have been a deficiency in their diet before we switched to 'all in one' feeding."

When it comes to illness, they don't come any bigger than parvovirus which hit the kennel in 1983 (see Chapter 4).

But given sufficient effort, even that was partially defeated with one of the sufferers, Westmead Account, going on to reach the Silver Collar and Scurry Finals and breaking the sprint clock at Oxford.

Westmead Chase was another who battled the disease and went on to win the Autumn Cup at Milton Keynes and reach the Scottish Derby Final.

Other problems: There are a variety of problems that can arise in rearing. The most likely is that, for some reason, the pups will lose their appetites.

Nick said: "In most cases, something minor has probably gone wrong – they've picked up a tummy upset and it will pass in a couple of days.

"Occasionally, it is something that requires veterinary attention and the use of medication. Teething can cause loss of appetite, or occasionally a virus might take hold.

"In the case of young pups, it might be that you have accidentally upset the dam's stomach and that has come through her milk.

"I no longer feed milk, cow's or powdered, to pups once they have gone on to solid food. I found that it caused scowering in some pups and wasn't necessary.

But good management isn't about just injuries. Sometimes a litter will not thrive for whatever reason.

Nick says: "It happens. You get picky eaters and you have to change the diet. Or they might need a tonic, or a blood test to find out if there is something seriously wrong.

"The alarm bells will always ring if I see a litter that looks lethargic and lacking in spirit.

"Whatever the problem might be, I will always attempt to rectify it, not just 'leave it to nature' and in most cases we get to the bottom of it."

REARING ELSEWHERE

"The Australians tend to rear differently to the British, Irish and Americans – at least those that I observed.

"For example, Paul Wheeler rears 25 pups of all ages in the same paddock. We wouldn't normally be able to do that for fear of them fighting – the most that I have reared together is 10 from the same litter - but the Australian paddocks are very much bigger, sometimes 10 acres, which appears to be the secret.

"It appears that the dogs form a sort of pack, much as they would in the wild, and because they have so much more space, they

MUM KNOWS: All Westmead broods are encouraged to spend time with their pups even after they have been weaned. The great Westmead Move seems keen on dishing out some advice.

don't encroach on each other.

"Other differences are down to climate. For example in the warmer states most rearer have a pond in the middle to allow the pups to cool off.

"The Americans tend to rear in long paddocks side by side. I am in no position to criticise because they get good results, but I prefer my pups to get the chance to twist and turn in wider paddocks.

"I was interested to see that Dutch Koerner, whose record as a breeder is one of the best in America, breeds to a system very much closer to my own. He operates in a much bigger way of course, though I know he was impressed when he came to see how we do things."

SCHOOLING

Nick says: "I think schooling is overrated. Since I've had the 'whirly' I hardly school them. Westmeads Joe and Lord each had just one trial at my track before they ran their qualifying trials.

Because the pups are virtually unschooled, there is invariably plenty of scope for improvement from the first trial to the 'completed article'. But two dogs stood out from the moment of their first trials.

Nick said "Phantom Flash and Westmead Merlin both did open class times in their first ever trial. In each case I thought to myself "My God what have I got here?"

It is often said that the Westmead schooling

track has been a major factor in producing so many champions. Nick doesn't agree.

He said: "If I had my time again, I wouldn't build a track. The time and expense of maintaining it are way out of proportion to its benefit.

"It might be justified if you were running a schooling track commercially, but I never wanted to go that way. It would have been much easier to use someone else's schooling facilities. My track was an expensive mistake!"

FEEDING

The two biggest factors in rearing are feeding and exercise, and in each case no compromises are made.

Nick said: "Over the years my feeding methods have changed for the racing dogs, so they also did for the pups. All our pups have always been fed from the same batch of food as the racers (see 'Training'). I would never have imagined doing it differently.

"Having visited many good breeders I am sure that there is no 'one way' to feed. Feeding varies greatly, but you can still get excellent results providing that you don't compromise on quality."

"For example, Paul Wheeler, who breeds the hugely successful 'Bale' dogs, feeds his dogs on a stew of kangaroo meat and barley.

"He told me, 'my father had great success using this method and I see no reason to change'."

SPOTTING A CHAMPION

So can a good dog man pick out the best pup in the litter?

Every breeder has tried it. They might take a shine to a bold pup when they are first born. More likely, selections will be made

through fencing as pups chase each other around the paddock.

Nick clearly remembers his early attempts at future champion spotting as the ultimately successful Clonalvy Pride/Cricket Dance litter went through their paces.

He said: "Westmead Silver used to be the hare. They would chase her and she would run them into the ground. From what I saw of her in the paddock, she was probably the fastest in the litter."

But while entertaining, champion spotting is a very inexact science.

Nick says: " I certainly couldn't look back at dogs like Phantom Flash or Sonic Flight and say that I knew they would be champions before they got on the track. I don't think it can be done. "If anybody can show me how to pick the best in the litter at three months I'd pay him.

"I remember the great Joe Booth coming to Mels Pupil for a mating and offering me a pup *en lieu* of the fee.

"The pup he sent me, Westmead Hall, turned out to be the best of the litter. If anyone could have spotted the best in the litter while it was still a pup, it would have been Joe."

"As they get older, if you spend a lot of time with them, you can start to form an opinion, so by the time they were ready for schooling I'd like to think I would know which would be the best.

"But even then, when you put a clock on them for the first time, you can still discover that you made a mistake, particularly with slow developers and stayers."

Conversely, Nick will sometimes make up his mind about a whole litter in a negative way, even when they are only a few months old.

He said: "It is not a good sign when you get bad behaviour among pups. Some litters just don't know how to behave. They wet their beds, or misbehave on the leads. They might be cowardly and standoffish. They might bark a lot, basically have no manners.

"All our pups are reared in the same way. These traits must come from the parents and if a particular bitch has produced two or three good litters and suddenly a bunch of misbehaved pups, the obvious blame must go to the sire.

"I remember when we had the Tico litter out of Westmead Move. They were quite disruptive, and they didn't even look like nice greyhounds. It is hard to put into words, but they just didn't look as though they had any class about them.

"It is very rare that a litter that has displeased me ultimately goes on to prove me wrong."

But that doesn't mean that all well-behaved dogs will be fast. "A good example was the Hondo Black litter out of Westmead Aoife. They were stunning to look at, had perfect behaviour in every way, but turned out to be minor open class at best.

"The champions though are invariably model greyhounds. Ask anybody who has been lucky enough to train a special dog and they invariably tell you that the dog does nothing wrong. Well, that star quality is usually visible in the rearing paddocks.

The only factor in picking the best pup is luck – as was demonstrated so very early in the Westmead story with the four 'least wanted' pups out of Cricket Dance (see chapter 3).

For many years Bob Morton has taken his choice of whatever pups are born at the kennel. There are any number of Westmead stars who were snapped up by other owners, including Phantom Flash, Westmead Merlin, Right Move, Westmead Harry, and Westmead Surprise.

The broods who were sold out of the kennel included Westmeads Kim and Seal (both later returned), Westmead Flight and Westmead City (dam of 'The Manorvilles')

Nick says: "People always used to say 'he always keeps the best for himself' but it doesn't always work out that way.

"I remember Brian Turner wanted to buy a couple of pups and he asked what was available. There were three bitches and I said the only one that I didn't want to let go was the fawn because Natalie had taken a shine to her.

"He said, 'if Natalie likes her that's good enough for me' and he insisted that I keep my promise and give him the pick.

"The fawn never made it, the other two that he didn't want were Westmead Call and Westmead Move."

But compared to one of the kennel's longest established owners, Brian Turner is Midas.

Nick laughs: "Poor old Barrie Bolton. I have never seen a man be so unlucky. The times he has had pick of the litter and always picked the worst one, is uncanny."

There is a rumour that the other owners insist the "Allglaze" man get first pick to give themselves more chance.

At least Turner got Olivers Wish from the Move litter that also included Westmead Wish and Westmead Whisper. BB got the forgettable Allglaze Chelsea.

In the litter that included Westmead Claim and Charm, BB got the moderate

HANDSOME IS. . .Westmead Odd was a breeding anomaly being as undershot as a bulldog. A litter brother to Westmead Chick he nevertheless became a prolific sprint open race winner.

Allglaze Crystal (who was later sold and became a good brood).

The list of misses goes on and one. Left to choose two from three pups he rejected Mistley Trojan... and he also turned down Westmead Striker.

But maybe luck levels itself out! Westmead Chick's litter to Spiral Nikita were hugely disappointing. But Barrie held on to Westmead Wise, who went on to be a decent brood and produced Beatties Best (Sussex Puppy Cup) and Fear Robben (Puppy Classic).

One day Nick received a phone call from a well-spoken lady who asked if he had any pups for sale. Nick replied that he had two young litters and she would be welcome to view them.

The lady turned out to be Gill Cribbens who duly arrived with her husband, the comedy actor, Bernard.

Gill wanted two pups but couldn't choose between the two litters. Nick tried to help by recommending a brother and sister from the litter by Toms The Best out of Celtic Lady.

He says: "It was quite funny because Gill then became very suspicious at why I had recommended that particular pair. It was quite obvious that she wasn't sure she could trust greyhound people

"She started to question me, so I said, 'if you are not happy, take the other pair instead.'

"She seemed relieved that she still had the choice and decided to go with the first pair I suggested. They were only young babies and I had no idea how they would turn out."

In the following months, Gill became a regular visitor to the kennel, sometimes with her husband, sometimes on her own.

Nick said: "They both took a real interest in the pups and we became good friends, Gill was much keener than Bernard, though he was always very friendly and good company."

Unfortunately, things took a down turn when the pups were around nine months old. The bitch developed an aggressive form of bone cancer and had to be put to sleep.

The dog turned out to be Westmead Woofa, who won a string of competitions, including Nottingham's Puppy Classic, and the Diamond Stake at Shelbourne Park.

So what happened to the two pups that Gill originally rejected?

"They ended up as two graders," replied Nick.

To balance that story there was a day when Gail May asked Nick for some help choosing a pup.

He says: "She picked out a white and black dog. He didn't have any testicles and I tried to persuade her to take one of the others. But she was determined to stick to her choice. He turned out to be Spiridon Louis."

Epilogue

As we reach the end of the tale, it is autumn 2011, almost four years after we started.

Nick continues to train, albeit in a smaller way. Many of the better dogs have been sent to Fraser Black in Ireland, or former head girl Kelly Findlay.

Westmead Hawk landed his first UK sires title in 2010, sired the 2011 English Derby winner, and is Ireland's busiest stud dog.

There are pups in the Westmead paddocks, and, as, long as Nick's health holds out, there always will be.

Whether the most successful breeding kennel in the history of British greyhound racing will be around to celebrate its 50th anniversary in 2017 must remain a matter of speculation.

Looking back, Nick and Natalie have sharply contrasting views when asked 'was it all worth it?'

Natalie says: "No, not for me. The sacrifices have just been too great. When I think back to our time in Colindale, and imagine how our life style would have evolved, I do resent it if I'm honest.

"The clothing business was going well, we had a circle of good friends in the Greek community and would soon have a young family.

"The greyhounds were supposed to be a hobby, but Nick threw himself into it like he does with everything.

"The greyhounds just took up such a lot of his time, particularly when the girls came along. I spent a lot of time on my own."

Nick feels very differently. Ironically, the man

who only turned to breeding in desperation, after buying so many poor racing dogs, has long seen himself primarily as a breeder.

He has said, on many occasions, "I would rather breed a Derby winner than train one."

Not that success is an overriding factor. Given a choice of being presented with a Category One trophy live on TV, or taking a litter of pups for their qualifying trials, Nick would opt for the trials session every time.

Former head girl Kelly Findlay said: "I think the only reason Nick trains at all is so that he can be sure his pups have been given the best possible treatment."

Owner Gail May said: "I will sometimes come to the kennel and catch Nick just watching the pups running around the paddocks. He is totally contented. After all these years, rearing pups has never lost its magic for him."

Reflecting on his life-changing decision to dedicate himself to greyhound racing, Nick says: "Greyhounds have been an addiction to me. I was never a gambler, but I remain fascinated with the dogs and I have given them everything I possibly could. It has been 100-per-cent commitment.

"I accept that sacrifices were made, huge sacrifices, but I made them gladly.

"I am sometimes aware that people look at our success and think 'they've been lucky'.

"But it was all hard-earned. If I had paid for all the trophies a hundred times over, it would have been cheaper than winning them.

"If you look around at the successful open race kennels, they have all put much more into the greyhound industry than they have ever taken out.

"Trainers like Charlie Lister, Barrie Draper and Harry Williams have subsidised their kennels by their other businesses. Before them, the De Mulders did the same thing; Joe Cobbold calculated that it cost him £100,000 to win the trainers championship and that was back in the early 1980s.

"I know, beyond any doubt, that if I had stayed in the rag trade I would have become a multi-millionaire

"But money was never my motivation. I fell in love with greyhound racing, and, despite all the ups and downs, that feeling is just as strong as it has ever been.

"So, no, I have no regrets – I would do it all over again."

Appendix 1
ROLL OF HONOUR

1969

Catford Breeders Stakes	Westmead Villa	Owned/bred

1970

Cobb 700	Westmead Villa	Trained/bred

1972

Summer Cup	Westmead County	Trained/bred
The Test	Westmead Lane	Trained/bred
Cesarewitch	Westmead Lane	Trained/bred
Christie Stayers Trophy	Westmead Silver	Trained/bred

1973

Breeders Forum St.	Drynham Rocket	Trained/bred
Bookmakers Marathon	Westmead Mia	Trained/bred
Scottish Marathon	Westmead Mia	Trained/bred
Ladbroke Marath. Champ.	Westmead Pride	Bred
Gt London Challenge T.	Westmead Pride	Bred
Jubilee Marathon	Westmead Pride	Bred

1974

Buckinghamshire Cup	Delrony Leader	Trained/bred
TV Trophy	Stage Box	Trained
Catford Breeders Stakes	Westmead Moss	Bred
Scurry Gold Cup	Westmead Valley	Bred

1975

Longcross Cup/GRA St.	Westmead Bounty	Bred

1976

GRA Stakes	Westmead Satin	Trained/bred
Spring Cup	Drynham Star	Trained/bred
Playboy Bookmakers St.	Westmead Land	Trained/bred
Whitbread Trophy	Westmead Land	Trained/bred
Regency	Westmead Champ	Bred
Jubilee Stakes	Drynham Star	Trained/bred
Essex Vase	Westmead Myra	Trained/bred
St Leger	Westmead Champ	Bred
Gold Collar	Westmead Champ	Bred
Gold Vase	Drynham Star	Trained/bred
Playboy Match	Westmead Myra	Trained/bred
Midland Flat	Westmead Border	Trained/bred
Whitbred Challenge	Ka Boom	Trained
Milton Keynes Derby	Westmead Satin	Trained/bred
Mercury Trophy	Westmead Melody	Trained/bred

1977

Gold Collar	Westmead Power	Trained/bred
Mercury Trophy	Westmead Melody	Trained/bred
Midland Classic Potential	Westmead Velvet	Trained/bred

East Anglian Derby	Westmead Dance	Bred
N. Canes Puppy Derby	Westmead Chief	bred
Top Dog Stake	Westmead Melody	Trained/bred

1978

Hunt Cup	Westmead Manor	Trained/bred
GT London Challenge Cup	Westmead Spring	Trained/bred
BBCTV Trophy	Westown Adam	Trained
Steel City Cup	Westmead Manor	Trained/bred
Mullard Stakes	Westown Adam	Trained
St Leger	Westmead Power	Trained/bred
Stow Marathon	Westown Adam d/h	Trained
W Hill Marathon C'ship	Westown Adam	Trained
Winter Trophy	Westmead Bound	Trained/bred

1979

W Hill Hurdle Champion	Westmead Manor	Trained/bred
Golden Jacket	Westmead Bound	Trained/bred
Britvic Marathon	Westown Adam	Trained/bred
Supreme Marath. C'Ship	Westown Adam	Trained/bred
Mecca Marathon	Westmead Tina	Trained/bred

1980

Canada Dry Marathon	Westmead Tina	Trained/bred
British Breeders St.	Panview	Trained/bred
Milton Keynes Derby	Westmead Prince	Trained/bred
Buckinghamshire Cup	Rikasso Pancho	Trained
Catford Breeders Stakes	Panview	Trained/bred

1981

Gold Cup	Westmead Prince	Trained/bred
Buckinghamshire Cup	Westmead Seal	Trained/bred
Wimbledon Puppy Derby	Special Account	Trained

1982

Guys & Dolls	Westmead Badger	Trained/bred
The Test	Westmead Gem	Trained
SCOTTISH DERBY	Special Account	Trained

1983

North'land Puppy Cup	Westmead Milos	Trained/bred
Sporting Life Juvenile	Westmead Milos	Trained/bred

1984

International	Westmead Milos	Trained/bred
GRA Stakes	Westmead Dena	Trained/bred
The Olympic	Westmead Milos	Trained/bred
Jack Berry Puppy Cup	Westmead Chase	Trained/bred
Autumn Cup	Westmead Chase	Trained/bred
Classic Select	Mistley Trojan	Trained/bred

Anglo-Irish (Wimbledon)	Mistley Trojan Trained/bred	

1985

Romford Puppy Cup	Cannonroe	Trained

1986

Upton Rocket Stake	Westmead Move	Trained/bred
Produce Stakes	Westmead Cannon	Trained/bred
Wessex Vase	Westmead Call	Trained/bred
Gold Collar	Westmead Move	Trained/bred
Bedfordshire Derby	Westmead Call	Trained/bred
Grand Prix	Westmead Move	Trained/bred
Manchester Puppy Cup	Olivers Wish	Trained/bred
Cosmic Puppy Stake	Westmead Gold	Trained/bred

1987

Westmead British Cup	Westmead Gold	Trained/bred
Midland Oaks	Westmead Move	Trained/bred
Brighton Belle	Westmead Move	Trained/bred
The Circuit	Flashy Sir	Trained
Stewards Cup	Olivers Wish	Trained/bred
Grand Prix	Olivers Wish	Trained/bred
Laurels	Flashy Sir	Trained

1988

Stewards Cup	Westmead Move	Trained/bred
Midland Oaks	Westmead Move	Trained/bred
Derby Invitation	Westmead Claim	Trained/bred

1989

Eclipse	Westmead Harry	Trained/bred
Bookmakers Puppy Trophy	Westmead Lodge	Trained/bred
International Club Trophy	Maggies Magic	Trained/bred
Thousand Pounder	Westmead Harry	Trained/bred
Thousand Pounder	Westmead Cruise	Trained/bred
Anglo-Irish (Shelbourne)	Bens Baby	Trained/bred

1990

Bookmakers Grand	Westmead Cruise	Trained/bred
Valentine Trophy	Bens Baby	Trained/bred
Blue Riband	Westmead Harry	Trained/bred
Archie Scott Mem.	Phantom Flash	Trained/bred
SCOTTISH DERBY	Westmead Harry	Trained/bred
Brighton Belle	Westmead Chloe	Trained/bred
Sussex Cup	Phantom Flash	Trained/bred
Produce Stakes	Phantom Flash	Trained/bred
Anglo-Irish (Wimbledon)	Phantom Flash	Trained/bred
Walter Prince Invit.	Phantom Flash	Trained/bred
Anglo-Irish (Shelbourne)	Westmead Harry	Trained/bred

1991

Westmead Eddie Puppy St.	Right Move	Trained/bred
SCOTTISH DERBY	Phantom Flash	Bred
Wimbledon Puppy Derby	Right Move	Trained/bred
Sunderland Puppy Derby	Right Move	Trained/bred

1992

Gold Cup	Westmead Suprise	Trained/bred
Bedfordshire Derby	Next Move	Trained/bred
Gold Collar	Westmead Suprise	Trained/bred
Grand Prix	Westmead Darkie	Trained/bred
English Laurels	Balligari	Trained/bred
Produce Stakes	Westmead Spirit	Trained/bred
Breeders Forum Stakes	Next Move	Trained/bred
Fosters Choice Stake	Westmead Darkie	Trained/bred
Boxing Day Marathon	Westmead Gypsy	Trained/bred

1993

Bookmakers Invitation	Westmead Darkie	Trained/bred
Walthamstow Test	Westmead Mount	Trained/bred
Gone To Dogs Trophy	Stylefield Law	Trained
Champion Stakes	Westmead Suprise	Trained/bred
Swaffham Derby	Stylefield Law	Trained
Dean Jackson Mem.	Stylefield Law	Trained
Ron Bazell Puppy Stake	Westmead Chick d/h	Trained/bred
Autumn Puppy Cup	Westmead Mystic	Trained/bred
William Hill Guineas	Staplers Jo	Trained
Action Line Trophy	The Great Gonzo	Trained
Boxing Day Marathon	The Great Gonzo	Trained

1994

The Arc	Westmead Chick	Trained/bred
The Olympic	Westmead Chick	Trained/bred
Brighton Belle	Westmead Chick	Trained/bred
Life Triple Challenge	Westmead Merlin	Trained/bred
Produce Stakes	Westmead Merlin	Trained/bred
Midland Flat	Westmead Chick	Trained/bred
English Oaks	Westmead Chick	Trained/bred

1995

The Arc	Westmead Merlin	Trained/bred
Midland Puppy Derby	Staplers Jo	Trained
Gymcrack	Staplers Jo	Trained
Derby Invitation	Westmead Chick	Trained/bred
Moral Standard Stakes	Westmead Merlin	Trained/bred
Midland Gold Cup	Westmead Chick	Trained/bred
Champion Stakes	Westmead Merlin	Trained/bred
Wey Plastics	Westmead Chick	Trained/bred
Produce Stakes	Staplers Jo	Trained
Guineas	Staplers Jo	Trained
Anglo Irish (Hackney)	Staplers Jo	Trained
Dundalk International	Westmead Merlin	Trained/bred

1996

Cesarewitch	Elbony Rose	Trained
English Oaks	Annies Bullet	Trained
Boxing Day Marathon	Elbony Rose	Trained

1997

Pepsi Cola Marathon	Elbony Rose	Trained
Gorton Cup	Aztec Travel	Trained
Nixon Bookmakers Stake	Elbony Rose	Trained
Peterboro' Grand National	Im Henry	Trained
Champion Hurdle	Westmead Panda	Trained/bred
English Derby Consolation	Toms The Best	Trained
Midland Gold Cup	Toms The Best	Trained
Wey Plastics	Larkhill Jo	Trained
Sussex Cup	Toms The Best	Trained
St Leger	Tralee Crazy	Trained
Select Stakes	Larkhill Jo	Trained
Cesarewitch	Tralee Crazy	Trained
Eclipse	Larkhill Jo	Trained
Boxing Day Marathon	Tralee Crazy	Trained
IRISH DERBY	Toms The Best	Trained

1998

Rhodes Mem. Marathon	Tralee Crazy	Trained
SCOTTISH DERBY	Larkhill Jo	Trained
ENGLISH DERBY	Toms The Best	Trained
Coldseal Puppy Classic	Sarah Dee	Trained
Wimbledon Puppy Derby	Sarah Dee	Trained
English Oaks	Sarah Dee	Trained

1999

Blue Riband	Droopys Merson	Trained
Greenwich Cup	Westmead Leo	Trained/bred
Sussex Cup	Curley Tresa	Trained
St Leger	Dilemmas Lad	Trained
P Post Fest. Standard	Larkhill Bobby	Trained

2000

William Hill Stayers Classic	Texs Lady	Trained
Quicksilver Stakes	Dilemmas Lad	Trained
Queen Mother Invit.	Last Flight	Trained/bred
Puppy Classic	Westmead Woofa	Trained/bred
Chinn Memorial	Westmead Woofa	Trained/bred

2001

Lincoln	Sonic Flight	Trained/bred
Scottish Derby	Sonic Flight	Trained/bred
Derby Plate	Toms The One	Trained/bred
Derby Invitation	Carhumore Cross	Trained
Select Stakes	Sonic Flight	Trained/bred
Northern Flat	Carhumore Cross	Trained
Doc Burns Trophy	Mossley Pusher	Trained
Irish Laurels	Sonic Flight	Bred
Waterford Masters	Sonic Flight	Bred
Chinn Memorial	Westmead Woofa	Trained/bred
Diamond Stakes	Westmead Woofa	Trained/bred
Midland Puppy Derby	Droopys Hewitt	Trained

2002

Freephone Trophy	Droopys Hewitt	Trained

2005

Greyhound Stud Book Tr	Westmead Hawk	Trained/bred
Ladbrokes Summer Classic	Westmead Hawk	Trained/bred
ENGLISH DERBY	Westmead Hawk	Trained/bred
Star Racing Maiden Derby	Westmead Aoifa	Trained/bred
Produce Stake	Westmead Hawk	Trained/bred
Bedfordshire Puppy Derby	Westmead Joe	Trained/bred

2006

Blue Riband	Westmead Joe	Trained/bred
Prestige	Westmead Olivia	Trained/bred

ENGLISH DERBY	Westmead Hawk	Trained/bred
Summer Stayers Classic	Westmead Aoifa	Trained/bred
Select Stayers	Westmead Aoifa	Trained/bred
Swindon Produce St.	Westmead Joe	Trained/bred
Gold Cup	Westmead Joe	Trained/bred
Hall Green Produce St.	Dilemmas Flight	Trained/bred
English Oaks	Dilemmas Flight	Trained/bred
Coventry St Leger	Westmead Swift	Trained/bred

2007

Peterborough Puppy Derby	Westmead Prince	Trained/bred
Paddy Dunne Memorial	Westmead Lord	Trained/bred
Regency	Spiridon Louis	Bred
TV Trophy	Spiridon Louis	Bred
ENGLISH DERBY	Westmead Lord	Trained/bred
VC Puppy Standard	Westmead Keawn	Trained/bred
Select Stayers	Spiridon Louis	Bred
St Leger	Spiridon Louis	Bred
Romford Puppy Cup	Westmead Keawn	Trained/bred
Totesport Puppy St.	Westmead Tina	Trained/bred
VC Marathon	Spiridon Louis	Bred
Romford Gold Cup	Westmead Aoifa	Trained/bred

2008

Ocean Trailers Puppy St.	Westmead Osprey	Trained/bred
Greyhound Stud Book Tr.	Westmead Lord	Trained/bred
Swindon Produce	Westmead Osprey	Trained/bred

2009

Wimbledon Puppy Derby	Westmead Logan	Trained/bred

2010

Henlow Derby	Westmead Guru	Bred
Northern Puppy Derby	Westmead Maldini	Trained/bred
Henlow Puppy Derby	Westmead Shaw	Trained/bred
Irish Derby Plate	Westmead Bolt	Bred

2011

Monmore Puppy Derby	Droopys Greg	Trained
Primus Gold Cup	Westmead Maldini	Trained/bred
Brighton Belle	Westmead Melanie	Trained/bred
Henlow Silver Salver	Westmead Palace	Bred

Appendix 2

WESTMEAD LITTERS 1968-2010

2010	Droopys Vieri-Westmead Olivia Nov 10	2d 2b
	Droopys Scolari-Westmead Swift Nov 10	3d 2b
	Top Honcho-Westmead Liz Jul 10	2b
	Droopys Vieri-Westmead Aoifa Feb 10	5d 4b
	Top Honcho-Westmead Olivia Jan 10	3d 4b
2009	Ballymac Maeve-Westmead Liz Mar 09	6d 5b
	Ballymac Maeve-Westmead Swift Mar 09	3d 5b
2008	Droopys Maldini-Mega Delight Dec 08	2d 2b
	Hondo Black-Westmead Aoifa Oct 08	3d 1b
	Tyrur Ted-Westmead Swift Jul 08	3d 3b
2007	Droopys Vieri-Westmead Swift Nov 07	3d 6b
	Droopys Scholes-Westmead Nicole Nov 07	2d 2b
	Droopys Scolari-Mega Delight Nov 07	7d 2b
	Toms The Best-Westmead Oak Jun 07	4d 7b
2006	Westmead Hawk-Droopys Jean Nov 06	7d 3b
	Droopys Kewell-Mega Delight Jan 06	2d 6b
2005	Droopys Kewell-Mega Delight Jun 05	3d
2004	Larkhill Jo-Mega Delight Feb 04	4d 6b
2003	Sonic Flight-Mega Delight May 03	4d 4b
	Jamaican Hero-Early Flight Mar 03	2d 9b
2002	Larkhill Jo-Lochbo Jenny Jun 02	3d 8b
	Top Honcho-Early Flight Apr 02	1d 2b
2000	Deep Decision-Lochbo Jenny Jun 00	3d 5b
	Spiral Nikita-Westmead Chick Jun 00	3d 3b
1999	Sonic Flight-Westmead Chick Dec 99	1d 2b
1998	Toms The Best-Celtic Lady Sep 98	5d 3b
	Toms The Best-Westmead Chick Sep 98	6d 2b
	Frightful Flash-Westmead Flight Feb 98	2d 4b
1997	Thorgil Tex-Westmead Amour Dec 97	1d 5b
	Daleys Denis-Westmead Chick Aug 97	5d 6b
	Shanless Slippy-Celtic Lady Mar 97	2d 6b
	Head Honcho-Westmead Chick Jan 97	1d 2b
1996	Staplers Jo-Westmead Chick Jul 96	5d 5b
	Boyne Walk-Westmead Suprise Mar 96	4d 3b
	Westmead Hazzard-Celtic Lady Jan 96	3d 3b
1995	Deenside Spark-Westmead Chick Nov 95	2d 5b
	Staplers Jo-Westmead Mystic Aug 95	1b
	Chet-Celtic Lady May 95	3d 5b
	Chet-Westmead Suprise May 95	5d 4b
	Westmead Hazzard-Duffys Pearl May 95	5d 2b
1994	Murlens Slippy-Westmead Suprise Jul 94	6d 3b
	Murlens Slippy-Westmead Move Jun 94	3d 4b
	Daleys Gold-Celtic Lady Apr 94	3d 4b
1993	Murlens Abbey-Westmead Chloe Nov 93	4d 4b
	Daleys Gold-Westmead Chloe, Ap 93	3d 2b
	Slaneyside Hare-Just Flash Mar 93	6d 4b
	Daleys Gold-Westmead Move Mar 93	7b
1992	Aussie Flyer-Just Flash Aug 92	4d 8b
	Right Move-Westmead Chloe Aug 92	3d 6b
	Flashy Sir-Westmead Kim Mar 92	1d 3b
	I'm Slippy-Westmead Move Jan 92	3d 2b
	I'm Slippy-Westmead Chloe Jan 92	4d 4b
1991	Daleys Gold-Westmead Flow Dec 91	3d 3b
	I'm Slippy-Just Flash Nov 91	5d 1b
	I'm Slippy-Westmead Move May 91	1d 3b
1990	Airmount Grand-Westmead Move Sep 90	7d 2b
	Greenpark Fox-Westmead Alva Sep 90	4d 2b
	Westmead Havoc-Lucky Empress Jun 90	5d 4b
	Daleys Gold-Westmead Move Jan 90	5d 6b
	Flashy Sir-Westmead Alva Jan 90	3d 4b
1989	Tico-Westmead Move Mar 89	1d 10b
1988	Fearless Champ-Westmead Alva Jul 88	2d 5b
	Flashy Sir-Westmead Tania Jul 88	2d 3b
	Flashy Sir-Westmead Seal Jul 88	3d 1b
1987	Fearless Champ-Westmead Move Nov 87	4d 4b
	Flashy Sir-Westmead Seal Nov 87	1d 2b
	Flashy Sir-Westmead Alva Nov 87	7d 3b
	Flashy Sir-Westmead Tania May 87	3d 3b
1986	Fearless Champ-Westmead Tania Sep 86	2d 5b
	Whisper Wishes-Westmead Alva Jul 86	3d 6b
	Cooladine Super-Westmead Seal Jan 86	4d 3b
1985	Special Account-Westmead Tania Jul 85	6d 2b
	Glenroe Hiker-Westmead Seal May 85	4d 5b
	Mathews World-Westmead Alva Jan 85	3d 4b
1984	Whisper Wishes-Westmead Tania Nov 84	5d 3b
	Ks Prince-Westmead Alva Apr 84	2d 2b
1983	Glenroe Hiker-Westmead Satin Feb 83	3d 3b
	Special Account-Westmead Seal Mar 83	4d 1b
1982	All Wit-Westmead Satin	
1981	Glenroe Hiker-Westmead Satin Apr 81	6b
	Knockrour Brandy-Westmead Damson Mar 81	4d 3b
1980	Westmead Pancho-Westmead Damson Aug 80	4d 1b
1979	Linacre-Westmead View May 79	1d 2b
	Wired To Moon-Westmead Satin Feb 79	6d 2b
1978	Westmead Pancho-Westmead View Oct 78	2d 2b
	Westmead Pancho-Westmead Damson Oct 78	3b
	Westmead County-Westmead View Apr 78	4d 1b
	Fionntra Frolic-Westmead Damson Apr 78	1d 3b
1977	Fionntra Frolic-Cricket Dance Aug 77	1d
	Fionntra Frolic-Westmead Silver Aug 77	4d 2b
	Monalee Champion-Westmead Land	3d 1b
	Westmead County-Westmead Damson Jan 77	3d 2b
	Prince Champion-Westmead Satin	
1976	Prince Champion-Westmead Silver Nov 76	2d 4b
	Mels Pupil-Cricket Dance Nov 76	1d 2b
	Fionntra Frolic-Westmead Damson May 76	3d 3b
	Fionntra Frolic-Westmead Silver Mar 76	2d 6b
	Fionntra Frolic-Cricket Dance Feb 76	4d 2b
1975	Westmead County-Westmead Damson Aug 75	1d 2b
	Westmead County-Hacksaw Jun 75	2d 2b
	Mels Pupil-Westmead Silver Apr 75	3d 4b
	Mels Pupil-Cricket Dance Apr 75	5d 2b
1974	Westmead Lane-Hacksaw Nov 74	3d 4b
	Myrtown-Westmead Silver Jul 74	4d 4b
	Clohast Rebel-Cricket Dance Jun 74	1d 3b
	Westmead County-Hacksaw Apr 74	2d 2b
	Westmead County-Westmead Hi Mar 74	4d 2b
1973	Westmead Lane-Hacksaw Aug 73	3d 6b
	Westmead County-Westmead View Mar 73	5d 3b
1972	Westmead County-Hacksaw Dec 72	4d 3b
	Cash For Dan-Westmead Hi Aug 72	6b
1971	Carry On Oregon-Cricket Dance Jul 71	5d 4b
	Newdown Heather-Hacksaw Jul 71	5d 2b
	Discretions-Pincano Apr 71	2b
	Newdown Heather-Westmead Hi Mar 71	2b
	Faithful Hope-Cricket Dance Jan 71	2d 1b
1970	Discretions-Pincano Oct 70	2d 1b
	Franks Tower-Hacksaw Apr 70	4d 3b
	Deneholme Hunter-Pincano Mar 70	3d 3b
	Clonalvy Pride-Cricket Dance Jan 70	7d 3b
1969	Boro Parachute-Pincano, Jun 69	2d 4b
1968	Maryville Hi-Pincano Jan 68	4d 5b